DEFINING HINDUISM

A Reader

Edited by

J. E. Llewellyn

LONDON

Published by

Equinox Publishing Ltd.
Unit 6
The Village
101 Amies St.
London
SW11 2JW
www.equinoxpub.com

First published 2005

British Library Cataloguing-in-Publication Data
A catalogue record for this book is available from the British Library.

ISBN   1 904768 73 3   (paperback)

Typeset by ISB Typesetting, Sheffield
www.sheffieldtypesetting.com

Printed and bound in Great Britain by Antony Rowe Ltd, Chippenham, Wiltshire

To Margaret and Bridget

Blackbird singing in the dead of night
Take these broken wings and learn to fly

CONTENTS

ACKNOWLEDGMENTS

I am grateful to the publishers of the essays included in this book for the permission to reproduce them. The publishers retain the copyright to them. The original publication information is:

Halbfass, Wilhelm. 1991. "The Idea of the Veda and the Identity of Hinduism." In *Tradition and Reflection: Explorations of Indian Thought*, ed. Wilhelm Halbfass, 1–22. Albany: State University of New York Press. Copyright © 1991 State University of New York Press. All rights reserved. Reprinted with the permission of State University of New York Press.

Lipner, Julius J. 1996. "Ancient Banyan: An Inquiry into the Meaning of 'Hinduness.'" *Religious Studies* 32: 109–26. Copyright © 1996 Cambridge University Press. Reprinted with the permission of Cambridge University Press.

Lorenzen, David N. 1999. "Who Invented Hinduism?" *Comparative Studies in Society and History* 41/4 (October): 630–59. © 1999 Society for Comparative Study of Society and History. Reprinted with the permission of Cambridge University Press.

Sweetman, Will. 2001. "Unity and Plurality: Hinduism and the Religions of India in Early European Scholarship." *Religion* 31: 209–24. Copyright 2001, with permission from Elsevier.

Smith, Brian K. 1998. "Questioning Authority: Constructions and Deconstructions of Hinduism." *International Journal of Hindu Studies* 2: 313–39.

Frykenberg, Robert E. 1993. "Constructions of Hinduism at the Nexus of History and Religion." *Journal of Interdisciplinary History* 23/3: 523–50.

Searle-Chatterjee, Mary. 2000. "'World Religions' and 'Ethnic Groups': Do These Paradigms Lend Themselves to the Cause of Hindu Nationalism?" *Ethnic and Racial Studies* 23/3: 497–515.

Omvedt, Gail. 1995. "Introduction." In *Dalit Visions: The Anti-Caste Movement and the Construction of an Indian Identity*, ed. Gail Omvedt, 1–6. Hyderabad: Orient Longman.

Fitzgerald, Timothy. *Problems with "Religion" as a Category for Understanding Hinduism*. Decatur, IL: International Institute of India Studies, Canada, and Millikin University Department of Religion, USA.

I am also grateful to the authors of these essays for their fine work on the originals and for their generous willingness to help me with this book. Russell McCutcheon made substantial suggestions for improving my introduction, and he is the editor of the series in which the book appears. In large measure this book is the product of the many years of conversations that we have had—for which no expression of gratitude would be sufficient. I owe a debt to Vishal Agarwal, Greg Bailey, Jeff Brackett, Brad Clough, Richard S. Cohen, Gavin Flood, Andrew Fort, Luis Gonzalez-Reimann, Linda Hess, Alf Hiltebeitel, Amod Lele, Robert Menzies, Sushil Mittal, Laurie Patton, Deepak Sarma, Arvind Sharma, Will Sweetman, and Shrinivas Tilak for making suggestions about what material should be included in the book. Thanks to Janet Joyce and the staff at Equinox for their patience and professionalism. Finally, I am grateful beyond measure to my wife, Eileen, for her support while I was working on this book and over the past eighteen years.

INTRODUCTION:
THE PROBLEM OF DEFINING HINDUISM

J. E. Llewellyn

This is a book about "Hinduism," that is, about the term. It is also a book about Hinduism, the thing to which the term refers. It is concerned not only with what Hinduism is but also with what it has been, with the history of the religion and of the term. Some of the authors included here make political or ideological claims, so they are also interested in what Hinduism *should* be. The book is composed of nine essays originally published over a ten-year period between 1991 and 2001. These are only some of the most important and interesting examples of the growing literature on the problem of defining Hinduism. This is obviously a critical subject for students of South Asia, given that Hinduism is the dominant religion in that region. Since Hinduism is almost always counted as one of the major world religions, its definition is also significant for religious studies generally.

The reader will find that this book includes essays that argue that Hinduism is at best an umbrella term that covers a variety of religions, and not just one religion. By this logic, it might be appropriate to place the word Hinduism in quotation marks wherever it occurs, but I will not follow that rule. If an author used quotation marks in the original version of an essay, I have retained them here. Where they are found, the marks sometimes mean that the essay is talking about the word Hinduism, as opposed to the thing. In other contexts they seem to indicate that the author does not really believe that there is a Hinduism, though other people may. So in that case "Hinduism" is equal to "so-called Hinduism." And there may also be passages in which the quotation marks are a sign that the author has decided to defer the question of whether or not there is a Hinduism. Given the possible confusion over what these marks are intended to convey, I have largely eschewed them in this introduction. At any rate, since postmodernism has convincingly demonstrated the problematic relationship between language and meaning, the theoretically correct practice might be to put every word in quotation marks.

The nine essays that make up this book are divided into four parts. The middle two parts are historical. The second part contains essays by David N. Lorenzen and Will Sweetman that analyze descriptions of Hinduism in writings before India became a British colony. In the third part, Brian K. Smith and Robert Eric Frykenberg reach back to the precolonial era, but extend the argument into the British period and independent India. At the beginning and the end of the book are thematic parts, the first on definitions of Hinduism and the last on caste. Because Wilhelm Halbfass and Julius J. Lipner base their definitions of Hinduism largely on evidence from classical Hindu culture, Part I belongs before Part II chronologically. Still, these authors certainly do not limit the applicability of their definitions to that earlier time; rather, they understand them to be relevant today. The relationship between Hinduism and caste is one of the subjects of the essays in the fourth part of the book by Mary Searle-Chatterjee, Gail Omvedt, and Timothy Fitzgerald. Caste is an important issue in contemporary Indian politics, of course, but it has also shaped South Asian society for centuries. Because there is an "Orientation" at the beginning of each part of the book, I will not summarize the essays in this introduction. Here I only intend to introduce some of the significant themes of this book, to give the reader a purchase on threads that weave these essays together. As a background, I will begin with one site where there is considerable confusion about the definition of Hinduism, that is, in world religions textbooks.

The Trouble with the Textbooks

The map of the "Religions of India" in Lewis Hopfe's *Religions of the World* illustrates the problem with Hinduism (Hopfe 2001, 73). At first glance it appears that there is hardly any territory at all in South Asia in which there is a Hindu majority, since the solid shading that the legend says represents that demographic area is only to be found in a few small patches. On further reflection it becomes obvious that the map marks most of India as Hindu-majority, but this is obscured because Hinduism's solid gray is overlaid on most of the map with the vertical bars of the "Significant Muslim minority," and in a few areas with the diagonal bars of the "Significant Buddhist minority." The map also identifies regions that have a majority religion other than the Hindu, that is, Sikh, Muslim, Buddhist, and Christian. There are two obvious and fairly substantial errors in the map. In the northwestern part of India, most of the Punjab is marked by the horizontal bars of the

"Sikh majority"—but not against a white background, as the legend would have it, but against Hinduism's solid gray. So this part of the map is identified as *both* Hindu majority and Sikh majority. The other problem is that Sri Lanka is included in the map in Hinduism's gray, and not in the same charcoal color that separates off the countries which are not India. The casual reader might come away with the impression that Sri Lanka is also a Hindu-majority country, a particularly poignant misapprehension given that island nation's recent history of violent conflict between the Sinhalese Buddhist majority and the Tamil Hindu minority. Regardless of these errors, for the purposes of this book the most striking thing about this map is that in it Hinduism is so hard to see. It is the nearly invisible background on which India's minority religions are inscribed.

Similarly, in textbooks which survey the world religions, Hinduism is often distinguished by what it is not. S. A. Nigosian opens his chapter on Hinduism with "Unlike most other religions of the world, Hinduism has no identifiable founder" (Nigosian 2000, 20). He later notes another significant absence: "Although hundreds of sacred texts are considered authoritative [by Hindus], there is no equivalent to the Christian Bible or the Muslim Qur'an, that is, no single definitive text" (27). Actually this is apparently a case of Hinduism having too much and too little at once—it has too many scriptures but lacks a central one. Carmody and Brink divine in Hinduism a peculiar doctrinal flexibility. "More than such religious traditions as the Jewish, the Christian, the Muslim, and the Buddhist, whose basic doctrines have been relatively uncontested, Hindus have admitted variety ... into the core of their religious culture" (Carmody and Brink 2002, 130).

The textbooks generally agree that one of the distinguishing features of Hinduism is its extreme diversity. Lewis Hopfe says simply that "It is probably the most diverse and varied of all religions" (Hopfe 2001, 71). An explanation that is frequently advanced to account for this complexity is that Hindus have been unable or unwilling to jettison old religious ideas and practices as they progress. "The long past is still present in India. Much has been poured into the melting pot of Indian culture over the centuries and millenia [*sic*], but little (except Buddhism) has been lost. The earliest continues alongside the latest" (Ellwood and McGraw 1999, 93). And the sheer size of India's population is also proffered as an explanation for Hinduism's variety. For example, Warren Matthews admits that "Hinduism has approximately 800 million adherents, so we can expect to find many different ways of understanding it" (Matthews 1999, 83). A considerable expansion upon this idea is made by Mary Pat Fisher, who in her criticism of the Hindu nationalist V. D. Savarkar points to "the historical evidence that Sanatana Dharma [Sanskrit for 'eternal religion'] is a noncentralized, evolving composite of variegated ways of worship, with as many ways to the Ultimate as there are people" (Fisher 2002, 124). For Matthews there must be many different understandings of Hinduism because there are eight hundred million Hindus. By Fisher's logic there must be eight hundred million different understandings, since there are "as many ways to the Ultimate as there are people."

An interesting solution to the problem of Hinduism's complexity is suggested by a couple of the survey texts that have already been quoted. Ellwood and McGraw suggest that one of the reasons that the goal of Hinduism is so variously described is because it is beyond ordinary language. "Let us first look ahead to the goal of Hinduism. It may be given many labels—God-realization, identification with the absolute, supreme bliss, cosmic consciousness—but it is perhaps best spoken of by more negative terms such as release, liberation, or freedom. For it is really beyond all concepts and labels" (Ellwood and McGraw 1999, 60). A similar logic is expressed by Nigosian when he writes: "Religious truth, according to Hinduism, is not conceived necessarily in dogmatic terms, because truth transcends all verbal definitions" (Nigosian 2000, 20). And this follows and is an answer to Nigosian's observation that

> The chief concern of Hindu religious conviction is not the existence or nonexistence of God or whether there is one God or many gods. Hindus can choose to be monotheists, polytheists, pantheists, atheists, agnostics, dualists, monists, or pluralists. They may or may not follow strict standards of moral conduct, spend time on everyday religious rituals, or attend a temple. Magic, fetishism, animal worship, and belief in demons coexist, supplement, and accompany profound theological doctrines, asceticism, mysticism, and esoteric beliefs (Nigosian 2000, 20).

In other words, it may seem as if there should be a logical contradiction caused by the inconsistencies of these very different theologies and religious practices, but that is not a problem in Hinduism, since the truth transcends logic anyway.

Though this kind of argument would seem to obviate the necessity of identifying any core beliefs or practices in Hinduism, most college textbooks do try to describe the essence of that religion. A kind of hard social definition is offered by Carmody and Brink: "Having had many forms of divinity, Hinduism has had many worldviews. The membership requirements are quite simple: As long as one accepts the divine inspiration of the Vedas and the caste system, one can be called a Hindu" (Carmody and Brink 2002, 139). There is evidence for the centrality of the Vedas as authoritative texts and Brahmans as their interpreters in most of the textbooks reviewed here. Often this is only betrayed indirectly. For example, Fellows only spells out that "orthodox Hindus of every level in traditional Hinduism do not question Brahminism and the Vedas," in the context of distinguishing Hinduism from the "heterodox systems," Buddhism and Jainism (Fellows 1998, 50). It is as if we are back to Hopfe's map of the "Religions of India," in which Hinduism can only be seen in contrast to the minority religions of South Asia.

In a few of these textbooks what unifies Hinduism is unity itself. This idea is expressed by Carmody and Brink when they write that:

> How, overall, does Hinduism seem to configure reality for its adherents? What is the center, or summarizing pattern, that the Hindu "ways" appear to depict? It seems to us that the Hindu center is an alluring sense of unity. From the time of the Vedas, reflective personalities in India sought to put together the many disparate facets and forces of reality. Thus *Rig-Veda* hymns, the *Upanishads*, and the later theistic cults all proposed a mystery, or ultimate reality, or god that stood behind things, promising the devout adherent, or the self-disciplined yogi, a satisfying peace (Carmody and Brink 2002, 140).

These authors see an agreement in the belief in an ultimate reality, despite the apparent disagreement over the nature of that ultimate reality. The most insistent partisan of the unity argument is Ward Fellows, who begins his chapter on Hinduism by writing that "'Oneness' is not the one word to describe the essence of Hinduism, but it is as close as we can get to a one-word characterization. For there is a strange and fascinating unity to this religion of the nation and people of India" (Fellows 1998, 41). Because the precise nature of this oneness is not spelled out very clearly, I suspect that there is a kind of circular or tautological reasoning operating: what unifies Hinduism is, well, its unity.

The Hinduism chapters analyzed here are remarkable for their similarity. They all cover more or less the same topics in more or less the same way. Especially given that, even more remarkable is the lack of consensus on a definition of what Hinduism is. Some of these authors don't even take a stab at defining the term. Most acknowledge the importance of the authority of the Vedas and of Brahmans, but sometimes only indirectly. Some attempt more speculative definitions, but they impress me as analytically insubstantial.

Themes in Defining Hinduism

So this is the problem: Hinduism has been variously and confusingly defined, where it has been defined at all. All of the essays in *Defining Hinduism* address this problem in one way or another. Before confronting that issue, I want to suggest some other themes that emerge repeatedly throughout this book.

The Politics of Hinduism

The most significant political development in India in the last two decades of the twentieth century was the rise of the Hindu right. The most notorious sign of this change was the destruction of the Babri Masjid in 1992 and the subsequent riots. Because this mosque was said to occupy the space where a Hindu temple had stood, the very spot where the God Ram was born, a campaign was begun at least a decade earlier to demolish the Muslim house of worship in order to rebuild the Hindu one. Finally, a mob took matters into its own hands and tore down the mosque. This, in turn, sparked riots across north India in which hundreds were killed, both Hindus and Muslims, but more Muslims than Hindus (Llewellyn 1996).

As shocking as this event was, it is not as important as the transformation that was taking place at the same time in Indian politics. In 1996 the Indian National Congress fell. The Congress was at the center of the struggle for independence from British rule and it had controlled the central government for the first half century of the life of independent India. The Congress was the party of Mahatma Gandhi (1869–1948), the father of independent India, and Jawaharlal Nehru (1889–1964), the first prime minister. Soon after the Congress was ousted from power in 1996, a coalition took over led by the Hindu nationalist Bharatiya Janata Party. During its long reign, the Congress was led by high-caste Hindus, but its electoral majority depended upon lower-caste groups and religious minority communities. Their support was secured in part through the reservations system, which included seats set aside in legislatures, in the government bureaucracy, and in schools for lower-caste people and religious minorities. The stated rationale for reservations was not to secure votes, of course, but to extend a helping hand to people who were economically disadvantaged and who had been discriminated against in the past.

Though the Bharatiya Janata Party (BJP) has certainly not abolished this system of affirmative action, the perspective of it and other Hindu nationalist groups is fundamentally antithetical to that of its Congress architects. These reservations are based on the liberal conviction that it is the members of lower caste groups and religious minorities, prominently the Muslims, who are the aggrieved parties. For the Hindu nationalists, by contrast, the victims are the Hindus themselves, who, despite being the majority, have been neglected by a government which has bent over backwards for the benefit of others. For centuries, India had been dominated by foreign powers: the British (who controlled Indian politics beginning in the middle of the eighteenth century) and before them the Mughals and earlier Muslim dynasties (founded in north India beginning in the eleventh century), with their foreign religions, the Hindu nationalists argue. Even in independent India, the oppression of the indigenous people and their religion had continued. Now it is time to give the Hindus their due and to put others, especially Muslims, in their place. This is the logic that connects the politics of the BJP to the demolition of the Babri Masjid.

By this point it would be appropriate for the reader to ask what all this has to do with defining Hinduism. Though scholars have long puzzled over this problem, the issue was forced into something of a crisis with the rise of the Hindu right. The essays in this book are one of the results of that crisis. About half of them have something to say about Hindu nationalism, generally something unfavorable. Typical is Julius J. Lipner's criticism of "extremist Hindu rightwing elements." Near the other end of this book, but at the same end of the political spectrum, is the essay by Mary Searle-Chatterjee. Its point is to expose the improper reification of the Hindu religion *because that serves the interests of the Hindu nationalists.* For Lipner and Searle-Chatterjee, and for Robert Eric Frykenberg, too, these politicos have improperly redefined and narrowed Hinduism.

A radical dissent from this position is expressed by Brian K. Smith in Chapter 5. He argues that the Hindu nationalists have not produced some Hinduism that is rated R for restricted. On the contrary, since they have sought to attract a large following, the politicians have had an interest in building "a version of 'Hinduism' that is as inclusive, and vague, as possible." Despite his disagreement on this point, I believe that Smith would go along with Searle-Chatterjee, for example, in condemning the Hindu nationalist movement. In fact, part of the reason why he advances a scholarly definition of Hinduism in his essay is to wrest control over it from the Hindu right. This political debate is mixed up with the theme that is the subject of the next section of this introduction.

The Problem of Orientalism

If the great political development in the last two decades of the twentieth century in India was the rise of Hindu nationalism, the great intellectual development among scholars who study South Asia was postcolonialism. The publication of *Orientalism* in 1978 was the watershed. In this book the literary critic Edward Said analyzes the western discourse about the Orient. Westerners, according to Said, created an image of the Orient as the Other, the opposite of the west, primitive as opposed to advanced, mystical as opposed to rational, passive as opposed to active, and so forth. Though Said focused on the Middle East, his work had a profound effect on South Asian studies, with scholars working to expose stereotypes about Indian culture. This has been more than just an academic exercise. Rather, the goal has also been political, to liberate India from colonialist ways of thinking, which endured long after the colonizers themselves had been kicked out.

Though postcolonialism is sometimes mentioned in a positive light in the essays included in this book, it more often comes in for criticism. Robert Frykenberg takes the postcolonialists to task for overemphasizing the power of the colonizers in their interactions with the colonized. He writes that "Denigrators of Orientalism give too much credit to Europeans and too little to hosts of Native Indians (mainly Brahmans and others imbued with Brahmanical world views; but also Muslims imbued with Islamic world views) for the cultural constructions (and reconstructions) of India." According to Wilhelm Halbfass and Brian Smith this is not a problem confined to the nineteenth century, as contemporary postcolonialists arrogate to themselves the right to speak for those Indians who are supposedly still locked in their Orientalist mental prison. Both Halbfass and Smith call this kind of theorizing "presumptuous."

There is an irony here in the politics of these criticisms. The postcolonialists see themselves as giving Indians back the agency that was denied them by the colonizers, who not only dominated them politically but also erased them culturally by substituting for India the west's alter ego. Yet Frykenberg suggests that the process was more complicated. The people of India did not take colonization lying down, but actively participated in it, trying to secure their own interests as best they could in a rapidly changing political and economic world (Llewellyn 2002). Halbfass and Smith seem to think that contemporary Indians also need not be presumed to be so supine. The postcolonialists' caricature of the process of colonization assigns all of the power to the colonizers in a way that does not give the colonized the capacity to act as agents. If the goal is to cast the people of South Asia as actors in their own history, then the postcolonialists are outmaneuvered by some of the authors in this book into being a part of the problem, not a part of the solution. In this way, the criticism of the postcolonialists is also political, like the criticism of the Hindu nationalists discussed earlier in this introduction.

Religion

In some of the essays in this book the problem with the Hindu religion is not with the Hindu part but with the religion part. In the textbooks analyzed earlier in this introduction, Hinduism is taken as a species of the genus religion. Though this practice is so common that it may seem commonsensical, there is no doubt that the notion of religion itself is a modern phenomenon which plays a specific role in contemporary thought. In this book Timothy Fitzgerald argues strongly that religion as a category of social analysis does not "pick out the finer distinctions" that scholars should unearth. Mary Searle-Chatterjee quotes an earlier essay by Fitzgerald approvingly and writes disparagingly of the "religionists" in the same vein. On the other side of the fence on this issue is Brian K. Smith, who argues for a definition of Hinduism specifically designed to bring that tradition into line with the other world religions.

A somewhat more conservative position is occupied by Will Sweetman. He insists that the premodern European observers of South Asian religion cannot be convicted of reifying Hinduism in line with the modern notion of what a religion is if that notion only developed after their time. In other words, we cannot critique our ancestors for trimming South Asia to fit the procrustean bed of the modern idea of religion if that bed itself had not yet been built. Sweetman's argument here is not *politically* conservative as opposed to being politically liberal; rather, it is conservative in the sense of being more modest. His point is about the way that the term religion has been used. Fitzgerald, Searle-Chatterjee, and Smith have arguments not only about the rhetorical work that religion has done, but also about the scholarly work that religion should do.

Caste

A fourth major theme in this book is caste. It is the focus of Part IV, but it can be found throughout. As on other questions, Robert Frykenberg stakes out a radical position when he argues that the different caste groups have been so deeply divided over the course of the history of South Asian society that it makes no sense to speak of them having a common religion, Hinduism. Timothy Fitzgerald shares Frykenberg's conviction that caste is king in India, but then makes a different point on the basis of that conclusion. Specifically, Fitzgerald argues that Hinduism is no *religion*, because when scholars adopt that term then they separate the spiritual from the social in a way that leaves out caste, India's "core ritual symbolic structure." Perhaps Frykenberg would be willing to accept Fitzgerald's conclusion on this point. They might agree that there is something that all South Asians have in common: they must abide by caste rules. However, they do not have any common religion.

Contrary to these kinds of deconstructionist arguments, according to Wilhelm Halbfass and Brian Smith there is a Hindu religion and it is a religion that has been shepherded by the priestly caste, the Brahmans. The emphasis in Halbfass's essay is on the Vedas as the center of Hinduism, but he acknowledges that the traditional masters of the Vedic tradition were the Brahmans. Halbfass seems to have a fairly positive view of caste, arguing that it was not just about "relationships of exclusion and subordination," but also about "a shared structure of mutual relations, which assigns different forms of participation to different groups." I am not sure that Smith would accept Halbfass's relatively rosy assessment of caste. At one point he calls the Brahmans' formulation of Hindu orthodoxy "extremely self-serving." Yet Smith insists that, as a practical matter, if scholars are going to treat

Hinduism as a world religion like the others, then they must acknowledge the role of the Vedas as scripture and the authority of the Brahmans as South Asia's priestly religious elite.

The political implications of the problem of caste are particularly clear in Gail Omvedt's essay in this book. She agrees with Halbfass and Smith in acknowledging Brahman dominance in Hinduism, but then she advances the argument of the Dalits, anticaste activists who condemn this religion as oppressive toward members of lower-caste groups. This Brahmanical Hinduism is the religion of the Brahmans themselves, which has been imposed upon others in South Asia. In theory the religion of the lower castes has been, or at least should be, different. I think that the antipathy to caste oppression that is articulated by Omvedt is probably shared by most of the authors in this book. Some of the essays shine a spotlight on caste, not just because it is a very important social reality in India, but also because it is an instrument of exploitation which must be exposed.

Defining Hinduism

The one problem that all of the essays in this book address, and about which they clearly disagree, is whether there even is a Hinduism. Now, none of the authors argues that Hinduism itself does not exist, that it is just an illusion, the phantasm of some febrile Orientalist. Rather, the debate concerns the unity of Hinduism. So the question is not: *Is* there a Hinduism? The question is: Is there *a* Hinduism? Halbfass and Lipner not only reply in the affirmative, but each also provides a definition of it, though their definitions are quite different. Lorenzen also argues strongly for a Hinduism, presenting evidence that a more or less clear depiction of it can be traced in texts from the past millennium. Sweetman's conclusion on this question is less clear, but he seems to come down against the unity of Hinduism, since he writes that some precolonial missionaries did not see a unity there. Smith maintains that there is a Hinduism, while Frykenberg finds only the various religions of the disparate castes. Claiming that the reification of Hinduism is politically pernicious, Searle-Chatterjee's essay falls into the anti-unity category. For Omvedt there may be one Hinduism that belongs to the upper castes, but this is not to be confused with the religions of all of the people of South Asia. So I would count her vote against the unity of Hinduism. Finally, Fitzgerald argues that Hinduism is not a religion at all, but ironically he might still belong in the unity camp, since he does see a certain kind of caste structure that has been pervasive and enduring in South Asia. As I have summarized the position of the authors in this paragraph, this informal poll ends up close, with five for the unity of Hinduism and four against. These authors are all experts in the religious history of South Asia. How is it possible for them to disagree so strongly on such a basic point?

One problem concerns the nature of the data. In this book, Wilhelm Halbfass quotes Heinrich von Stietencron that Hinduism is "an orchid bred by European scholarship. ... In nature, it does not exist" (Küng and Stietencron 1987, 25–26). I certainly do not agree with Stietencron's point here if what he means is that unlike Hinduism, other religions, say Christianity or Islam, do exist in nature. All religions are cultural, and not natural. Religions are often passed down in families, but they are not passed down genetically. There are no separate Islamic or Hindu genes.

That is not to say that there is no separate Islam or Hinduism, but only that those religions exist as social groups. For the purposes of analysis, the easiest kind of group to isolate is one that carefully polices its own membership. Of course, it is also possible to study a group that is not self-consciously distinct. For example, I'm not sure that the members of generation X realized how much they had in common until they were enlightened about that by social scientists. There are even cases in which it makes sense to pick out a group contrary to the self-understanding of its members. On surveys a broad range of Americans label themselves middle class, for instance, including many who are wealthy. Still, for some kinds of economic analysis, it may be more productive to treat the rich middle class as if they are upper class. However such social groups are delimited, just as there are no natural generations or classes, so there are no natural religions. Therefore, defining Hinduism is not like identifying the genetically determined, invariant characteristics of a species of tree.

That there are millions of people in India and around the world who call themselves Hindu is undeniable. How long this has been the case is debatable. Some variant of the word Hinduism first appeared as early as the middle of the first millennium BCE, but it seems that its usage was not religious but geographical and ethnic, referring to the South Asian subcontinent and the people who lived there (Sharma 2002, 2). In this book, David Lorenzen argues that Hinduism was recognized as a distinct religion by an outsider almost a thousand years ago, with the first use of words related to Hinduism as a self-description dating to the fifteenth century. Of course, it may be that something like what we now know as Hinduism existed before that time, even if this label wasn't used for it, and this is the position of Halbfass's and Lipner's essays in this book. At this point we are not talking about a social group that rigorously maintains its own boundaries. So Halbfass and Lipner cannot produce constitutions or membership rolls to delimit their Hinduism. Rather, they write about a kind of community of discourse, a group that has shared certain beliefs (in Halbfass's case) or a certain way of thinking (for Lipner) over time. It is impossible finally to prove or disprove the existence of such beliefs and ways, since either argument involves summarizing what millions have said and done over the course of centuries. There will always be more evidence that might be cited pro or con. This is one of the reasons why the opinions of scholars on this point conflict.

Another source of disagreement in this book concerns the biases of the analysts. An earlier generation of the students of the religions of South Asia might have gotten it all wrong because of the prejudices that determined their work. This kind of argument involves not only analyzing the data, but also analyzing the analysts of the data. In this book, detecting these biases is often itself more or less political. On the one hand, Robert Frykenberg deconstructs the unity of Hinduism to save it from the reifications of the Orientalists and their Hindu nationalist descendents. On the other hand, David Lorenzen restores to Hinduism the unity which has been robbed from it by the postcolonial theorists. In both cases, there is an effort not only to set the record straight but also to balance the scales, to derail someone else's juggernaut.

In this book Will Sweetman quotes with approval Jonathan Z. Smith's dictum that "Religion is solely the creation of the scholar's study" (J. Z. Smith 1982, xi). I would not be willing to go so far as to concede that Hinduism is solely the creation of the scholar's study for the authors found in this book. They frequently cite evidence from the history of the religions of South Asia, and critique other scholars on the basis of that evidence. If Hinduism were *solely* the creation of the scholar's study, then scholarship itself would be reduced to a kind of solipsism in which there are only various contemporary arguments with nothing behind them. However, I am willing to allow that Hinduism is *partly* a creation of the scholar's study, and all of these authors indicate this, too, when they critique the biases of other researchers. What each of them does is to use the evidence available to create a Hinduism and then to demonstrate why her or his creation is superior to earlier ones.

The reader who hoped that I'd resolve all of the confusion in this introduction by positing my own definition of Hinduism will be disappointed. If I could distill the essence of Hinduism from the essays included in this book and comprehensively and briefly restate it here, then there would be no point in reading the rest. The essays make too many conflicting arguments to allow for such a distillation. What is more, there are theoretical reasons that block such a move. If I could escape my own biases, to step outside of the history that conditions the thinking of everyone else, then I could issue the final verdict about whether or not there is a unitary Hinduism and how it might be defined. But that is obviously not possible. So in this introduction I have not sought to rise above the essays that this book contains. These essays are too interesting and important for that. I have merely sought to provide a way into the conversation, even if I don't have the last word.

Part I

Definitions of Hinduism

ORIENTATION

We begin with two very different proposals for defining Hinduism by Wilhelm Halbfass and Julius J. Lipner. The thesis of "The Identity of the Veda and the Identity of Hinduism" is expressed at the beginning of the essay, when Wilhelm Halbfass describes the Vedas as "a focal point of Hindu self-understanding." Halbfass earned his Ph.D. at the University of Göttingen and was a professor at the University of Pennsylania at the time of his death in 2000. His major works were on Indian philosophy (1988, 1991, 1992; see also Franco and Preisendanz 1997). The Vedas are the oldest Hindu texts, and belief in them has sometimes been identified as the litmus test of orthodoxy in the Hindu tradition. Yet Halbfass's argument in this essay is still surprising because scholars long ago noted that most Hindus now and throughout history have not known the Vedas well. Despite acknowledging that problem, the author insists that the Vedas have provided Hinduism with "its most significant point of reference and departure, and with a basis of its tenuous continuity and identity." Halbfass is particularly intent to maintain this claim against the critics of Orientalism, who argue that Hinduism is nothing but "a European invention." Halbfass believes this position to be not only historically inaccurate but also "presumptuous," with the current generation of western scholars patronizingly giving back to Indians the agency which an earlier generation of western scholars stripped from them. In the end, Halbfass concludes that "the idea of a comprehensive unity of the tradition, and of a common ground of orthodoxy, is inseparable from a vision of, and commitment to, the Vedic revelation."

In addition to allegiance to the Vedas, "The Identity of the Veda and the Identity of Hinduism" also discusses dharma, something else that has been suggested as definitive of Hinduism. Dharma very nearly plays this role for Halbfass, too, since about it he writes, "We cannot reduce the meanings of *dharma* to one general principle; nor is there one single translation that would cover all its usages. Nevertheless, there is a coherence in this variety; it reflects the elusive, yet undeniable coherence of Hinduism itself, its peculiar unity-in-diversity." It is significant that Halbfass stages his defense of dharma in response to critiques of Orientalist notions of Hinduism as casteist. The argument with which Halbfass takes issue says that traditional accounts of the beliefs and practices of all Hindus are actually only those of the Brahmans who were the Orientalists' chief informants. The strong formulation of this claim is that the Brahmans hoodwinked the Orientalists into accepting a version of the Hindu "tradition" which they invented to give themselves power. It is against this backdrop that Halbfass asserts the centrality of the notion of dharma. It is significant that Halbfass confesses that the essays in his book "are primarily based upon philosophical and normative literature in Sanskrit, that is, on texts which were for the most part composed by Brahmins" (Halbfass 1991, 16). Clearly evidence based on such elite sources cannot effectively answer the charge that the Orientalist understanding of Hinduism was caste-biased.

When Wilhelm Halbfass describes the Vedas as the center of Hinduism, it is sometimes difficult to determine whether he is talking about a thing or about a process. In Julius Lipner's essay, "Ancient Banyan: An Inquiry into the Meaning of 'Hinduness,'" the emphasis is clearly on a certain kind of process. Lipner, who obtained his Ph.D. from the University of London and is currently a reader at the University of Cambridge, has written several works about Indian thought (1986, 1994, 1997, 1999). Here he focuses on Hinduness rather than Hinduism, in an attempt to avoid a "closed construct" in favor of an "an open construct, that is, an intrinsically plural phenomenon." At the beginning of the essay, before he has introduced his shift to Hinduness, Lipner describes Hinduism as "macrocosmically one though microcosmically many, a polycentric phenomenon imbued with the same life-sap, the boundaries and (micro)centers seeming to merge and overlap in a *complexus* of oscillating tensions." In the context of this book, the best illustration of this complicated sounding idea is the arguments that Hindus have made about scripture. Lipner notes that it is not unusual to find later texts making the claim that they are the Vedas or are equal to the Vedas. These texts do not replace the Vedic canon, in Lipner's reading, but establish themselves as "alternative forms of the originals." So that what results is "a multicentrism of scriptural authority." Unlike Halbfass's essay, here the point is not that accepting the authority of the Vedas is a central tenet of Hinduism; rather, Lipner is merely using the Vedas as one example of a *process* which he maintains is characteristic of Hinduism. This polycentric Hinduism, Lipner says, is like the banyan tree, which has many apparent trunks, but no clearly identifiable center.

The primary conception of Hinduism against which Lipner is arguing in this essay is that of "extremist Hindu rightwing elements." For them, "Hinduism" has a "fixed, non-negotiable meaning," which is "divisive" and "religiopolitically preferential." By contrast, Lipner's Hinduism is marked by "an insightful aversion to dogmatism" and "a healthy dose of relativism." Apparently this tolerance is not so great that it will allow for the narrowness of the Hindu right itself, for Lipner labels it "un-Hindu." Ironically, there is no place for religious nationalism even under the capacious canopy of the banyan tree that is Lipner's Hinduism.

1

THE IDEA OF THE VEDA AND THE IDENTITY OF HINDUISM

Wilhelm Halbfass

Introduction

Louis Renou has characterized the role of the Veda in traditional Hinduism in a memorable and familiar statement: Even in the most orthodox circles of Hinduism, reverence for the Veda was nothing more than a "tipping of the hat," a traditional gesture of saluting an "idol" without any further commitment (Renou 1960, 2).[1] Against incautious identifications of Vedic and Hindu religiosity, Renou invokes Max Weber's observation that "the Vedas defy the *dharma* of Hinduism."[2]

Indeed, the role the Veda has played in Indian tradition appears paradoxical, ambiguous, and no less elusive than the "teachings" of the Veda itself. There seems to be a blatant contradiction between the proclamations of its sacredness and authority, and its factual neglect by the Hindu tradition. While it is often invoked as the criterion of Hindu "orthodoxy," its actual presence in Indian thought and life seems to be quite limited. Its oldest and supposedly most sacred sections, in particular the Rig Veda itself, have become most obscure and obsolete. For the "reality" of later Hinduism, they seem to be nothing more than a distant, barely recognizable echo of a different world.

The Vedic texts contain no Hindu dogma, no basis for a "creed" of Hinduism, no clear guidelines for the "Hindu way of life." They offer only vague and questionable analogues to those ideas and ways of orientation that have become basic presuppositions of later Hinduism. It may suffice to recall here the cyclical worldview, the doctrine of karma and rebirth, the ethical principle of *ahimsa* and the soteriology of final liberation. For all of this, the oldest and most fundamental Vedic texts provide no clearly identifiable basis. The Hindu pantheon, the forms of worship and devotion, and the temple cult are not Vedic. The traditional "order of castes and stages of life" *(varnashramadharma)* is far removed from the Vedic beginnings. Regardless of all retrospective glorification of the Veda, even the "orthodox" core of the tradition, as represented by the exegetic Mimamsa and the Dharmashastra, follows largely un-Vedic ways of thought and is oriented around a projection or fiction of the Veda. This is also true for those philosophical systems of Hinduism whose "orthodoxy" is defined by their recognition of the authority of the Veda. While proclaiming the sanctity of the Veda, the Hindu tradition seems to be turning away from the Vedic ways of thought and life. The preservation and glorification of the text seem to coincide with its neglect and the obscuration of its meaning.

Renou himself says that the history of the Veda in India is ultimately a history of failure and loss, and that the recitation of the text, in particular the mantras, and the preservation of its phonetic identity, occurred at the expense of a living exegesis and appropriation. From an early time, the Veda ceased to be "a ferment of Indian religiosity"; in the end, the Vedic world was nothing but "a distant object" (Renou 1960, 77). Is this the final word on the role of the Veda in India? Are Vedism and Hinduism essentially different religions and worldviews, held together only by an ideology of continuity and correspondence? Is the Veda, which the Dharmashastra and the "orthodox" systems of Hindu philosophy present as a measure of orthodoxy, actually a projection and a fiction?

In addition to his research on the Veda as such, Renou has done much to document and explore the ways in which the Veda is present in the later Hindu tradition. His study *Le destin du Veda dans l'Inde* ("The Destiny of the Veda in India") contains much useful information on the role of the Veda in post-Vedic India, such as the forms in which the Veda was preserved, the attitudes towards the Vedic word, and the application, interpretation, and critique of the Veda at various levels of religious life and philosophical reflection. Regardless of his statements on the merely ceremonial role of the Veda, Renou also refers to its "real extensions" in later Hinduism (Renou 1960, 3). Somewhat casually, he notes that the very essence of the Vedic world found its way, in a process of transformation, into "the living substance of Hindu practice and speculation" (Renou 1960, 77). What is the meaning of these "real extensions," and how do they relate to the ceremonial gestures and retrospective projections? How can the statements concerning the real "transformation" of the Vedic world be reconciled with those about its loss and obscuration? Renou's survey provides helpful clues, but not much explicit hermeneutic reflection concerning these questions.

What Renou calls "the destiny of the Veda in India" is a wide-ranging phenomenon of extraordinary complexity and ambiguity. His survey makes reference not only to the literary traditions of the Hindu sects, Tantrism, Dharmashastra, the Epics, Puranas, iconography, rituals, traditions of secular learning, methods of preserving the Vedic texts, techniques of recitation and memorization, Vedic schools and auxiliary sciences, Vedic commentatorial literature, and the "orthodox" systems of Hindu philosophy, but also to the anti-Vedic critique and polemics of the Buddhists, Jains, and Materialists. We are dealing with semantic as well as nonsemantic approaches, with ritual and magical usages of Vedic words and formulae, with myths and theories concerning the unity and totality of the Veda, with forms of archival preservation, with definitions and reinterpretations, and with comprehensive attempts to establish the Veda as the source and framework of the entire tradition. In spite of the growing distance and obscuration, an idea and vision of the Veda emerges not only as a focal point of Hindu self-understanding, and a center for the precarious unity and identity of the tradition, but also as a prototype for its inner variety and potential universality.

In dealing with the Veda, the Hindu tradition combines strict commitment to textual and phonetic details with an extraordinary freedom of speculation. In one sense, the Veda is the sum total of its words and sounds. In another sense, it can be summarized in a few "great sayings" (*mahavakya*), or fundamental ideas. On the one hand, there is the idea that no single sound or syllable is dispensable. On the other hand, there is a persistent belief that this verbal multiplicity may be reduced to an original unity (such as the Rig Vedic *akshara*, van Buitenen 1959) or transcended towards one ultimate essence, that is, the *brahman* and its closest linguistic approximation, the *om* or *pranava* (Parpola 1981 and Svaminathan 1970/1972).

The orthodox traditionalists of the Mimamsa and of some related schools try to establish the Vedic texts as timeless, unalterable linguistic constellations, texts without divine or human author, and thus beyond the range of error and deception. They also try to demarcate once and for all the extent of genuine Vedic "revelation" (*shruti*), and to distinguish it from merely human and traditional additions or accretions. According to the most common definition, "revelation" in the strict sense comprises the Mantras and Brahmanas; that is, the collections of hymns and ritual formulae in the Rig, Yajur, and Sama Veda, together with their accompanying Brahmanas, Aranyakas, and Upanishads. While the status of the Atharvaveda remains somewhat precarious, more significant debates focus on the internal differentiation of the Vedic revelation, its modes of discourse, the different kinds of linguistic entities contained in it (*vidhi, arthavada, mantra, namadheya*), and the different types of meaning and levels of authority associated with its injunctive and factual statements.[3]

The theistic traditions, on the other hand, view the Vedas as the word of God, and as a stage in an open-ended process of revelation (Oberhammer 1974 and Heesterman 1974). In this view, they are susceptible to, and even call for, continued revisions, explications, adaptations, and other forms of divine supplementation and renewal. Furthermore, there is also room for the idea that the present Vedas are not the Veda per se, that is, its true and real archetype.[4] The "real" and original Veda is thus contrasted with the extant Vedic texts and invoked against their "orthodox" and inflexible guardians, and a dynamic sense of tradition is brought into confrontation with a static and archival one.

The Veda as Text and Reality

Understanding the role of the Veda in Indian thought involves more than textual hermeneutics. It also involves what we may call the hermeneutics of an event. The different approaches to the Veda are not just different interpretations of a text, and commitment to the Veda is not only, and not even primarily, acceptance of a doctrine. In another and perhaps more fundamental sense, it means recognition of a primeval event, and a response to a fundamental reality. In the understanding of those who accept it, the Veda itself is beginning and opening par excellence. It not only speaks, in its own elusive fashion, about the origin and structure of the world and the foundations of society; it is also their real and normative manifestation and representation.

The language of the Veda *is* primeval reality. Bhartrhari says that the Veda is the "organizing principle" (*vidhatr*) of the world, that is, not only its "teacher" or principle of instruction (*upadestr*), but also its underlying cause and essence (*prakrti*, Bhartrhari 1977, 1, 10). This may be an extreme and somewhat unusual form of expression, but the basic viewpoint it articulates is by no means isolated. The *Manusmriti*, as well as other dharma texts, characterize the Veda as an organizing and sustaining principle, and even as the real basis of the social and natural world.[5] It would be wrong to view such statements as merely metaphorical. The Veda *is* the foundation of language, of the fundamental distinctions and classifications in the world, and of those rituals which are meant to sustain the social and natural order. It is itself the primeval manifestation of those cosmogonic occurrences which establish the dharma (Halbfass 1988, ch. 17). Text and world, language and reality, are inseparable in this worldview and self-understanding.[6] The "text" itself opens and sustains the "world" in which it appears, to which it speaks, and by which its own authority has to be recognized and sustained.

Commitment to the Veda in this sense means, above all, accepting one's ritual obligations, one's dharma; that is, one's duty to renew and perpetuate the primeval occurrences represented by the Veda, and to uphold the structure of the world established by it. The recitation, memorization, and exegesis of the Vedic texts, just as the correct usage of the Sanskrit language in general, has ritual implications. The "rehearsal" (*svadhyaya*) of the Veda not only supplements the actual physical rituals, but to some extent may even replace them (Malamoud 1977).

In a sense, the Veda precedes or transcends the entire semantic dimension. This applies specifically, but not exclusively, to its mantra portions. According to Kautsa's controversial thesis, the mantras have no semantic status at all. Authoritative advocates of the tradition, such as Yaska, Shabara, and Sayana, reject Kautsa's notion of the "meaninglessness" (*anarthakya*) of the mantras.[7] Yet even they recognize the protosemantic dimension of the Vedic language, specifically of the mantras, a reality of the Vedic word that is more fundamental than any semantic functions, and that precedes the dichotomy of "word" and "meaning." Even though the mantras may not be "meaningless," the amount of information they provide is not their most significant aspect. They are, above all, "real" components of a mythical and magical world, and basic ingredients of the rituals necessary to uphold this world. As such, they have to be employed and enacted, not "understood."[8]

From the perspective of later Hindu thought, the entire Veda is sometimes associated with the idea of a protosemantic presence of "words" and "sounds." In this view, the Veda is "primarily word" (*sabdapradhana*) and thus distinguished from the Puranas, which are said to be *arthapradhana*, that is, texts in which "meaning" and "information" predominate (Renou 1960, 83 and 25, n. 8).

What then is the role and "destiny" of the Veda in later Hindu thinking and self-understanding? What are the basic hermeneutic positions and presuppositions in dealing with the Veda? What are the basic forms and patterns of its preservation and neglect, its interpretation and misinterpretation? What is implied in the "transformations" of the Vedic world to which Renou refers? What kind of continued presence does the Veda have within such transformations? What is the relationship between preservation, transformation, obscuring, and loss? Are there modes of presence and elements of continuity that remain unaffected by the growing distance and obscuring, and inherent in all the later fictions and superimpositions? In what sense is the relegation of the Veda to the distant past, this inapplicability and obsoleteness, compatible with its continued recognition and authority? Is such withdrawal from the actual world of living Hinduism, such remoteness and transcendence, perhaps a peculiar manifestation of sanctity and authority?

How can we distinguish the "real extensions" of Vedic thought and life from later projections and reinterpretations? Is there any inherent connection between these "real extensions" and the later myths and fictions *about* the Veda? Why did the Veda become the focus of so many fictions and superimpositions? Why were so many ideas that seem to be foreign to, or even incompatible with, "real" Vedic thought projected into the Veda? Does the Veda provide a genuine basis for the processes of superimposition?

In order to deal with these questions, and to account for the fictions and projections that post-Vedic India has associated with the Veda, inevitably, one must examine the extra-Vedic components of later Hinduism. But regardless of such external accretions, how does the Veda lend itself to these later developments?[9] Is there a sense in which the Veda itself has been conducive to the superimpositions and fictions attached to it? Are there reinterpretations, fictions or myths, and perhaps even forms of rejection and neglect, that are at the same time genuine effects and "real extensions" of the Veda?

Whatever the answer to these questions may be, and regardless of the highly elusive and ambiguous nature of the historical relationship between the Veda and Hinduism, the Hindu tradition has, for many centuries, defined itself in relation to the Veda. The Veda, or the idea of the Veda, has provided one indispensable focus for Hindu self-understanding. It may be true that "the Vedas defy the *dharma* of Hinduism"; yet it is also true that they have provided this dharma with its most significant point of reference and departure, and with a basis for its tenuous continuity and identity. We may even say: There would be no Hinduism without the Veda; its identity and reality depends upon the idea, or fiction, of the Veda. But what is the "reality" of Hinduism?

"Orientalist Constructions" and the Problem of Authenticity

It has often been stated that Hinduism has neither a well-defined, clearly identifiable creed nor a coherent organizational structure, and that it is not a religion in the sense of Christianity and Islam. More recently, this observation has been radicalized in various ways. There has been a tendency to call the reality of Hinduism itself into question, or to challenge the legitimacy and authenticity of the concept of Hinduism. W. Cantwell Smith says: "There are Hindus, but there is no Hinduism" (W. C. Smith 1963, 65). In his view, this concept is nothing but a foreign—Islamic and European or Christian—superimposition upon the "luxuriant welter" of a tradition that "is not a unity and does not aspire to be," and an inappropriate attempt "to systematize and congeal the spontaneous" (W. Smith 1963, 66).[10] Similarly, H. von Stietencron states that "Hinduism" is a European invention, "an orchid bred by European scholarship. ... In nature, it does not exist" (Küng and Stietencron 1987, 25).[11]

Stietencron's statement echoes P. Hacker's observation that Hinduism is nothing but a "collective label," which was produced by western scholars of religion in order to have a common designation for "the innumerable, partly cognate, partly divergent religious phenomena of one geographical and historical region" (Hacker 1978b, 480 and 290, n. 43). According to Hacker, the similarities and common denominators that can be found in this "group of religions" are primarily due to contacts and coexistence in the same area of South Asia (Hacker 1978b, 496 and 790).

From a different angle, various Indian authors have also rejected or criticized the concept of Hinduism, as well as its characterization as a religion.[12] Yet, since the early nineteenth century many other Indians have asserted the unity and identity of Hinduism, and they have tried to establish it as a religion fully commensurable with Christianity and Islam (Halbfass 1988, 341ff.). Others (and this may be the more characteristic approach) have tried to define the "essence" of Hinduism not in terms of a specific religion, but as a more comprehensive and inclusive constellation of religious thought and life, and as a potentially universal framework for religious plurality. According to this view, such religions as Islam and Christianity should not be compared to Hinduism itself, which appears as a kind of "metareligion," but to the sects or sectarian "religions" within Hinduism, such as Shaivism and Vaishnavism (Halbfass 1988, 341ff.; Halbfass 1991, ch. 3; and Radhakrishnan 1968).

Are both of these modern conceptions radical deviations from the tradition? Are they expressions of a nonauthentic self-understanding, a borrowed sense of identity, an adoption of western ways of objectifying the life and thought of the Indians? Is such a sense of "religious" identity and such an allegiance to "Hinduism," or "the Hindu way," without genuine precedent in premodern, or at least pre-Islamic, India? This is indeed the case, according to critics such as P. Hacker. In Hacker's view, questions concerning the "essence" of Hinduism have meaning only from the standpoint of Neo-Hinduism; the idea of such unity and essence is motivated by, and inseparable from, the modern Indian search for national identity (Hacker 1978b, 790).

Other, even more radical denunciations of the concept of Hinduism are associated with the critique of "Orientalism" and scholarly "discourses of domination," which has gained momentum in recent years. This movement of critique and "deconstruction" tries to expose links between the scholarly exploration and the political subjugation of India and the "Orient," to identify and eliminate Western constructs and superimpositions, and to provide a comprehensive revision of the conceptual apparatus of Oriental and Indian studies. Western Orientalists, according to such critics, have tried to "represent" the Orient, to deprive it of a genuine self-understanding, to project it as a sphere of "otherness," to objectify, categorize, and classify it in accordance with European interests of domination. More specifically, Indologists have categorized, redefined, or even invented "much of India's ancient past" (Washbrook 1988, 83). In a more or less explicit alliance with the British colonial administration, and in consonance with such measures as the census reports, they created the "caste system" in its currently accepted sense, and "Hinduism" as a clearly definable religious category. If there is a connection with premodern India, it is through the conceptualizations and theoretical norms of the Brahmans, whose writings provided the source materials for the scholars as well as the colonial administrators. Through this unholy alliance, colonialism "elevated Brahmanic formulations to the level of hegemonic text" (Raheja 1988, 498), while "Indological discourse" continued to project "the essence of Indian civilization" as "just the opposite of the West's"; that is, as the caste system and the "religion that accompanies it, Hinduism" (Inden 1986, 402). In the hands of the colonialists, "caste became an administrative tool to arrange and register Indian society into a definable sum of parts," and "helped to transform brahmanical hypocrisy into an established social fact" (Rosel 1982, 101).

There can be no doubt that the time for such critique concerning the premises, goals, and ramifications of Indian and "Oriental" studies has come. Yet it is equally obvious that its own premises and procedures, too, call for critical reflection and clarification. This may be exemplified by referring to the most famous and influential contribution in this field, Edward Said's *Orientalism* (first published in 1978).

In a broad and general sense, Said claims "that all academic knowledge about India and Egypt is somehow tinged and impressed with, violated by, the gross political fact" (Said 1979, 11) and that Orientalism as an academic discipline is "a kind of Western projection onto and will to govern over the Orient" (95). "Orientalism overrode the Orient. … Can any other than a political master-slave relation produce the Orientalized Orient?" (96). The positivism of western research appears itself as an ideology of domination; philology is a symptom of the western will to power: "There is an unmistakable aura of power about the philologist" (132). Europeans have not tried to understand the Orientals; they have tried to articulate or prescribe a self-understanding for them: "They cannot represent themselves; they must be represented."[13]

Said's book deals specifically with certain French and British approaches to the Islamic "Orient" since the end of the eighteenth century. However, these approaches appear as symptoms of much more pervasive European attitudes and of much deeper links between thought, speech, and power. In Aeschylus's drama *The Persians*, which was written after the battle of Salamis in 480 BC, Said finds a programmatic summary of the central motifs of Orientalism: "Europe is powerful and articulate; Asia is defeated and distant. Aeschylus *represents* Asia. … It is Europe that articulates the

Orient" (Said 1979, 57). What is more, F. Nietzsche and M. Foucault are invoked to enhance such critique with even more general suggestions concerning the nature of truth and the inherent connections between language, power and illusion.[14]

The rhetorical qualities of Said's procedure are obvious; its contribution to historical understanding and conceptual clarity is, however, questionable and elusive. Said merges different levels of argumentation and analysis; he confounds highly selective historical observations with broad philosophical generalizations. The specter of "Orientalism" he conjures up is a combination of very specific and very general traits. Much of what he says applies only to the European treatment of Islam, but not of other parts of Asia or the nonwestern world; other statements, though meant to depict "Orientalism," apply equally to European ways of dealing with Occidental, European phenomena. And finally, a very substantial part of what he says applies by his own admission to the encounter of civilizations and to human group behavior in general, and thus to "Oriental" as well as "Occidental" ways of dealing with "the other" and his otherness.[15] At the end, "Orientalism" emerges as a historical and conceptual hybridization that is no less a construct and projection than the so-called Orient itself.

Said does not deal explicitly with European approaches to India. This has been done by other authors. For instance, R. Inden has criticized "Orientalist constructions of India" and ways in which "Indological discourse" has denied to Indians "the power to represent themselves" and thus reinforced processes of alienation and subjugation (Inden 1986, 440). Indology, too, has projected its objects into a sphere of "otherness," has "reified" and "essentialized" them in its own way, and "has appropriated the power to represent the Oriental, to translate and explain his (and her) thoughts and acts not only to Europeans and Americans but also to the Orientals themselves" (408). In particular, it has construed the caste system as the "essence of Indian civilization" (402).

Inden's critique of Indology is by no means a mere extrapolation of Said's procedure, yet it raises some analogous questions. It, too, blends specific historical issues, concerning specific European misinterpretations and false "essentializations" of Indian phenomena, with fundamental epistemological and metaphysical questions concerning the role of essentialization and conceptual representation and construction in general. Such specific issues as the role and meaning of "castes" in medieval India require empirical historical research and efforts of understanding; so does the genesis of European constructions or misconstructions of the "caste system." The epistemological and metaphysical issues concerning "representation" and "construction" per se; that is, ultimately the very structure of our world of appearance, demand an essentially different approach. The commensurability and mutual applicability of the two sets of problems can certainly not be taken for granted;

greater efforts of reflection and clarification are called for. Moreover, what is the role of essentialization and representation in the critical process itself? What are the standards to expose false constructs and superimpositions? To what extent are "Orientalism," "Indology," and the other targets of criticism themselves constructs and imposed essences?

Another question to be addressed is: What is the relationship between European and non-European, specifically traditional Indian modes of conceptualizing and "representing" others in their otherness? It may be true that there is something unprecedented about the European ways of objectifying and representing others, and this something may have to do with what has been called the "Europeanization of the Earth." Yet in order not to be parochial and naïve, "xenological," "heterological" reflection requires a comparative perspective.

Self-questioning and the critique of Eurocentric preconceptions are necessary ingredients of any responsible study of India. However, the attempt to eliminate *all* western constructs and preconceptions and to liberate the Indian tradition from all non-Indian categories of understanding would not only be impractical, but also presumptuous in its own way. Although it would seem to be diametrically opposed to the Hegelian Eurocentric method of subordinating and superseding non-European traditions, it would raise the problem of a "reverse Eurocentrism."

"The capacity to have true knowledge and to act have to be, as it were, returned to the many Others from whom Western practices have taken it. We cannot claim to accord independence of action to a sovereign, independent India while still adhering (whether intentionally or not) to presuppositions that deny the very possibility of it" (Inden 1986, 445). The west has imposed its methods of research, its values and modes of orientation, its categories of understanding, its "epistemic absolutism" upon the Indian tradition and alienated the Indians from what they really were and are (444).[16] It now takes the liberty to remove such superimpositions, to release the Indians into their authentic selfhood, to restore their epistemic and axiological sovereignty. This self-abrogation of Eurocentrism is at the same time its ultimate affirmation.

What kind of "authenticity" would the Indian civilization have once it has been freed from "Orientalist constructions" and western "discourses of domination"? Would it be a reality and identity free from all constructs and essentializations? Would it be a reality left to indigenous, Indian, and thus "legitimate" constructions? Could it still be subject to inappropriate and illegitimate, though indigenous, constructions and superimpositions? Does the tradition itself have its own modes of alienation and epistemic subjugation?

We have referred to the argument that there has been an unholy alliance between the Brahmans and the colonialists, and that Brahmanical constructions of Indian society were adopted and translated into social reality by colonial administrators or misinterpreted as truthful descriptions of Indian society by Indological scholars. Accordingly, the exposure of western "Orientalist constructions" would have to be combined with a critique of internal, Brahmanical superimpositions and "discourses of domination," as found, for instance, in the Dharmashastra texts or the Mimamsa literature.[17]

The desire of the early "Orientalists" to find in the normative and theoretical dharma literature factual accounts of Indian society and its governance was obviously mistaken. But does this mean that such texts and their teachings are inauthentic and insignificant as far as the *reality* of the Indian civilization is concerned? Where the earlier reading may have been too literal and naïve, more recent approaches have gone to the opposite extreme, tending to explain and dismiss these texts as documents of wishful thinking and theoretical constructs, and to overlook their real authentic role in the multilayered totality of the Indian tradition.

At this point, we cannot and need not discuss to what extent the norms and precepts found in these texts have been applied or implemented, and in what sense their schemes and theories correspond to actual occurrences in society. Whatever the answer to these questions may be, the texts themselves, as well as their "theoretical" constructions, have an overwhelming presence among the extant records of the Indian civilization. Whether or not they have much value as "descriptions" of this civilization, they certainly are its products and reflections. They may be expressions of wishful thinking, attempts to legitimize divisions of society and relationships of exclusion and subordination. Yet, they are also expressions of a sense of identity and community that transcend such divisions and relationships of exclusion. They reflect a commitment to a shared structure of mutual relations, which assigns different forms of participation to different groups; that is, they are expressions of a self-understanding and sense of identity which is characterized by the idea of dharma.

The Idea of Dharma and the Coherence of Hinduism

What are the premodern antecedents of the modern ideas of "Hinduism," the "Hindu way," and so forth? Is there a traditional sense of identity or coherence that pervades what Hacker calls the "innumerable religious phenomena" of South Asia? Is there, or was there, a "reality" of Hinduism over and above the "reality" of individual Hindus? In order to answer or clarify these questions, no concept is more significant than the concept of dharma.

In the history of traditional Hinduism, *dharma* is one of the most pivotal, most symptomatic concepts. It is the key-term of "Aryan" self-understanding. Its uses exemplify the basic orientation, but also major changes, reinterpretations, and tensions in the tradition. The term refers to the primeval cosmogonic "upholding" and opening of the world and its fundamental divisions, and then to the repetition and human analogues of the cosmogonic acts in the ritual, as well as the extension of the ritual into the sphere of social and ethical norms. Subsequently, there is increasing emphasis on the "upholding" of the social and religious status quo, of the distinction between hereditary groups and levels of qualification (i.e., the *varnashramadharma*), and on the demarcation of the *arya* against the *mleccha*. The rituals and social norms which were once associated with the upholding of the universe are now primarily a means of upholding the identity and continuity of the Aryan tradition. An ancient cosmogonic term becomes a vehicle of traditionalism and ethnocentrism.

We cannot reduce the meanings of *dharma* to one general principle; nor is there one single translation that would cover all its usages. Nevertheless, there is coherence in this variety; it reflects the elusive, yet undeniable coherence of Hinduism itself, its peculiar unity-in-diversity. There is no *one* system of understanding *dharma*, but a complex network of interactions and tensions between different usages. Various groups and movements have laid claim to this fundamental term. They have reinterpreted it in different ways, and they have used it in order to challenge the "orthodox" core of the tradition. Yet these reinterpretations and competing usages were in most cases indebted to, and oriented around, the "orthodox" Brahmanocentric usages. It is easy to argue that Mimamsa and Dharmashastra do not represent the totality of the Hindu tradition; but it is also easy to underestimate their central and paradigmatic role (Halbfass 1988, 332–33).

This is not the place to discuss the specific developments that have led to the modern notion of "Hinduism," to its interpretation as a "religion," to the Neo-Hindu reinterpretations of dharma, and to the lexicographic equation, or at least coordination, of dharma and "religion" (Halbfass 1988, ch. 18). The changes are obvious and significant. It is important, however, not to overlook the traditional, premodern dimensions of unity and identity, contextuality and coherence, and the centripetal and inclusive elements in what W. Cantwell Smith calls the "luxuriant welter" of traditional Hindu life. To be sure, this is not the dogmatic and institutional identity of an "organized religion"; but on the other hand, it is neither an "Orientalist construction," nor can it be reduced to a Brahmanical fiction or projection.

It has often been suggested that in traditional India a sense of religious identity and allegiance comparable to what we have in Christianity and Islam may be found in the "sectarian" movements of Shaivism and Vaishnavism, but not with reference to "Hinduism" as such.[18] Indeed, such movements may represent self-contained religious constellations and much more immediate and obvious domains of religious commitment and identification than the wider field of "the Hindu tradition." Yet the manner in which the theoreticians and literary representatives of these theistic formations relate and refer to one another, juxtapose or coordinate their teachings, and articulate their claims of mutual inclusion or transcendence, indicates the presence of this wider field. It reflects a wider sense of identity, a sense of coherence in a shared context and of inclusion in a common framework and horizon, and it refers us to some fundamental implications of the elusive reality of "Hinduism" (Halbfass 1988, ch. 19).

The commitment to unity and identity, and the idea of one comprehensive structure and framework for the variety of Indian religious thought and life, is much more explicit and compelling in the work of such "suprasectarian" theoreticians and ideologists of the Hindu tradition as Bhartrhari, Kumarila, Shankara, Sayana, and Madhusudana Sarasvati.[19] In all these cases, the idea of a comprehensive unity of the tradition, and of a common ground of orthodoxy, is inseparable from a vision of, and commitment to, the Vedic revelation. The Veda is invoked as the source and focus of the unity and identity of the tradition, but also as the prototype of its inner variety. It is invoked against the internal, sectarian disintegration of the tradition, as well as against the "external" (*bahya*) and "heterodox" (*nastika*) challenges of Buddhism, and so forth.[20]

The modern idea of "Hinduism," or of the "Hindu religion," is a reinterpretation of the traditional ideas and, in a sense, a hybridization of the traditional self-understanding. Yet it is by no means a mere adaptation of western superimpositions. It is also a continuation of the tradition, an expression and transformation of that self-understanding which articulates itself in its commitment to the Vedic revelation. It is this commitment that provides the focus for traditional Hindu self-understanding, and that provides a paradigm and exemplary precedent even for those movements that pay little attention to the Vedic revelation, or try to supersede and replace it.

Notes

1. Renou's study has been translated into English by D. R. Channa. This translation is so awkward and unreliable that it seemed advisable to disregard it.
2. Cf. Weber 1967, 27. The German original quoted by Renou (1960, 3, n. 3) expresses such "defiance" even more strongly: "der Veda schlagt dem Dharma des Hinduismus geradezu ins Gesicht."
3. On the definition and analysis of the Veda, see, for instance, Medhatithi on Manu II, 6; Sayana's introduction to his commentary on the Rig Veda (together with Oertel 1930); Madhusudana Sarasvati, *Prasthanabheda*; Laugaksi Bhaskara, *Arthasamgraha*.

4. See, for instance, *Bhagavata Purana* IX, 14, 48: *eka eva pura vedah pranavah sarva-vanmayah.*
5. Cf. Manu II, 76ff.; III, 75; XII, 99. But see also II, 7, where the epithet *sarvajnana-maya* should be construed with *veda*, not *manu*; cf. Wezler 1982, specifically 90ff., on Medhatithi's explanation of the Veda as *sarvajnanamaya.*
6. The Veda itself frequently presents itself as a cosmic or cosmogonic reality. See, for instance, *Rig Veda* X, 90, 9; for numerous other references, cf. Muir 1976, III, 3, ff.
7. On the Kautsa controversy, cf. Renou 1960, 68ff. The most important references are Yaska, *Nirukta* I, 15f.; Sabara on MS I, 2, 31–53; on Sayana, cf. Oertel 1930, 15–26, 53–72. See also Alper 1989.
8. Cf. the role of the *dharani* in Tantrism; in various significant ways, the Tantric approach to the reality and real power of words, and their association with cosmogonic events, continues the Vedic tradition.
9. We should, of course, not forget that the Vedic texts do not necessarily present a full picture of the religious thought and life of the Vedic period. What we tend to regard as "later" elements of Hinduism may, to some extent, have coexisted with what is documented in the Vedic texts.
10. Above and beyond his specific critique of the concept of Hinduism, Smith rejects any attempt to "reify" or "essentialize" the personal faiths of human beings, and he considers the very idea of "religions," and of "religion" itself, as inadequate; see Baird 1971, 91–106.
11. For further valuable and challenging comments on this issue, see Stietencron 1997.
12. Halbfass 1988, ch. 18 (on Bankim Chandra Chatterji and S. V. Ketkar); see also Joshi 1948.
13. This quote from *The Eighteenth Brumaire of Louis Bonaparte* by K. Marx serves as the motto of Said's book. In Marx's own context, the sentence has no reference to the "Orient."
14. Cf. Said 1979, 203 (Nietzsche on language and truth), 94 (Foucault's concept of discourse), but see also 23: "Yet unlike Michel Foucault, to whose work I am greatly indebted, I do believe in the determining imprint of individual writers upon the otherwise anonymous collective body of texts constituting a discursive formation like Orientalism."
15. Said himself notes casually (1979, 204) that "imperialism, racism, and ethnocentrism," which his book associates very specifically with the *European* phenomenon of "Orientalism," are, in fact, common attributes of the way in which "human societies, at least the more advanced cultures" have dealt with "other" cultures.
16. Inden wants "to produce a world that is more egalitarian and multi-centered" (1986, 445); this project in itself is obviously rooted in European ideals and ideologies and "Eurocentric" in its own way.
17. The idea of an internal Indian "Orientalism" has, indeed, been suggested by Pollock 1993a.
18. For their part, Indian authors have often argued that the western notion of religion has fundamentally sectarian connotations and corresponds to what has been called *sampradaya* in the Indian tradition; see, for instance, Ketkar 1988, 155.
19. Among these authors, Shankara himself has become one of the symbols of the fundamental unity of Hinduism; he appears in this role, perhaps in response to the Islamic challenge, in such works as the *Sankaradigvijaya* by Madhava-Vidyaranya.
20. On the use of the term *bahya* see, for instance, Medhatithi on Manu II, 6 (Manu 1972–1985, 168); on the distinction between *nastika* and *astika,* see Halbfass 1988, ch. 19.

2

ANCIENT BANYAN: AN INQUIRY INTO THE MEANING OF "HINDUNESS"

Julius J. Lipner

This is by way of an experimental, and hence exploratory, paper.[1] The evidence as I see it, however, has been accumulating for some time, not only from my own researches, but from the work of other scholars in the field. The time has come to test this hypothesis in the forum of public scrutiny. If this proves worthwhile, it may be fruitful to continue the analysis, for I offer nothing less than a Garuda eye view, from one perspective, of my subject and a proposal for its further study.[2]

My evidence is drawn mainly from the Sanskritic textual tradition, examined from a historical-philosophical point of view. Of necessity, because it is still being collated and space is limited, it is here sketchy and incomplete. Still, I have tried to give a representative sample sufficient to make the hypothesis worthy of serious consideration. Its Sanskritic nature may be a distinct advantage in so far as this would indicate a dominant *mentalité* of the Hindu traditions which may well be expected to seek practical applications. Indeed, there is reason to believe that this form of *theoria* seeks wide-ranging expression in practice.[3] Strictly speaking, the practical implementation of my thesis is a separate issue—*theoria* does not necessarily work out or work into *praxis*—but if apparently supportive ethnographic evidence is forthcoming, this at least may not detract from my position and indeed may be explained by it. Finally, comparative study will be required to show whether the putative distinctiveness of "Hinduism" suggested here is also *unique*, if not in kind then at least in degree.

Here an analogy might be useful. Consider the magnificent banyan tree (*Ficus bengalhensis*) of the Calcutta Botanical Gardens. As a banyan, it has the characteristic of sending down aerial shoots, many of which have grown

thick and strong to resemble individual tree trunks. As an ancient and pro-
liferating banyan, it resembles an interconnected collection of trees and
branches without any obvious botanic center.[4] Put simplistically, the conception of Hinduism I wish to propose is something like this: it is macrocosmically one though microcosmically many, a polycentric phenomenon
imbued with the same life-sap, the boundaries and (micro)centers seeming to
merge and overlap in a *complexus* of oscillating tensions. Further, unlike the
botanic model, the Hindu banyan does not appear uniform to view. Rather,
it is a network of variety, one complex shading into another and so forming
a multifaceted unity.

The advantage of this analogy is twofold. First, it helps us to side-step the
objection that we may be arguing in a circle. In other words, the analogy
helps us to see how the examples I will adduce in this paper to substantiate
my thesis are uncontroversially integral to what passes for Hinduism, certainly in the world of scholarship.[5] We do not first have to justify some definition of "Hindu" in order to be able to adduce the examples! Second, the
analogy provides a living, visualizable and pervasive basis for the conceptual
and abstract arguments I deploy.

My paper is divided into two unequal parts. In Section I, I shall make
some clarificatory comments about the plural nature of religion in general (or
at least of the so-called world-religions), of which Hinduism is a particular
instance.[6] This will help us to distinguish between "Hinduism" and "Hinduness," at least for the purposes of this paper. In Section II, I shall explore
and argue for (minimally) a, if not *the*, chief characteristic of Hinduness,
that is, of what it means to be Hindu, in terms of this distinction.

I

I think it is generally accepted, and indeed must be accepted from the evidence at hand, that the major religious traditions of the world are both
extrinsically and intrinsically plural. They are extrinsically plural in the
obvious sense that we label them differently, as Buddhism, Christianity,
Hinduism, Islam, Judaism, Sikhism, and so forth. Though it is true that the
boundaries between some of the phenomena thus labeled differently are
blurred (so that hyphenated labels sometimes seem more appropriate), and
that it would be misguided to submit, as many do, to the tyranny of some
religiocultural labeling game, there is a proper sense in which these labels
are separately applicable, both inside and outside the world of scholarship.
This paper is properly about "Hinduism" and not about "Judaism." Without the signposting such names provide, it would be impossible not only to
undertake and communicate research about religion, but also to function
religiously. I need not labor the point.

But these religious traditions are also intrinsically plural. We are familiar with the fact—their ongoing conflict-ridden narratives are all too salient—that each comprises different denominations clustering under the same label. What does this mean? That each denomination is a species of an underlying, homogenizing essence or genus? Wilfred Smith, in his seminal *The Meaning and End of Religion,* has pointed out that this is not so. We must abandon the western tendency of "reification," he admonishes, of "mentally making religion into a thing, gradually coming to conceive [of] it as an objective systematic entity" (W. Smith 1978, 51, and chs. two and three). It would be misguided to impose an essentialist understanding on these religious phenomena.

Here another analogy might be helpful, one which enables us to introduce the element of heterogeneity in our (Hindu) banyan model. According to this analogy, the various designations for the world religions may be regarded as cluster-terms for different families comprising what may be described as "belonger" traditions.[7] Just as in an extended family individual members, not excluding distant cousins, may be identified as belonging to that family on the basis of shared characteristics in various permutations and combinations, so in the different families of religions individual traditions may be identified as belonging to a particular family on the basis of shared characteristics. These characteristics may include a distinctive form of discourse, a particular set of symbols and/or myths, a specific pattern of behavior, and so on. This analogy allows for the difference-in-identity that is the mark of the major religious traditions. It is also open-ended in that it accommodates the, to some extent arbitrary, element of decision. We know that it is sometimes necessary to decide, that is, to impose criteria, as to whether a particular individual belongs to a particular family or not. Similarly, it may be necessary to decide as to the identity of a particular religious tradition. In other cases, this decision may be left open. Either way, the point of all this is that it must be recognized that we can no longer write descriptively about a particular religious tradition under such titles as "The Hindu View of Life,"[8] where one tradition/denomination among many is made to assimilate or act as the standard for the others. Because religions are intrinsically plural phenomena, such works must be recognized for what they are: prescriptive and/or programmatic approaches to their subject-matter.

From these comments it would be reasonable to infer, I think, that Hinduism is a distinctive and heterogeneous phenomenon. We must now distinguish, for the purposes of this paper, between "Hinduism" and "Hinduness." In our reckoning, "Hinduism" is not a cover-term for a reifying process, the expression of some closed construct; this would be to distort methodologically the reality it seeks to designate. Since many people (including scholars) seem to use the term in this way, it has been suggested that we do away with such abstract religious designations altogether.[9] But this is both impracticable and undesirable. If we use the term and its colleagues (e.g., "Christianity," "Buddhism," etc.) to express an open construct, that is, an intrinsically plural phenomenon, it can continue in useful service, making a virtue of what has become a practical necessity.

In this usage the term "Hinduism" refers to a family of religious traditions whose kinship is based on the distinctive characteristic of "Hinduness." "Hinduness" denotes a particular orientation in the world, a specific way of being, a distinctive *mentalité*. It is the purpose of this paper to seek to identify at least *a* chief mark of Hinduness.[10]

At this stage it will be helpful to inquire into the Sanskrit terminological equivalent of "Hinduness." For the rationale underlying this Sanskritic construction will help us to see how we might properly set about our task of exploring the nature of Hinduness. In Sanskrit, the terminological equivalent of "Hinduness" is either *hindutva* or *hinduta*. Terminologically both mean exactly the same thing. *Hindutva* or *hinduta* is a perfectly regular construction formed by the application of a well-known grammatical rule in Sanskrit, that is, rule 5.1.119 in the grammarian Panini's magisterial work, the *Ashtadhyayi*. Introducing the (*taddhita*) suffixes *-tva* and *-ta*, Panini comments: *tasya bhavas tvatalau.* This may be construed as follows: "The abstract noun formed when either the suffix *-tva* or the suffix *-ta* is added to a nominal stem denotes a state or condition as identified by that nominal stem."

We could say that the abstract noun thus formed denotes a property. Linguistically, no implicit statement is being made about the kind of thing that that property may be. Rather, a statement is being made about a specific way of being of the property-possessor. Thus, to predicate *sat-ta* or "beingness" of something, is not, on the basis of its linguistic construction, to imply that the property "beingness" is some thing; it is only to say that its property-possessor exists in a certain way, that is, really rather then notionally. Again, to say that someone has "blindness" (*andha-tva*) is not *ipso facto* to make some metaphysical statement about blindness, for example, that it is a kind of thing. Rather, it is to say that the person who has blindness—that is, the blind person—exists in a certain way, the way that we understand to be identified by the use of the (Sanskrit) nominal stem for "blindness."

Determining the metaphysical status of the property identified by the particular *-tva* or *-ta* suffix is a further question, a task for the philosophers. And indeed there has been a protracted and sophisticated debate in the Sanskritic philosophical tradition, between "Hindus," Buddhists, and Jains, about the status of properties thus denoted (Bhattacharyya 1990, especially ch. 3; Matilal 1985, especially ch. 2). Similarly, to speak of *hindutva/-ta* is not, on the basis of the construction alone—if the spirit of Panini's rule is to be followed—to make a metaphysical statement, to pronounce on the kind of thing that *hindutva/-ta* ("Hinduness") might be; it is only to refer to a way of being, to an orientation or stance in the world.

However, in the political arena in India today, the grammar of the term *hindutva* is being misused precisely in the way suggested above. For this term is being appropriated by extremist Hindu rightwing elements to refer, apparently *ipso facto*, not only to a way of being, but also to a kind of thing, "a reality in its own right ... for which followers are prepared to fight and even die, and which can be used as a weapon to beat the opponent with" (Lipner 1992, 7). And if it is used to refer to an attribute, then this is an attribute whose reality-status enfranchises the attribute-possessor and disenfranchises everybody else.[11] It is for this reason that I eschew the use of *hindutva* for "Hinduness" in this essay, and suggest, for the purpose of value-neutral discourse, not only in this essay but in general, the use of *hinduta* for "Hinduness."

My purpose in this paper, then, is to make neither a metaphysical nor an ideological statement, but, taking my cue from the term *hinduta*'s open-ended grammatical origins, to inquire into the kind of way of being, of life-orientation, that it seems to intimate.

II

We can now survey some of the evidence collated. Let me start with the philosophical theology of the classical Vedantin, Ramanuja (eleventh–twelfth century CE). Ramanuja is an extremely influential thinker for a number of Hindu schools from his time to the present day, so we are not inquiring into views that are marginal to the multi-currented stream of Veda-based Hinduism. A key concept in Ramanuja's thought is that the "world" is the supreme Being, Brahman's, "body." Both "world" and "body" here are to be understood in a special sense. "World" stands for the aggregate of individual, finite beings. For Ramanuja, each individual substantival being, as well as the aggregate of such beings, is the "body" of Brahman. And that is the "body" of Brahman which depends on Brahman in a threefold relationship: (i) it exists to be supported (*adheya*) by Brahman which is its support (*adhara*); (ii) it is to be controlled (*niyamya*, *sic*) by Brahman which is its controller (*niyanta*); and (iii) it is the accessory or "remainder" in respect of Brahman, its "whole," or "goal," or "end" (*sheshin*).

I have argued, in my book on Ramanuja, that the various aspects of his body-of-God theology can best be understood in terms of a system of polarities.

By "polarity" here I mean a more or less stable tension between two (possibly more) poles such that this tension is resolvable into two mutually opposing but synchronous tendencies. One tendency is "centripetal," whereby the poles are attracted to each other; the other is "centrifugal," keeping the poles apart. Each tendency by itself is destructive of the polarity as a whole, but as simultaneously corrective of each other the tendencies work towards preserving the dynamic equilibrium of the system. The centripetal and centrifugal tendencies comprising a polarity can each be articulated in terms of a distinctive but mutually complementary mode of discourse. Each polarity itself is translatable into its own appropriate and more or less self-contained pattern of speech which ultimately ... must be integrated into the universe of discourse of the polarity-system as a whole (Lipner 1986, 134).

Let us give one or two examples to clarify my point. Consider Brahman's originative (i.e., "creative") causality in Ramanuja's thought. For Ramanuja, Brahman is simultaneously the *upadana-karana* (the "resource" or "material" cause[12]) and the *nimitta karana* (the "efficient" cause) of the world, that is, of the aggregate of individual beings, and of each individual being considered separately.

The *upadana-karana* is that out of which something arises; thus clay is the *upadana-karana* of the clay pot. On the basis of salient Upanishadic texts (e.g., *Chandogya Upanisad* 6.1.4f.), Ramanuja says that Brahman is the *upadana-karana* of the world.

This accentuates the identity between infinite and finite being in Ramanuja's theology of "identity-in-difference." Now this way of talking can be said to be "centripetal" in that it tends to collapse the Brahman-pole and the world-pole into each other by its "kenotic" emphasis. It empties out, in a manner of speaking, Brahman's reality into the world, identifying the reality of the cause too closely with that of the effect. By seeking to do justice to the utter derivativeness of the world's being, it threatens the transcendence of that being's originative cause (Lipner 1986, 135).

Indeed, Ramanuja goes so far as to describe the world from this perspective as "the effected Brahman" (Lipner 1986, ch. 5). The problem of this mode of discourse for the theist that Ramanuja indubitably was is that it seems to entail the supreme being's pantheistic involvement with the world's natural limitations and imperfections.

To counter this, Ramanuja provided "centrifugal" correctives. The main such corrective was to speak of Brahman as the *nimitta-karana* or efficient cause of the world. In traditional Hindu philosophical discourse, the *nimitta-karana* is that which, while remaining ontologically distinct from the effect, brings the latter about; thus, the potter is the *nimitta-karana* of the clay pot. By referring simultaneously to Brahman as the world's *nimitta-karana* (as well as its *upadana-karana*), Ramanuja wishes to stress the difference between infinite and finite being in their "identity-in-difference" causal relationship.

As the world's efficient cause, Brahman initiates and sustains the action which brings the world into being. This mode of discourse is "centrifugal" since the Brahman-pole and the world-pole are sought to be kept apart and "the way is open for that distinctive theological talk which is mindful of the Lord's essential transcendence, perfection and ontological sovereignty in relation to the world" (Lipner 1986, 135). These two modes of discourse fall under the first, that is, "supportive" (*adhara-adheya*), constitutive relationship of Ramanuja's body-of-God theology. For both indicate—and it is their combined effect that is crucial here—the peculiarly intimate yet transcendent way in which Brahman ontologically supports the world, in its totality and in its individual components.[13]

Ramanuja acknowledges that objects of empirical experience cannot simultaneously be *upadana* and *nimitta karana* with respect to the same effect. But then experience and knowledge of Brahman is based on scripture, and Brahman is *vijatiya*: not akin to objects of everyday experience. It is not my purpose here to defend this conception of the supreme being. We are concerned rather with the kind of theologizing that Ramanuja is about. Ramanuja's God is not some substantival, monocentric being: philosophically, a congealed Absolute depicted as intrinsically utterly self-bounded and self-sufficient ("infinite" in contrast to "finite"); theologically, a fortress-God, existing in personal, self-reflexive bliss from whose distant stronghold of transcendence acts of creation, judgment or salvific grace variously emanate.[14] Ramanuja's God, though personal, is a fluid reality, pouring out creative, compassionating being into and, indeed, as the world from one point of view, and yet from another, distinct from the world's evils and natural limitations. This is what it means to say perspectivally that the world is Brahman's "body." For Ramanuja, Brahman's central attributes extend to the limits of its outreach as metaphysically creative, epistemically pan-referential, and salvifically fruitful, in such a way as to "in-form" finitude without violating its alterity. In this sense, Ramanuja's God is a polycentric reality who yet remains the subject of devotional, theistic discourse as creator, sustainer and savior.

Let us note one more example of this multicentrism, or of Ramanuja's polarity theology. This concerns the *shesha-sheshin* ("remainder-fulfiller") relationship of the tri-relational body-of-God scheme. This mode of discourse accommodates reference to Brahman as causal and devotional Lord (*ishvara*), Sovereign over all. "The *shesha-sheshin* relationship in all cases is as follows," says Ramanuja. "That whose proper nature is to exist in subservience to the due superiority of another is the *shesha*; that other is the *sheshin*" (Lipner 1986, 174, n. 24). To be the *sheshin* of something then is to be the fulfillment or goal of that thing. A value judgment is implied here. The *sheshin* is the value-bestower, the *shesha* is what is "remaindered" in the relationship. Paraphrasing words of Krishna, the supreme being who had descended in human form, to his devotee Arjuna, under *Bhagavad Gita*

6.47, Ramanuja describes a universal aspect of the *shesha-sheshin* relationship as follows: "[Serve and worship] Me ... as illumining the whole world by My unlimited and surpassing luster, gladdening the Universe by the beauty of My self" (Lipner 1986, 174, n. 31). In other words, the Lord is the jewel, that is, the seat of value, the aesthetic focus, in the setting of our lives and of the world.

This kind of language is explicitly "centripetal," tending to assimilate all worth and beauty to the divine being. But it would also convey "centrifugal" resonances to any attuned hearer. For *shesha* has connotations of the "remnant" or "leavings" in traditional worship.[15] In the context of devotional worship, the remnant functions as the medium by which the deity and devotee are (temporarily) identified (see, e.g., Fuller 1992, ch. 3, esp. pp. 72f.). So from this standpoint, in Ramanuja's theology, the worshipper and/or the world, as God's body, is the (divinized) locus of beauty and value *per se*. As Ramanuja makes clear, on the microcosmic level this valorizing principle is the human spirit (*atman*), which in all its inter-subjective relationships (including relationships with the deity) must be treated as an end-in-itself. So again, the qualities of the divine center pervade the boundaries in terms of an equilibrating tension between centripetal and centrifugal regulators of perspective and discourse. This kind of de-centering conceptual tendency on the one hand and its concurrent counterpart, a perspectival (and potentially plural) re-centering on the other, this dynamic polycentrism—which may well generate characteristic social, moral and behavioral consequences—is, I contend, at least *a* chief distinctive mark of Hinduness (*hinduta*) and the focus of this essay.

In characteristic Hindu fashion, *hinduta*, thus identified, itself manifests variously. We have begun with a particular instance; we can now go on to more wide-ranging examples. Consider the sense and symbolism implied by the term Veda. Originally Veda referred to that sacrificial knowledge which brings about relative or ultimate human fulfillment, and to the fourfold textual repository of that knowledge, that is, the Rig, Yajur, Sama and Atharva "Vedas." This canon, usually divided into two parts (the *karmakanda* or ritual section and the *jnanakanda* or wisdom section), took about a millennium and a half to develop (from about 1200 BCE to 200 CE), and, as is to be expected, was subjected to different interpretations. Be that as it may, Vedic knowledge, however interpreted, in the Sanskritic tradition became the preserve of *dvijas* or twice-born males, that is, those who had undergone a second, accredited ritual birth. Excluded from this category were all females and those males regarded as *non-dvija* or Shudra.

In time, other texts developed, also described as "Veda," which were regarded by their votaries in the Sanskritic tradition as salvific for all, not excluding females and Shudra males. These texts included the *Puranas*, folk-loric in content (from about the third century CE in their present form), a nd a voluminous epic, the *Mahabharata* (c. fourth century BCE–fourth century CE).[16]

The point is that when these other texts are described as "Veda" or are explicitly equated with it, they are not being set up as rivals of the originals, but are being posited as in a real sense alternative forms of the originals, en- capsulating their saving/fulfilling knowledge in a more accessible way. The originals continue to function as the standard symbol of (orthodox) scrip- tural authority which the "alternative" Vedas supplant in a representative capacity. Thus the authority of the originals is not lost or lessened; rather, it is enhanced in so far as it is seen as being exercised undiminished in the alternatives. How this simultaneously de-centering and re-centering process— this equilibrating strategy—in respect of Veda-polycentrism takes place is ex- pressed variously. Let us consider one or two examples.

The first is taken from the still important Shaiva Siddhanta tradition, which has had a long history. This tradition has a fourfold scripture: "the Vedas ... the twenty-eight *Shaiva* Agamas, the twelve *Tirumurai*, and the fourteen *Meykanta Shastras*" (Dhavamony 1971, 4). Briefly and simplisti- cally, the Agamas, composed in Tamil and in Sanskrit, give guidance for the Shaiva Siddhanta way of life; the *Tirumurai* (c. twelfth century but containing much earlier material) are devotional compositions in Tamil by poet-mystics; and the *Meykanta Shastras* (c. twelfth–fourteenth centuries) are theological treatises. Here we are interested in the relationship posited between the Vedas and the other three groups of scripture.

The *Tirumurai* are on occasion referred to by Shaiva Siddhantins as the Tamil Veda. This seeks to legitimize their content as salvific as a kind of extension of or alternative to the traditional Veda. The *Agamas* too are invested with Vedic authority, notwithstanding the fact that they contain a number of remarks which imply a rejection of the religion of the traditional Vedas in favor of wholehearted devotion to Shiva. Dhavamony quotes Tiru- mular, one of the contributors to the *Tirumurai*, as saying: "The Vedas and the *Agamas* are both true and both are the word of God. The first is a general treatise and the second a special one. When examined and where difference is perceived by some between the Vedanta and the Siddhanta, the wise will perceive no such difference" (Dhavamony 1971, 4). The strategy here is to validate the *Agamas* as a later, "special revelation" of the Vedas. According to this reasoning, they make explicit, for a particular clientele, the more obscure salvific content of the Veda. Understood aright, they re-present the Veda more clearly in and for a different context; they are not antagonistic to the Veda.

Again, we are told that the theologian Shrikantha Shivacarya declared that there was no salvific difference between the Vedas and the *Shaiva Agamas*: "Shaiva Agama is twofold, one being intended for the three higher castes, the other being intended for all. The Vedas are intended for people of the three classes, and the other for all" (Dhavamony 1971, 4). This time the Vedas are socioreligiously a more restricted form of the "same" revelation as in the egalitarian *Agamas*. Either way, whether the distinction is based on general or special revelation or on more or less restricted access, apparently extra-Vedic or anti-Vedic texts are assimilated to the traditional Vedas. The boundaries of accredited canonical scripture have been extended so that a multicentrism of scriptural authority is set up, a multicentrism that diffuses but does not emasculate the authority of any one center. Indeed, a consequence is an interactive polarization between these centers. In our example, the *Agamas*, the *Tirumurai* and the Vedas are properly comprehended (at least in theory) only in terms of simultaneous mutual cross-referencing. Theoretically, no one pole dominates interpretatively. The "polycentrism" here is a de-centering/re-centering oscillatory process. Such Veda-polycentrism, articulated variously, is an extensive phenomenon in Hindu tradition. We need not dwell on it further (for more examples see Lipner 1994, 58–62). Instead let us turn to another example of the facet of *hinduta* under discussion.

This time we inquire into the key term *dharma*, which may be translated as "that which supports right living." This stands for a pervasive notion in the Sanskritic tradition, of course, but one way to derive a leading insight into the way the term signifies on a popular level in the textual tradition is to fix upon what appears to be a seminal text of Sanskritic folklore and explore the connotations of the term in that text. We have chosen the dicing incident in the *Mahabharata* for this purpose. By general consent, the *Mahabharata* has a central place in the Hindu tradition, and the dicing incident is pivotal for the unfolding of the *Mahabharata* narrative.[17]

Briefly, the episodic story is as follows.[18] King Yudhishthira, eldest and head of the five Pandava brothers (all of whom, unusually for Sanskritic literature, are married to the same woman, Draupadi) has been invited to a game of dice by his cousin and rival, Duryodhana, the eldest brother of the Kaurava scions. Duryodhana plans to win the game by cheating, at heavy cost to Yudhishthira, as a way of exacting revenge for humiliations suffered earlier when he was a guest of the Pandavas. The game is to be played in the assembly hall of the Kauravas, and the Pandavas and their common wife, Draupadi, duly arrive for the "friendly" match. As the story develops, the dicing match turns out to be anything but friendly. In a highly dramatic narrative, Yudhishthira loses inexorably to Duryodhana's uncle Shakuni, a master trickster who plays on Duryodhana's behalf. Yudhishthira progressively loses his kingdom, his brothers, himself and their joint wife, Draupadi. After Draupadi has been staked and lost, some of the leading Kauravas seek to humiliate her in the assembly hall. But miraculously she is saved the final humiliation of being publicly stripped. The *dharma* of her status, in terms of the burning question, "Was Draupadi rightfully staked, seeing that Yudhishthira had gambled himself away *before* he staked her?" is hotly debated in the assembly. Ultimately Draupadi is vindicated by the turn of events, their kingdom and their freedom are restored to the Pandavas, and together with Draupadi they return home, the scene having been set for the fateful continuation of the main story.

In keeping with the polycentric method of which we speak, there is more than one focus for the exploration of the meaning of *dharma* in the narrative. There are, among others, the Kauravas, especially Duryodhana and Shakuni, and the Pandavas, especially Yudhishthira and Draupadi. Let us ourselves focus on Yudhishthira, significantly called "Dharmaraja," Dharma-King. At the nadir of his desperation, when all seems to have been lost, he is portrayed as passive and helpless, bound, the text suggests, by the noose of *dharma*.

Consider the dharmic pulls—the multiple nooses—of which he is a nodal point. He is described as a virtuous king, a man of his word, with a weakness for gambling. Yet it is precisely with this in mind that Duryodhana invites him to a game of chance with the intention of cheating him. Yudhishthira does not know (but suspects) that he is being cheated; so, is his word his bond as he takes on fate (*daiva*), with all the dire consequences of such a game? Yudhishthira did not have to gamble everything progressively away, yet how free was he in the circumstances, granted that he had a passion for gambling in the first place and that the dice were loaded? As a kingly member of the Kshatriya or warrior caste, he was particularly constrained by the dharmic pull of abiding by the agreed stakes honorably, and yet—as king, eldest brother and cohusband—of protecting the relevant individuals under his charge (especially his brothers and Draupadi). The pulls of free-will and of fate, of being a Kshatriya and a king, of being the eldest brother and cohusband, and of a final dubious stake in a dubious game of chance—these are some of the main dharmic nooses exerting their pressures on the hapless "Dharma-King." In this whirl of circumstances, what was the *dharma* of the situation where he was concerned? As if in response, the text says through several characters that *dharma* is subtle (*sukshma*) and hard to fathom. The message is clear: *dharma* is not a monolithic concept with a hard center, susceptible of being cracked interpretatively in problem-situations with unambiguous certitude. On the contrary, it is a fluid notion analyzable into interactive semantic polarities, and generally applicable in life's complexities with only ambivalent or tentative certainty.

The text itself seems to recommend this interpretation of *dharma*. An impasse is reached in the assembly-hall during the debate on the *dharma* of Draupadi's predicament. The impasse is breached not by some dharmic answer tailor-mode for the situation, but by an unexpected intervention. A jackal howls during a ritual being conducted in the vicinity. This and other inauspicious signs bring Dhritarashtra, the blind paterfamilias of both the Kauravas and the Pandavas, to his senses. Acknowledging Draupadi's violated innocence, he offers her three boons in compensation. She accepts two, and secures the release of the Pandavas (and herself included). In addition, their kingdom is restored to them by Dhritarashtra.

Interpretatively, no attempt is made to untie the Gordian knot of the dharmic problematic generated by the episode. Rather, it is severed at a stroke by the literary device of the unexpected boons. The teaching is that *dharma* cannot be absolutized; there is no master-solution to life's apparently intractable problems. Each one must decide, amid the conflicting dharmic pulls experienced, as to what is righteous in the circumstances. *Dharma* is a polycentric concept, and its responsible implementation in a particular case is the result of a personal decision arrived at within the existing rational and other guidelines available. This is what it means to say that *dharma* is "subtle" and hard to understand.[19]

What we have sought—all too briefly—is a revealing glimpse into the semantic heart of *dharma* at what may be called the precritical level, that is, in the embeddedness of folkloric narrative. This is why we have had recourse to a key text of the *Mahabharata*.[20] For it is at this level, and not at that of reconstructive ideologies or theories, that we may presume to make contact with the most basic semantic content of the term. At this level it seems, then, that *dharma is* semantically open-ended in the way we have described.

In a more explicitly ideological context, we can see distortive pressures at work on the meaning of the term. Consider the use of the expression *sanatana dharma* (i.e., "eternal *dharma*") by some militant rightwing Hindu groups in India today. For these groups, *sanatana dharma* has a fixed, non-negotiable meaning. It is accorded a creedal, divisive function, identifying those who subscribe to this creed as religiopolitically preferential to those who do not or cannot. As we all know, attempts to enforce this distinction have been highly destructive. I suggest they have also been un-Hindu.

Another example of the ideological use of *sanatana dharma*, this time on a philosophical plane and in less sinister circumstances, has been that of the well-known thinker, S. Radhakrishnan (1888–1975). For Radhakrishnan, the expression becomes the Hindu equivalent of *philosophia perennis*, and refers to a way of life ("the Hindu way of life") based on an Advaitic or monistic outlook, which he regards as normative for human spiritual development.[21] It is hard to see how such ideological appropriations of the semantics of *dharma* can accommodate the much-vaunted claim of traditional Hindu tolerance, whether doctrinally or otherwise. On the contrary, it would seem that it is our own semantically fluid interpretation of *dharma*, for which we claim historical, textual authenticity, which is most conducive to behavioral and doctrinal tolerance.

Significant work by other scholars on other themes also approximates to what I have tried to articulate in this essay. In her book, *Banaras: City of Light*, Diana Eck makes a telling comment on the way sacred space tends to be structured in (religious) Hindu lives and writings (a phenomenon in evidence far beyond the obvious limits of the Sanskritic tradition). After having stressed the "most widely acclaimed" nature of Kashi (Banaras) as an ancient *tirtha* or sacred ford for Hindu pilgrims across the denominational divides, Eck writes:

> A place such as Kashi is important, even supreme, without being unique. ... To celebrate one god or one *tirtha* need not mean to celebrate *only* one. Far from standing alone, Kashi, like a crystal, gathers and refracts the light of other pilgrimage places. Not only are other *tirthas* said to be present in Kashi, but Kashi is present elsewhere. [As examples, she mentions the "northern Kashi" at the headwaters of the Ganges, and a southern Kashi and a Shiva Kashi in the Tamil South.] This kind of "transposition of place" is a common phenomenon in Indian [i.e., Hindu] sacred topography ... the affirmation is that the place itself, with its sacred power, is present in more than one place. ... In a similar way, the River Ganges is a prototype for other sacred waters (Eck 1983, 39–41).

Eck speaks of the phenomenon of something sacred being perceived by Hindus to exist crystal-like, not only synchronously, but also diachronically. In other words, as in the case of the Vedas discussed earlier, one prototypical reality—a ford, the transcendent being (or indeed, a deity), a river—extends itself polycentrically, through a tracery of multiple and interactive self-referencing presences.[22]

Lack of space, primarily, constrains us to give only one further example of Hindu polycentrism. I refer to David D. Shulman's well-known work, *The King and the Clown in South Indian Myth and Poetry*, which has only recently come to my attention. Shulman writes with a different end in view, but his argument can be seen to favor my thesis. In his study, which derives much inspiration from the work of J. Heesterman, Shulman analyses, in depth, king and clown figures mainly in Tamil and Sanskrit texts. Though the main scope of his book is ostensibly the Chola rulers in the area corresponding to present-day Tanjore district from the mid-ninth to the late thirteenth centuries (described by Shulman as "a classical apogee" in literature and the arts), it is significant how time and again he is drawn to generalized conclusions based on corroborative analyses of texts and events well beyond this focus.

It may well be that Shulman tends to overinterpret some of his material (the section on Kama [Shulman 1985, ch. 7.7] seems to be a case in point), but I believe that the overall rigor and plausibility of his analysis is undeniable. The upshot of his study, as I understand it, is that over a range of texts and times, kings, clowns and Brahmans, described as pivotal characters in the predominantly Hindu culture considered, emerge as essentially unstable figures which articulate their fluid identities in a nexus of polycentric relationships. These:

> major symbolic types ... are composite figures incorporating multiple personae, which come into view and then dissolve in relation to other such identities. ... In conjunction with one another, [they] appear to unfold their hidden aspects in kaleidoscopic patterns; isolated, they recede before our gaze or disappear into their own antithesis (Shulman 1985, 39).

Painting a "synthetic portrait of the medieval South Indian state," Shulman contends that in this state "no single center exists ... the state has no real boundaries. Instead, [one] would gradually become aware of a varied, shifting series of centers of different kinds and functions, connected with various interlocking networks" (21). Shulman lists various entities—local kings and supralocal ones, temples, deities, Brahmanical academies, local heroes and so on—which function as shifting centers in a polyvalent system. It is in this general context of fluid identities and roles that he can speak of an "unending oscillation of poles, [a] creative and energizing imbalance" (128–29), of centers that are "ambiguous, open-ended, inclusive of ordered limits as well as of their transcendence, and given to dynamic movement and transformation" (195), of the clown's "habit of dissolving boundaries and categories ... and of producing incongruous combinations" (265), of the Brahman "basically divided into two related, tensely oscillating halves" (372), and of the king sporting "a chameleonlike parade of identities ... in his innermost being ... nothing but a melange of self-substitutes" (372). Once more, in a study of sustained analysis and depth, we come across an at least inchoate expression of that characteristic of *hinduta* that it has been the purpose of this essay to identify, a phenomenon which itself manifests with subtle variety and emphases in its concrete forms.

By trying to adduce evidence that in the end can only be cumulative, I have sought to intimate in a way that I hope encourages further inquiry and debate, what a chief attribute of Hinduness might be: a *mentalité*, a leading tendency, of simultaneously shifting yet equilibrating perspectives whose conceptual and behavioral focuses are more stages of semantic transition than points of stasis. Thus is engendered a religion, a culture, of calculated paradoxicality—of "fire and ice," to use W. D. O'Flaherty's (1973, 82) memorable phrase—where the cool detachment of shifting and pliable conceptual structures tempers the absolutist ardor of the quest for truth and value in a ceaseless and multifarious display of mutually corrective alternatives and possibilities; where, in short, the so-called weakness of systematic tentativeness belies the mature strength of the capacity to tolerate and to endure.[23]

This paradoxicality is calculated; there is no glorying in paradox for its own sake, no wanton flouting, at the level of reasoned discourse, of the laws of contradiction and identity (as if this jaded jibe at "Hindu logic" could be justified!). Even a perfunctory, if educated, glance at the traditional debates among Indian logicians—"Hindus," Buddhists and Jains—about sense and denotation, particular and universal, self and substance, cause and relation and so on, and at the nature of Hindu theological justification, would dispel this misapprehension.[24]

It is a paradoxicality that rises from an insightful aversion to dogmatism in articulating the findings of reason and experience, and from the nurtured desire to inject a healthy dose of relativism into our perception of things. It represents a paean to the liberative workings of myth rather than to the absolutizing dictates of doctrine (though there is plenty of doctrinal consolidation in Hinduism), to spontaneity and unpredictability in our relationships with the divine, to the necessarily ineffable in our studied graspings of reality. As such, this paradoxicality is an affirmation of the mature realization of the fact of change, of the bewildering aspect of life's endless metamorphoses, of the ubiquitous porosity of boundaries, rather than a recoiling from the robust challenges of life. It evinces an increasingly tried and trusted readiness to encounter the world head-on, rather than some retreat into the seductive embrace of prevarication.

This inquiry then, besides being an attempt to characterize a great civilization and an invitation to study it afresh, is also a call to dialogue. For there are other cultures and civilizations in our world, each presumably with its own identity that is distinctive at least through complexity of degree if not of kind. Are there more insistent emphases here on a linear teleology, on historical closure, semantic determinacy, unicentric stases and nomic universality, say, than I have been able to detect in general in Hinduism? If so, does this not call for a continuing, perhaps mutually corrective, dialogue-of-respect between the variously competing sides in what seems to be an increasingly shrinking, partisan and beleaguered world?[25]

We must now consider one final objection to my thesis before concluding. In an article entitled, "On the De-Construction in Indian Literature: A Tentative Response to Vijay Mishra's Article," the scholar Greg Bailey has subjected another interpreter, Vijay Mishra's, amplified endorsement of Shulman's work to a probing critique. It is not my purpose here to defend either Mishra or Shulman. I have already indicated that Shulman wrote with other ends directly in view. However, Bailey's critique may be interpreted as raising several questions in respect of my own thesis which it may be useful to consider. Indeed, it remains unclear as to whether Bailey rejects the Shulman-Mishra hypothesis or only requires further data for scrutiny.

Bailey speaks again and again of a "radical displacement of meaning," of "continual deferral of meaning," as characterizing the Shulman-Mishra stance. I suspect that he is doing an injustice to Shulman here. In any case, this is not the brunt of my own position. I do not wish to dwell exclusively on a radical decentering, in conceptual or behavioral structures, as distinctive of *hinduta*. A radical decentering *tout court*, semantic or otherwise, is an evanescent process with nowhere to go, and belies the evidence I have sought to adduce and interpret. In my analysis, any process of decentering is part of a larger process, within the same framework of discourse, of continuous recentering among a set of interactive polarities in dynamic tension.[26] This allows for forms of "progress," of identity-in-difference, in which both *theoria* and *praxis* have the scope to develop in terms of constructed (and where necessary, alterable) teleologies. The Hindu phenomena we have considered are not semantic black holes, susceptible merely of some radical deferral of meaning in which sense and reference are systematically swallowed up in deconstructive chaos. On the contrary, in my scheme of things, they are conductors both of the elusiveness and re-purchase of meaning in a continuous equilibrating tension. This is why I feel constrained to describe my interpretation as a "polycentrism" rather than as a "decentering" or "radical dispersal" *per se*.

Bailey further queries the scope of Shulman's analysis as capable of sustaining his implied universal conclusions. If there is a problem with Shulman here, I hope I have undermined a similar objection to my own study. The evidence I have adduced ranges from the particular to the more universal. As for the objection that my hermeneutic, "as the key to understanding the culture, might lead in turn to its reification as a kind of unifying concept which establishes a new integrated framework of meaning for the culture" (Bailey 1989, 91), we see no sting in it. As characterizing a process, the hermeneutic we have here addressed is less susceptible of reification than other strategies. Further, if it seems to work, to make more cohesive sense of a greater range of evidence, and to call for a re-evaluation, as Bailey would imply, of the (supposed) current dominant Dumontian dyadic interpretive key to Hindu culture expressed in terms of, say, the notions of *pravritti* (engagement with the world as the norm of life) and *nivritti* (the recommendation to withdraw from the world), let it be accepted for the apparently more successful heremeneutic it is. In the *wissenschaftlich* interpretive process, re-evaluation is an occupational hazard.

But even here, one suspects, not least from the ambivalent nature of the evidence Bailey himself adduces (and acknowledges as such), we may not be talking at cross-purposes. For the concepts of *pravritti* and *nivritti* might well be susceptible, as Bailey himself hints, of reappraisal in terms of a fresh approach to Hinduism—perhaps even the polycentric hermeneutic I here describe. It is not for me to attempt this reappraisal here. Here I do no more than commend for serious attention a fresh, perhaps re-inventive approach for the study of and dialogue with a potentially profoundly enriching world religion, culture and civilization.

Notes

1. It is a revised version of a plenary address delivered at the East-West Philosophers' Conference (August 12–15, 1994) at Massey University, Palmerston North, New Zealand. My visit to New Zealand was sponsored in part by a grant from the British Council (New Zealand), for which I am grateful.
2. Garuda is the giant bird-mount of God Vishnu.
3. It seems that some current anthropological discourse about Hindu phenomena is moving in this direction. See, e.g., Marriott 1989, which has inspired some of the ethnographic studies published in the same issue. Thus the category of "mixing" in Marriott's essentially triadic structuralist account, in which unfortunately "Indian" seems to be assimilated to "Hindu," "suggests the probability that any entity will be found nonself-sufficient, incompletely related to itself ... being to a greater or lesser degree open and dependent for its qualities and processes upon exchanges with others" (19). What Marriott's analysis has in common with mine is its stress on fluidity and perspectivalism in Hindu categories. His cubic metamodel I find opaque.
4. It is well over two hundred years old and has a canopy of about four acres.
5. Further support will be forthcoming from the integrity of the scholarship on "Hinduism" from which I draw.
6. I contend in my recent book, Lipner 1994, ch. 1, that to be Hindu is not necessarily to be religious. Nevertheless, since historically Hindus have collectively regarded religious activity as a chief concern and factor in shaping their identity, it is religious Hinduism that I mainly address in this essay.
7. A Wittgensteinian notion.
8. The title of S. Radhakrishnan's well-known book, first published in 1927, and subsequently reissued.
9. By W. C. Smith in the book mentioned. But see a rejoinder by Smart 1974. Similar problems would arise with the use of such terms as "Vaishnavism," "Shaivism," etc.
10. It might be objected here that the world "Hindu," from which "Hinduness" is derived, is originally an outsider-term, imposed in various senses on indigenous inhabitants of India. As such, especially through such abstract constructs as "Hinduism" and "Hinduness," it gives the misleading impression that the religion, culture, etc., of these people(s) is homogeneous. But it is disputable, to say the least, in what sense "Hindu" is an outsider-designation, since it seems to have arisen from the Sanskrit word *sindhu* ("river," with special reference to the Indus) which, it may be argued, played a significant role in determining Hindu identity from the inside. Further, "Hindu" has now been virtually universally appropriated by those we designate "Hindus" as a self-description (with different meanings, of course). My purpose in this essay (see further) is not to invest "Hindu" and its derivatives with tendentious meaning, but given the fact of their self-appropriated and common currency, to suggest how they might aptly be used, and more specifically, what a chief mark of "Hinduness" might be, based on an analysis of mainstream Hindu Sanskritic sources.
11. For a current discussion of this appropriation see, e.g., Basu, *et al.* 1993. For a conceptual analysis of this ideology, see Ram-Prasad 1993.
12. This is infelicitously translated, as I have myself done on occasion, as "substantial/substantival" cause. *Upadana* does not necessarily connote a substance, the Sanskrit equivalent of which is, philosophically, *dravya*. *Upadana* denotes appropriate or self-referencing being, the stuff or resource-material out of which changes take place (from *a-da*, to take to oneself, to appropriate, and the prefix *upa*). It is significant that, in Buddhist thought, *upadana* is generally denotative of attachment or change (see, e.g., Gethin 1986, esp. 37–39).

13. Brahman is also epistemologically the world's support, as I go on to discuss in the book.
14. Which is the general, traditional image of, e.g., the Christian God. By contrast, in Hindu art, Brahma, a demiurgic figure representative of the world as produced, is depicted as emergent on a lotus whose stalk arises from the navel, i.e., nub, of Vishnu, the supreme being. Such Hindu depictions suggest a far more intimate ontological nexus between originative cause and produced being than in corresponding Christian portrayals. On the classical understanding of the Christian God as substantivally monocentric, see, e.g., the theology of Thomas Aquinas as presented in Ward 1993. Ward starts off by noting that "the classical Christian idea of God ... reached its paradigm formulation in the work of Thomas Aquinas."
15. That is, the *ucchishta* or sacralized food, which is identified with *prasada* in devotional worship.
16. "This work," the *Mahabharata* says of itself, "is on a par with the Vedas and is supremely purifying. This ancient lore, praised by the seers, is the best of tales worth listening to [because of its universal purifying power]," 1.56.15.
17. In the Poona critical edition of the epic, the dicing incident is located in Book 2, chapters 43–65.
18. I have analyzed the connotations of *dharma* in this context at length in my book, *Hindus* (1994, ch. 8); here I can do no more than summarize.
19. See further Lipner 1994, ch. 8. *Dharma*'s interpretive elusiveness is attested to repeatedly in the Sanskritic tradition. It is implied, for instance, in the highly influential Law Code of Manu which requires that a group of experts, including a logician (*hetuka*), a dialectician (*tarkin*), and a semanticist (*nairukta*), deliberate on what is *dharma* in certain cases (Manu 12.111; see also 12.105–15). See further, Matilal 1989.
20. Rather than, say, of the other "epic," the *Ramayana*. As has been pointed out, the *Ramayana* seems to have been "composed *in the manner of* an epic," presumably starting out as a literary oral composition in epic style before succumbing to "processes of textual inflation" and Brahmanic literary redaction. This is why there is a tendency in Hindu tradition to refer to it as *kavya* or "poetry." The *Mahahbarata*, however, which is "most commonly referred to as *itihasa* [narrative]," seems to be an epic proper, having evolved from the diffuse nucleus of an orally transmitted tradition. Quotations taken from John D. Smith 1980, to which attention is directed for further discussion on this distinction.
21. For an analysis of Radhakrishnan's religious philosophy, see Lipner 1989.
22. A recent work providing particular ethnographic evidence of a polycentric approach to deity is Erndl 1993. But this is a characteristic approach, and in my view, reaches back to the origins of "Hinduism." It may well have given rise to the somewhat puzzled description of Vedic religion as *henotheistic*, by the well-known orientalist F. Max Muller (1823–1900), according to which "the god invoked is seen to be supreme [for the occasion] and ... there are no clear cut relationships of superiority and inferiority among the gods"; see Neufeldt 1980, 31. For tendentious reasons, Muller seems to have described as "henotheistic/polytheistic" what was and remains, in fact, polycentric.
23. I do not claim, of course, that in daily life Hindus are necessarily doctrinally or behaviorally tolerant, or even more tolerant than people of other cultures or faiths. In fact, experience can indicate the contrary, but then this would seem to be at variance with some of the tradition's fundamental normative insights.
24. See further, e.g., Mohanty 1992, and Bhattacharyya 1990 and Matilal 1985.
25. I offer thoughts on the groundwork for this urgent task in Lipner 1993, The Aquinas Lecture for 1993 at Blackfriars, Cambridge.
26. I am not speaking of grand dialectical movements across historical spectra of a particular culture or civilization.

Part II

Hinduism in the Precolonial Period

ORIENTATION

This part is composed of two essays about the understanding of Hinduism in the precolonial period. The author of the first, David N. Lorenzen, obtained his Ph.D. from Australian National University and is a professor at El Colegio de Mexico. He has written another essay following up on the one in this book (2003), as well as other works about Indian religious history (1972 [1991], 1991, 1995, 1996). In "Who Invented Hinduism?" his main argument is that "the claim that Hinduism was invented or constructed by European colonizers, mostly British, sometime after 1800 is false." Lorenzen describes the topics that are covered in an influential survey of Hinduism from the colonial period, and then argues that this same "standard model" can be found in earlier texts. His evidence here is essentially presented in reverse chronological order: precolonial European sources from the seventeenth and eighteenth centuries, Hindu sources from the fifteenth and sixteenth centuries, and Muslim sources, primarily al-Biruni, who lived in the eleventh century. From these works Lorenzen presents various lists of the elements of Hinduism which more or less correspond to the "standard model." The most succinct list comes in Lorenzen's analysis of a sixteenth-century text by Anantadas and includes "the major gods, avatars and goddesses, the life cycle rites, the six *darshanas*, the sacred bathing places, the Vedas, the touchability rules of caste, the sacred fire, and various seasonal observances."

Whatever resemblance there may be between these formulations of Hinduism, they are not based on textual borrowing, according to Lorenzen. On the contrary, these authors described Hinduism "directly on the basis of what they observed and what they were told by their native informants." And the Hinduism of their informants "already existed in their own collective consciousness." Lorenzen admits that this Hinduism did develop over time and he assigns a crucial role in the self-conscious articulation of this Hindu identity to the presence of Muslims in India, asserting that, "In practice, there can be no Hindu identity unless this is defined by contrast against such an Other." Yet it is also significant that Lorenzen sees the religions of South Asia "taking a recognizably Hindu shape in the early Puranas, roughly around the period 300–600 CE."

In the end Lorenzen seems to understand the definition of Hinduism as a process that required little positive work—the authors he analyzes just described what was there. Lorenzen betrays this when he calls the position that Hinduism was created by the nineteenth-century British "constructionist." There is a particularly interesting reprise of this theme in the rather obscure literary reference at the end of Lorenzen's essay, when he writes, "This Hinduism wasn't invented by anyone, European or Indian. Like

Topsy, it just grow'd." Topsy is the name of the slave girl in Harriet Beecher Stowe's *Uncle Tom's Cabin*, who replies when asked who made her, "I spect I grow'd. Don't think nobody never made me" (Stowe 1982, 282). Lorenzen's view of the development of Hinduism is not constructionist, but naturalist or organic—Hinduism wasn't built, but just grew.

In "Unity and Plurality: Hinduism and the Religions of India in Early European Scholarship," Will Sweetman focuses on a small part of the great canvas of history that Lorenzen paints. Sweetman is a lecturer at the University of Otago in New Zealand. This essay and his other publications developed out of his Ph.D. dissertation research at the University of Cambridge (1999, 2002). Here Sweetman analyzes the work of precolonial European missionaries, concentrating on texts by Roberto Nobili from the early 1600s and Batholomaus Ziegenbalg from the early 1700s. Over the course of the century that separates these two men, Sweetman discerns the beginning of a shift from understanding the religions of South Asia to be many, to understanding them to be one. Nobili is presented here as arguing for plurality in Hinduism, with one religion centering around Vishnu, for example, and another around Shiva. On the other hand, while Ziegenbalg sometimes described Vaishnavism and Shaivism as different religions, he also considered them a part of a larger "Malabarian heathenism."

In recounting this history Sweetman is arguing against the tendency in contemporary scholarship to see Hinduism as the product of the imposition of western categories on the religious diversity of South Asia. "Unity and Plurality" actually distinguishes between two versions of the tendency, one attributed to Richard King (1999), in which Hinduism is understood to have been squeezed into the modern unitary conception of a religion, and another attributed to Heinrich von Stietencron (1995), in which Hinduism is understood to have been squeezed into the premodern unitary conception of heathenism. The latter theory is disproven according to Sweetman on historical grounds—neither Nobili nor Ziegenbalg had the kind of simple notion of heathenism that readers of Stietencron would expect. And the former theory is also problematic historically, but for a slightly more complicated reason. These early missionaries did not operate with the kind of preconception about what a religion is that King would have predicted because that notion of religion itself had not been established.

Within the context of this book, it is important to underscore the contrast between Sweetman's history and Lorenzen's. In relatively similar descriptions of Hinduism in various sources over a long historical period, Lorenzen finds evidence for a single enduring conception of Hinduism. It is not clear from "Unity and Plurality" how Nobili's and Ziegelbalg's Hinduism fit Lorenzen's "standard model," but it is clear that Nobili at least, and perhaps even Ziegelbalg, did not conclude that this was just one religion.

3

WHO INVENTED HINDUISM?

David N. Lorenzen

... moreover if people of Arabia or Persia would ask of the men of this country whether they are Moors or Gentoos, they ask in these words: "Art thou Mosalman or Indu?" (Dr. Garia de Orta, quoted in Yule and Burnell 1968, 415).[1]

Over the past decade, many scholars have put forward the claim that Hinduism was constructed, invented, or imagined by British scholars and colonial administrators in the nineteenth century and did not exist, in any meaningful sense, before this date.[2] Prominent among scholars who have made this constructionist argument, if I can call it that, are Vasudha Dalmia (1995), Robert Frykenberg (1989), Christopher Fuller (1992), John Hawley (1991), Gerald Larson (1995), Harjot Oberoi (1994, 16–17), Brian Smith (1989), and Heinrich von Stietencron (1995 and 1997). W. C. Smith (1991) is sometimes identified, quite correctly, as a noteworthy precursor of these scholars. Romila Thapar (1985, 1989, 1996) and Dermot Killingley (1993, 61–64) have offered somewhat similar arguments, but both display greater sensitivity to historical ambiguities, distributing the construction of a distinctly modern Hinduism among British orientalists and missionaries and indigenous nationalists and communalists. Carl Ernst (1992, 22–29, especially 23) discusses early Muslim references to "Hindus" and their religion, but he joins the above scholars in claiming that the terms "do not correspond to any indigenous Indian concept, either of geography or religion." J. Laine (1983) agrees with Smith and his modern epigones that Hinduism was invented in the nineteenth century, but credits the invention to the Indians rather than to the British.

On the other side of the argument are several scholars who have directly questioned this claim from various points of view. They include Lawrence

A. Babb (1986), Wendy Doniger (1991), Gabriella Eichinger Ferro-Luzzi (1989), Alf Hiltebeitel (1991), Cynthia Talbot (1995, 694), Thomas Trautmann (1997, 64–80), Peter van der Veer (1994), and myself (1995, 11–13).[3] A recent review of the issue by Saurabh Dube (1998, 4–7) makes a valiant attempt to mark out a compromise position, but ends up, I think, straddling the fence rather than finding a new synthesis. In addition, it should be noted that most scholars of Indian religions who have not directly addressed this question—and even several who claim that Hinduism is a modern construction—continue to write about Hinduism as if it in fact existed many centuries earlier.

This essay argues that the claim that Hinduism was invented or constructed by European colonizers, mostly British, sometime after 1800 is false. The evidence instead suggests that a Hindu religion theologically and devotionally grounded in texts such as the *Bhagavad Gita*, the Puranas, and philosophical commentaries on the six *darshanas* gradually acquired a much sharper self-conscious identity through the rivalry between Muslims and Hindus in the period between 1200 and 1500, and was firmly established long before 1800. The obvious danger of this thesis is that it can be modified to provide support to a Hindu communalist argument that a self-conscious Hindu identity arose out of the violent persecution of Hindus by Muslims. In fact state-sponsored persecution was only sporadic and directed mostly at temple buildings, not people. Nonetheless, religious literature by Hindu poets such as Kabir, Ekanath, and Vidyapati (some of this quoted below) suggests that socio-religious conflict—occasionally violent conflict—did occur among people on a local level. In any case, only a recognition of the fact that much of modern Hindu identity is rooted in the history of the rivalry between Hinduism and Islam will enable us to correctly gauge the strength of communalist forces and wage war against them.

Inventing Hinduism

If what one means by Hinduism is simply the English word itself, then the claim that it did not exist before the nineteenth century is correct. Several scholars cite the date 1829 for the first known occurrence in English, in the form "Hindooism." W.C. Smith is sometimes given credit for this reference, but Smith cites the *Oxford English Dictionary* as his source (W. C. Smith 1991, 61, 253). In a search through several early nineteenth-century journals, I managed to find one example of the word "Hinduism" (with a "u") in a letter published in the 1818 volume of *The Asiatic Journal and Monthly Register* (London) and no less than seven examples (also with a "u") in an article by John Crawfurd on Hinduism in Bali, published in the 1820 volume of *Asiatick Researches* of Calcutta (Civis 1818, 107; Crawfurd 1820, 129,

135, 139, 147, 151). More significant are two appearances of the term in English language texts by Rammohan Roy published in 1816 and 1817, which have been noted and discussed recently by Dermot Killingley (1993, 62–63).[4] In 1816 Rammohan made this critical comment: "The chief part of the theory and practice of Hindooism, I am sorry to say, is made to consist in the adoption of a peculiar mode of diet." In 1817, on the other hand, he claimed that "the doctrines of the unity of God are real Hinduism, as that religion was practiced by our ancestors, and as it is well known at the present day to many learned Brahmins" (Roy 1978, 73, 90 as cited in Killingley 1993). This puts the proponents of the British construction of Hinduism in the embarrassing situation of having to admit that an India-born Hindu seems to have coined the label for this supposedly British construct.

It is true, however, that the word "Hinduism" became common in English only in the second quarter of the nineteenth century, and mostly in books by British authors. One important milestone was the publication of Alexander Duff's popular book, *India and India Missions: Including Sketches of the Gigantic System of Hinduism Both in Theory and Practice*, in 1839. M. Monier-Williams's introductory text, *Hinduism*, first published in 1877, also did much to popularize the term.

What contemporary scholars generally mean by the construction or invention of Hinduism, however, is not simply the coining of the name. What they claim is that the Europeans, and more specifically the British, imposed a single conceptual category on a heterogeneous collection of sects, doctrines, and customs that the Hindus themselves did not recognize as having anything essential in common. In this view, it was only after the concept of Hinduism was constructed by these Europeans that the Hindus themselves adopted the idea that they all belonged to a single religious community.

Although this argument about the construction or invention of Hinduism has a strong postmodern flavor, it was first developed by W. C. Smith in his 1963 book, *The Meaning and End of Religion*. Smith insists that religion must be analyzed using specifically religious categories, rather than through the medium of disciplines such as sociology, psychology, literature, or even philosophy and history. For this reason he strongly opposes any attempt by outside observers to impose their own categories and explanations on religious phenomena. In the case of Hinduism, he argues that the naming of this religion by Europeans was a mistake: there is no Hinduism either in the minds of the Hindus or in empirical reality itself.

> What exists cannot be defined. What obstructs a definition of Hinduism, for instance, is precisely the richness of what exists, in all its extravagant variety from century to century and from village to village. The empirical religious tradition of the Hindus developing historically in the minds and hearts and institutions and literatures and societies of untold

millions of actual people is not a form, but a growing congeries of living realities. It is not to be compressed within or eviscerated into or confused with any systematic intellectual pattern.

As an ideal "Hinduism" might conceivably be defined (though only by a Hindu), but not as an historical reality. The sheer facts, in all their intractable toughness, stand in the way.

"Hinduism" refers not to an entity; it is a name that the West has given to a prodigiously variegated series of facts. It is a notion in men's minds—and a notion that cannot but be inadequate. To use this term at all is inescapably a gross oversimplification.

To define Hinduism is to deny the Hindu his right to the freedom and integrity of his faith. What he may do tomorrow no man can say today (W. C. Smith 1991, 144–45).

Turning to more recent statements of similar positions, one of the wittiest is by John Hawley. He also comes close to identifying the construction of Hinduism with the coining of the word itself.

Hinduism—the word and perhaps the reality too—was born in the 19th century, a notoriously illegitimate child. The father was middle-class and British, and the mother, of course, was India. The circumstances of the conception are not altogether clear. One heard of the "goodly habits and observances of Hindooism" in a Bengali-English grammar written in 1829, and the Reverend William Tennant had spoken of "the Hindoo system" in a book on Indian manners and history written at the beginning of the century. Yet it was not until the inexpensive handbook *Hinduism* was published by the Society for Promoting Christian Knowledge in 1877 that the term came into general English usage (Hawley 1991, 20–21).

Brian Smith makes a similar argument in a more typically postmodern style. Here Hinduism is, to use two words much in vogue, simply "invented" or "imagined."

Just who invented "Hinduism" first is a matter of scholarly debate. Almost everyone agrees that it was not the Hindus. ... As a discrete Indic religion among others, however, "Hinduism" was probably first imagined by the British in the early part of the nineteenth century to describe (and create and control) an enormously complex configuration of people and their traditions found in the South Asian subcontinent. "Hinduism" made it possible for the British, and for us all (including Hindus), to speak of a religion when before there was none or, at best, many (B. K. Smith 1989, 5–6).

To give yet another example, Harjot Oberoi presents roughly the same argument, albeit in a somewhat more nuanced form, in the introduction to his recent work on the construction of a modern Sikh identity.

It is most striking that people we now call Hindus never used this term to describe themselves. The Vedas, the Ramayana and the Bhagavad Gita, which today are seen by many as the religious texts of the Hindus, do not employ the word Hindu. That term was first used by the Achae-menid Persians to describe all those people who lived on or beyond the banks of the river Sindhu, or Indus. Therefore, at one stage the word Hindu as an ethno-geographic category came to englobe all those who lived in India, without ethnic distinction. It was only under the Muslim rulers of India that the term began to gain a religious connotation. But it was not until colonial times that the term "Hinduism" was coined and acquired wide currency as referring collectively to a wide variety of reli-gious communities, some of them with distinct traditions and opposed practices. Communities like the Saivites, Vaishnavites, and Lingayats, each with their own history and specific view of the world, were tied together under the blanket category Hinduism (Oberoi 1994, 16).

Robert Frykenberg insists, with categorical bluntness, that even today "Hindu" and "Hinduism" are terms without any substantive content:

Unless by "Hindu" one means nothing more, nor less, than "Indian" (something native to, pertaining to, or found within the continent of India), there has never been any such thing as a single "Hinduism" or any single "Hindu community" for all of India. Nor, for that matter, can one find any such thing as a single "Hinduism" or "Hindu commu-nity" even for any one socio-cultural region of the continent. Further-more, there has never been any one religion—nor even one system of religions—to which the term "Hindu" can accurately be applied. No one so-called religion, moreover, can lay exclusive claim to or be defined by the term "Hinduism" (Frykenberg 1989, 29).

In order to present an alternative argument, we need to divide the topic into two separate questions. First, when did the British and other Europeans begin to conceptualize Hinduism as a single religious system? Second, when did the Hindus and other Indians begin to do the same? In both cases, the argument for a nineteenth-century construction of the concept does not agree with the available evidence. Before presenting this evidence, however, one other key issue has to be addressed: the meaning of the term "Hindu."

The Word "Hindu"

It is well known that variants of the word "Hindu" were current in Persian and vernacular Indian languages long before the nineteenth century. If this word always meant simply a follower of beliefs and practices drawn from the religion we now call Hinduism, then the constructionist argument would be refuted from the start. This would be the case even if no specific word or phrase equivalent to "Hinduism" could be identified. In point of fact, however, the religious sense of Hindu has long coexisted and over-lapped with an ethnic and geographical sense. What the constructionists are obliged to argue is that this ethno-geographical sense of Hindu remained overwhelmingly dominant up until the nineteenth century, and that only then did the religious sense become widespread as a result of the British invention of Hinduism.

Etymology clearly supports an ethno-geographical meaning of Hindu. Early European scholars, it is true, did sometimes claim either a biblical derivation from Hind, a supposed son of Ham and grandson of Noah, or a Sanskrit derivation from *indu* meaning "moon."[5] Now, however, everyone agrees that the word derives from Sindhu, the native name for the river Indus. There is also a consensus that the name Sindhu became "Hind" or "Hindu" in Persian languages and then re-entered Indian languages as "Hindu," originally with the sense of an inhabitant of the lands near and to the east of the Indus. Most proponents of the British construction of Hinduism not surprisingly begin by stressing this geographical etymology and then simply deny that use of the word "Hindu" in a religious sense was of any importance until the nineteenth century, without any close examination of the actual use in texts written before this date. Take, for example, the comments of Heinrich von Stietencron:

> The term Hindu itself is a Persian term. Used in the plural it denotes the people of Hind, the Indians, and in this sense it occurs in the inscriptions of Darius I and other rulers of ancient Persia from the sixth century B. C. onwards. It certainly goes to the credit of Persian scholars like Al-Biruni, Abu-l Qasim, al-Masudi, al-Idrisi and Shahrastani that they knew and distinguished different religions among the Hindus. Administrators were less exact or they saw no need for such differentiation between Hindus for taxation purposes. The British adopted the term from administrators, not from the scholars (Stietencron 1995, 77).[6]

Here Stietencron here quite blithely jumps from the sixth century BCE to the nineteenth century CE with virtually no discussion whatever of the intervening uses of the term "Hindu," either by foreigners or by native Indians. He admits that several Persian scholars did discuss the religions of the Hindus,

57

but implies that they never identified any one religion as *the* principal religion of this group. In the case of al-Biruni at least, this is simply not so, as we shall see. Finally, Stietencron asserts that the British, in any case, took the term "Hindu" not from these scholars but from administrators, who, he implies, were still using this term in the geographical sense found in the inscriptions of Darius I, written over 2400 years earlier.

If, however, the word "Hindu" had a purely geographical sense up until the nineteenth century, as Stietencron claims, then why were the foreign Muslims who permanently settled in India, or at least their descendants born in India, not called Hindus? He attempts to answer this objection by insisting that the Muslim rulers persistently maintained a foreign self-identity for generations, while the Hindus, that is, native Indians, just as persistently maintained a separate, indigenous identity:

> It was this feeling of superiority and the continuing linkage of social prestige to origins outside India which, even after centuries of settlement in the country, prevented upper class Muslims from considering themselves Hindus, i.e., indigenous Indians. The Hindus remained a separate population—natives the British would later call them—and, in spite of all differentiation according to caste and status, they continued to form a distinct entity characterized by their indigenous Indian origin. Whether caste Hindus, outcastes, or tribals, they were all designated as Hindus. It was a sad mistake of the British when they adopted this term from the Persian administrators, to believe that it was a religious term (Stietencron 1995, 78).

What then of the vast majority of Muslims in India who were indigenous converts of low-caste Hindu origin? If "Hindu" remained a purely ethnogeographical term, except perhaps in the eyes of a few Muslim intellectuals, at least these converts should have been called "Hindus" or "Hindu Muslims." There is in fact little or no evidence that this ever happened, but about this Stietencron has nothing to say.[7]

The Standard Model

Introductory books about Hinduism written by modern scholars tend to follow three different models or formats. Some books are organized primarily in terms of major metaphysical and theological concepts (karma, samsara, dharma, God, bhakti); some in terms of the textual history of gods, schools of thought, and rituals; and some in terms of a catalog of sects, beliefs, and practices.[8] Speaking more abstractly, these three models represent three different master narratives: one metaphysical, one historical, and one classificatory. Books in each of these three modes have been written both from the inside, by practicing Hindus, and from the outside, by followers of other religions and nonbelievers. A modern academic or textbook style—and an insistence on at least a minimum of historical plausibility and contextualization—does separate these books from traditional texts such as the Puranas and the *Bhagavad Gita*, but their authors have not invented or constructed anything radically new. Indeed, their main purpose is to represent observed Hinduism, both textual and contextual, as accurately as possible within the limits imposed by their varied ideological perspectives.

Since each of these three models or formats is obviously an ideal type, there is almost no text on Hinduism that follows any one model exclusively. Nonetheless, the dominant model is undoubtedly the historical one, and one of the first fully-developed examples of this model is presented in Monier Monier-Williams's influential book *Hinduism*, first published in 1877 and later reprinted in several revised editions. The importance of this text justifies, I think, taking its account of Hinduism as a "standard model" of the religion.

Monier-Williams begins with an analysis of what allows us to speak of Hinduism as one religion, rather than simply a motley collection of sects, beliefs, and practices. He claims to find the basis of unity in two historical factors: first, an origin in a "simple, pantheistic doctrine, but branching out into an endless variety of polytheistic superstitions"; and, second, the fact that there is "only one sacred language and only one sacred literature, accepted and revered by all adherents of Hinduism alike," namely Sanskrit. He identifies the founding principle as *"Ekam eva advitiyam*, 'There is but one Being, without a second'"* and makes this principle the basis of the first and highest of three ways of salvation in "popular Hinduism." These three are the well-known paths of knowledge, works and devotion (*jnana-marga, karma-marga*, and *bhakti-marga*) described in the *Bhagavad Gita* (Monier-Williams 1993, 11, 13). Monier-Williams here is undoubtedly influenced by the rising importance given to the *Bhagavad Gita* and to Advaita by Hindu reformers of the nineteenth century, but this is simply a process of selective emphasis, not invention.

Monier-Williams then runs though a step-by-step historical survey of the development of Brahmanism—the name he gives to the religion before the writing of the epics and Puranas—through Hinduism, properly so called, starting from these texts down to the present day. A list of the chapter titles will give a sufficient idea of how the author organizes the material: "The Vedic hymns; The Brahmanas and the sacrificial system; The Upanishads and Brahmanical philosophy; Brahmanical law, domestic usages, and caste; The Buddhistic movement, and its influence on Brahmanism; Development of Hinduism and the doctrine of triple manifestation (*tri-murti*); Development of Saivism, Vaishnavism, and the doctrine of incarnation; The doctrine of devotion (*bhakti*) as developed in the Puranas and Tantras; Medieval and modern sects; Modern castes; Modern idol-worship, sacred objects, holy places, and times"; and all this is followed by an appendix on the six schools of philosophy (*darshanas*), the *Bhagavad Gita*, Jainism, and the Carvakas.

The key chapters on Hinduism proper include discussions of the mythology of Shiva and Vishnu, including the latter's ten chief avatars; a brief summary of the *Mahabharata* and *Ramayana* epics; a list of the thirty-six major and minor Puranas and a summary of the five major topics ideally found in each; a discussion of the doctrine of the four yugas; and a summary of the major ideas of the Tantras including the importance of the female power of *shakti* and its embodiments in various goddesses, the infamous five *makaras*, and the importance of mantras, *yantras*, and *siddhis*. The chapter on Hindu sects includes a discussion of the different ideal types of devotion and of several orthodox Vaishnava sects, with brief mentions of Kabir and Nanak. About the division between Shaivism and Vaishnavism, Monier-Williams insists (1993, 97) that they "are not opposite or incompatible creeds. They represent different lines of religious thought ... quite allowable within the limits of one and the same system" (Monier-Williams 1993, 97). The chapter on idol worship discusses Hindu devotion to stone idols, cows, other animals and plants; pilgrimages to various sacred places (*tirthas*) and rivers; the twenty-seven astrological *nakshatras*; and various festivals. The earlier chapters on Brahmanism include, besides the topics mentioned above, summaries of the four Vedas, transmigration, the three qualities (*gunas*), the four stages of life (*ashramas*), the four social classes (*varnas*) and the twelve basic life-cycle rites (*sanskaras*).

This outline of what Monier-Williams regarded as the key characteristics of Hinduism can easily be read forward as the model, direct or indirect, for a host of later historical summaries of Hinduism, including those of A. L. Basham (1975), K. M. Sen (1961), Thomas J. Hopkins (1971), Klaus K. Klostermaier (1994), and even that of Benjamin Preciado Solis and myself (1996). The fact that many such books have been written by Europeans and Americans does not, I think, have anything to do with a European predilection for inventing things. Rather it reflects the need for textbooks in European and American universities, where basic Hinduism is more likely to be taught as an academic subject than in universities in India itself.

More interesting than a forward reading of Monier-Williams's text is a backward reading that compares his treatment of Hinduism with earlier European (Christian), Hindu, and Muslim attempts to summarize its more important characteristics. In what follows I will attempt to show how such earlier accounts, although generally more fragmentary, consistently embody substantial parts of Monier-Williams's standard model.

European Sources Before 1800

When, then, did British and other European observers first identify Hinduism—whether called Hinduism, Hindu religion, or religion of the Hindus—as a single set of religious beliefs and practices? I have already mentioned the 1820 article by John Crawfurd as one of the earliest sources to use the word "Hinduism." What is also interesting is the fact that Crawfurd uses the terms "Hinduism," "Hindu religion," and "Hindus" in the context of Bali, where the Hindus are clearly not Indians in any racial or ethno-geographical sense. What I want to show here, however, is that virtually all of the more scholarly observers among the European visitors and residents in India before 1800 had identified Hinduism as a diverse but identifiable set of beliefs and practices clearly distinguished from Islam and, less clearly, from the Sikh and Parsi religions as well.

Between 1775 and 1800, as the British commercial beachhead in Bengal transformed itself into an Indian empire, English language studies of Hinduism became more numerous and accurate, particularly after the founding of the Bengal Asiatic Society by William Jones and his friends in 1784. Noteworthy in this period are Nathaniel Brassey Halhed's *A Code of Gentoo Laws* (1776), Charles Wilkins's translation of the *Bhagavad Gita* (1785), several articles on Hinduism by William Jones and Henry Colebrooke in *Asiatick Researches*, and Charles Grant's *Observations of the State of Society among the Asiatic Subjects of Great Britain.*[9] Wilkins, Jones and Colebrooke all read and translated texts from Sanskrit, while Halhed worked with Persian texts.

Even scholars who acquired the linguistic competence to work directly with sources in Indian languages, however, regularly employed native intellectuals as teachers and informants. In most cases, the contributions of these native scholars to the construction of European knowledge about India and other Asian regions were never adequately acknowledged. Mohammad Tavakoli-Targhi (1996) has called this "orientalism's genesis amnesia," a criticism that is applicable not only to the original orientalists themselves but also to Edward Said and other modern opponents of traditional European orientalist scholarship. If Hinduism was invented, it was invented by European and Indian scholars working in tandem.

Of more interest here than the professional scholars such as Jones, Wilkins and Colebrooke, however, are two rather dilettantish writers, John Zephaniah Holwell and Alexander Dow, who wrote about Hinduism in the 1760s, before the East India Company regime was well-established and before its authorities had begun to sponsor more serious research (also in Marshall 1970). The accounts of Hinduism by Holwell and Dow display large gaps in their knowledge, mangle most Sanskrit words, and betray several mutual disagreements, but overall both their accounts contain the same basic elements found in any modern textbook variant of the standard model: the four Vedas; the social system of four *varnas*; the division of powers among the gods Brahma, Vishnu, and Shiva; goddess worship; basic elements of the mythology of these gods, including several of the avatars of Vishnu; the theory of the four yugas; some idea of the various *darshanas*; and the theodicy of karma, transmigration, and rebirth.

One curious word used to refer to Hindus in many eighteenth-century (and even earlier) English texts, including those of Holwell and Halhed (but not Dow), is "Gentoo" (Yule and Burnell 1968, 367). This term is not a corruption of "Hindu." "Gentoo" is derived from the Portuguese word *gentio*, meaning "gentile," "pagan," or "native." From the sixteenth century on, Portuguese texts regularly distinguish *gentios*, meaning Hindus, from both Muslims (*moros*) and native Christians.[10] The word *gentio* is in turn derived from *gentil*, which in Portuguese normally means "of noble descent" or "of good family." The collective noun *gentilidade* is sometimes used for Hindus in Portuguese texts. In early Italian texts about India, the word *gentile* (literally, "gentile" or "pagan") is regularly used for "Hindu." Similarly, in early Spanish texts the word *gentil* has this same sense.[11]

The Spanish language *Itinerario* of the Augustinian Sebastiao Manrique, published in 1649, identifies the *gentiles* with the Hindus (written as *Indus*) in a passage that is one of the earliest uses of the word "Hindu" in a European language, and one which gives the word a specifically religious, not a geographical, meaning.[12] Here Manrique quotes, with his own gloss in parentheses, the harsh words of a Mughal official in Bengal against a Muslim member of Manrique's party who had offended the Hindu population by killing a peacock: "Are you not, in appearance, a Bengali and a Muslim (which means 'Moor' and follower of the true law)? How did you dare, in a district of Hindus (which means *Gentiles*), kill a living thing?" (Manrique 1649, 319).[13]

Early European missionaries who wrote on Hindu religion before 1800, mostly in languages other than English, are of particular interest to our discussion since their observations were often recorded in territories outside the direct influence of colonial rule[14] and since the post-1800 British Orientalists who supposedly invented Hinduism were almost entirely unaware of what these missionaries had written about Hindu beliefs and practices. If we can show that the view of Hinduism presented by these pre-1800 Europeans closely resembles that of later British colonial scholars, then we have moved much closer to being able to say that Hinduism is not a colonial construct or invention, nor even a European one, but rather that European observers were attempting, with native help, to describe something that had a practical and conceptual coherence both for outside observers and the Hindus themselves.

The lives and writings of the European missionaries who worked in India in the seventeenth and eighteenth centuries have still not been adequately studied. The best-known of these missionaries is the Italian Jesuit Roberto de Nobili (1577–1656), who lived for many years in south India. Some of his works have been published and the modern Jesuit scholar S. Rajamanickam has written about him (1972a and 1972b).[15] The writings of four other early missionary intellectuals have also been at least partially published: the Portuguese Jesuit Goncalo Fernandes Trancoso (1541–1621; see 1973), the British Jesuit Thomas Stephens (1549–1619; see 1945), the Lutheran Bartholomaus Ziegenbalg (1683–1719; see Caland 1926), and the Italian Franciscan monk Marco della Tomba (1726–1803; see 1878).[16] One important unpublished text is a long dialogue between a Christian and a Hindu written in Hindi and Italian by another Italian Fransciscan, Giuseppe Maria da Gargnano, who was in North India from 1749 to 1761.[17]

The descriptions of Hinduism by these early missionaries, like those of Holwell and Dow, generally feature the same set of beliefs, gods, and practices found in the writings of later scholars associated with the British colonial project and the standard model. Since the missionaries had religious training and often knew the local languages, however, the scope and detail of their accounts rival those of the later colonial scholars. A few examples will have to suffice to illustrate this point. Although some of the concerns of both the precolonial and colonial writers are related to an implicit, or sometimes explicit, comparison with Christianity, on the whole they describe a Hinduism whose main features correspond to those found in the Puranas, supplemented by visual observations of temples, ascetics, pilgrimages, and daily or occasional rituals. Whether all of the early missionaries had any direct knowledge of the Sanskrit Puranas is uncertain—although at least de Nobili, Zeigenbalg and Marco della Tomba probably did—but most of them knew the local vernaculars well enough to get information about the Hindu beliefs, practices, and myths directly from local informants.

The Franciscan Marco della Tomba lived in various parts of northeastern India, especially the princely state of Bettiah just south of Nepal, from 1757 until 1773, and again from 1786 until his death in 1803. His writings include several essays on Indian religion and translations of various religious texts from Hindi to Italian. Among these translations is at least one chapter of Tulsidas's *Ramcaritmanas*. This is by far the earliest translation of this key Hindu text into any European language, but Marco has never been credited with the feat, since the few scholars who have commented on this translation, including Charlotte Vaudeville, all mistakenly took it to be based on an original text associated with the Kabir Panth.[18]

In an essay on the "Diversi sistemi della religione dell'Indostano," written in 1766, Marco refers to the Hindus as "Gentili" and contrasts their religion with that of both the Christians and Muslims (1878, 69–98). He divides up the "diverse tribes of men" that, he says, are believed to originate from the body of Brahma, and hence that are all in some sense Brahmans, into eight religious sects: the tribe of Brahmans and cows, the Vaishnavas (*Bisnuas*), the Ramanandis, the Shaivas, the Smartas (*Asmaetr*) of Shankaracarya, the Nastikas or atheists, the Pasandas or hedonists (according to Marco), and the Shaktas. He further subdivides the religious practitioners of these groups or sects, according to their style of observance, into Yogis, Vanaprasthas, Sannyasis, Nagas, Vairagis, and Avadhutas. Marco ends his essay with discussion of the Kabir Panthis (*Cabiristi*) and the Sikhs (*Nanekpanti*), two groups that he regards as somewhat separate from the other eight. In his discussion of the Sikhs (1878, 98), he quotes the Hindi phrase "Nanak fakir, hindu ka guru, musalaman ka pir" in order to show that the Sikhs had staked out a religious position combining elements of the religions of the Hindus and Muslims.

At first glance Marco's essay seems to confirm the constructionist view that there was no Hinduism, in the sense of a coherent set of beliefs and practices, before 1800, for what we have here is a heterogeneous collection of sects and ascetics, each with its own set of beliefs and practices. Against this I would argue that what is more significant is the clear distinction that he draws among the *gentili*, the Muslims, and Christians, and also the correctly ambiguous distinction that he draws between the *gentili* and the Sikhs and Kabir Panthis. In addition, another of Marco's essays, *Libri indiani* (1878, 99–127), contains a discussion of the four Vedas, eighteen Puranas, and different philosophical *darshanas* more in line with the standard model of Hinduism.

There is, however, an alternative way of looking at this question. A strong case can, I think, be made that Marco's conceptualization of Hinduism in *Diversi sistemi* represents a more specifically Christian construct than the standard model of Monier-Williams and his precursors. What could be more convenient from a Christian point of view than the idea that Hinduism was not really a single coherent religion at all, that it was not viewed as such by its followers, and that it was instead a heterogeneous collection of miscellaneous sects, beliefs, and idolatrous practices?

Since many later colonial scholars were also committed Christians and, even if not, had little good to say about Hindu beliefs and practices, it is not surprising that they sometimes adopted similar views. The locus classicus of arguments for the diffuse and incoherent nature of Hinduism is the famous study by H. H. Wilson, *Religious Sects of the Hindus*, first published in 1828 and 1832 in *Asiatic Researches*. Wilson begins his study with these words: "The Hindu religion is a term, that has been hitherto employed in a collective sense, to designate a faith and worship of an almost endlessly diversified description: to trace some of its varieties is the object of the present enquiry" (1972, 1). Here Wilson does accept some sort of overall Hindu unity, but the emphasis is clearly on internal divisions and differences. This sort of catalog approach to the conceptualization of Hinduism can be traced forward to imperialistic works such as John Campbell Oman's *The Mystics, Ascetics, and Saints of India* (1903) and the many semi-official studies of the "tribes and castes" of various regions, and also to more nuanced academic studies such as Sir R. G. Bhandarkar's *Vaisnavism Saivism and Minor Religious Systems* (1965), first published in 1913, Jan Gonda's *Der jungere Hinduismus* (1963), and Sudhakar Chattopadhyaya's *Evolution of Hindu Sects* (1970).

We cannot, however, correctly claim that even this catalog approach to Hinduism is wholly a Christian or colonial construct. H. H. Wilson (1972, 6) himself refers back to two earlier Sanskrit works—Madhavacarya's *Sarva-darshana-sangraha* and Ananda-giri's *Shankara-digvijaya*—as native precedents and sources for his own study. Other such early works can easily be cited. It is an empirical fact that the beliefs, practices, and human organization of Hinduism are less standardized and centralized than, say, those of Roman Catholicism or Sunni Islam. For this reason a description of Hinduism in terms of its various sects, gods, ascetics, and metaphysical doctrines is often appropriate and useful.

Half a century earlier than Marco della Tomba's essay, on July 29, 1717, Giuseppe Felice da Morro, another Italian member of the Franciscan mission, wrote a letter from Kathmandu, Nepal, that sets out a short account of Hindu religion closer to the standard model (Petech 1952–1956, part 1, 96–106).[19] Like Marco, he calls the Hindus "Gentili," and like most European writers, and many Sanskrit Puranas, he begins with the story of the creation of the world. He correctly notes that Hindus refuse to believe that God created the universe out of nothing, as Christian doctrine asserts. Instead, he claims, they insist that the souls of every person, the souls of every thing, and God himself are all one and the same. According to the somewhat curious account told to Giuseppe Felice by his Nepalese informant, God first created a woman named Manasa, who soon began to long for offspring.[20] God then created the gods Brahma, Vishnu, and Mahesha (Shiva). Manasa invited Brahma to mate with her, but he refused. Next she asked Vishnu and he too refused. Mahesha, however, accepted, provided Manasa would change her form to that of Parvati. Brahma, Vishnu, and Mahesha each assumed different functions: Brahma would concern himself with spiritual matters and scripture, Vishnu with conserving and governing, Mahesha with punishment and death.

Giuseppe Felice then notes the Hindus regard all the thirty-three crore male gods to be transformations of these three gods while the many goddesses are transformations of Manasa. He gives a list of the names of nine goddesses that corresponds roughly to the list of emanations of Devi found in the well-known Purana text, the *Devi-mahatmya*. Next, he turns to a discussion of the ten avatars of Vishnu, a standard topic of most Puranas. After this he gives a descriptive list of the gods associated with the various planets, the north star (Dhruva), eclipses (Rahu), followed by a list of some minor gods such as Yama, Kubera, Indra, Varuna, Agni, Vayu, Kumara, Ganesha, and the eight Bhairavas. The discussion then turns briefly to the Brahmans' veneration of the sacred cow, followed by the story of the origin of the Brahmans, the Kshatriyas, the Vaishyas, and the Shudras from God's mouth, shoulders, thighs, and feet respectively. Giuseppe Felice concludes his account with a description of the four yugas and the Hindus' belief in enormously long time periods.

One hundred years earlier, in the first part of the seventeenth century, the above-mentioned Jesuits de Nobili, Stephens, and Fernandes Trancoso were working and writing in south India, while the Augustinian Manrique worked in Bengal and elsewhere. Rather than review the works of these authors, however, I want to use the example of a less well-informed tract from about the same period, *A Discoverie of the Sect of the Banians*, published by the Anglican chaplain Henry Lord, in 1630. Lord describes, with mixed success, the beliefs and practices of some Banias he encountered during a stay at the East India Company factory at Surat in Gujarat in the early seventeenth century. He claims to have gone through their Bible, the so-called "Shaster," with the help of interpreters (Lord 1630, [A] 13).[21]

> I that thought my observance would bee well tooke, if I could present my Countreymen with any thing new from these forraigne parts, begun my worke, and essayed to fetch materials for the same out of their Manuscripts, and by renewed accesse, with the helpe of Interpreters, made my collections out of a booke of theirs called the Shaster which is to them as their Bible, containing the grounds of their Religion in a written word (Lord 1630, [A] 13).

Lord then presents those scattered bits of information that managed to pass through the filter of his interpreters. He begins with a confused account of God's creation of the world and of Pourous (Purusha) and Parcoutee (Prakriti) that reads like a twisted version of the creation in Genesis.

> For this cause that Almighty consulted with himselfe, about the making of this great worke which men call the world or Universe, and as the Ancient (say they) have delivered; the Lord made foure Elements as the ground-worke of this mighty frame; to wit, Earth, Aire, Fire, and Water, which foure Elements were at first all mingled together in a confusion, but the Almighty separated them in manner following.
>
> First, it is delivered, that by some great Cane or like instrument, hee blew upon the Waters, which arose into a bubble, of a round form like an egge, which spreading it selfe further and further, made the Firmament so cleare and transparent, which now compasseth the world about.

[God then created Earth, Sun, Moon, the points of the compass, and finally Man.] That this creature might not bee alone, who was made by nature socieable; God seconded him with a Companion, which was Woman; to whom not so much the outward shape, as the likenesse of the minde and disposition seemed agreeing: and the first mans name was *Pourous*, and the womans name was Parcoutee, and they lived conioyned together as Man and Wife, feeding on the fruites of the earth, without the destruction of any living creature.

Next Lord claims that the "Banians" have a social system based on descent from the four sons of Pourous and Parcoutee named Brammon, Cuttery, Shuddery, and Wyse (Brahman, Kshatriya, Shudra, and Vaishya). This account, however confused, seems to be indirectly based on the sacrifice of the primeval Purusha in the Rig Veda hymn 10, 90. Although Lord inverts the names of Vaishya and Shudra, his description of the division of labor among these four *varnas* is otherwise more or less accurate. He also manages a rather confused but recognizable account of the cycle of transmigration and its connection to vegetarian *ahimsa*; of the trio of gods Bremaw (Brahma), Vystney (Vishnu), and Ruddery (Rudra-Shiva); and of the four yugas. In his discussion of the Parsis, he also manages to recognize the basic differences of religion among the Banians (i.e., the Hindus), the Muslims, and the Parsis (Lord 1630, [D] 1):

Having declared the Religion, Rites, Customes & Ceremonies, of a people living in the *East Indies* called the *Banians*, a Sect not throughly publisht by any heretofore, whilst my observation was bestowed in such Inquiry, I observed in the towne of *Surratt* the place where I resided, another Sect called the *Persees*, who because I did discerne them to differ both fro the *Moore & Banian* in the course of their living, & in the forme of their Religion.

Even in Lord's rather garbled account, which was based on his visual observations and conversations with native interpreters (whose grasp of English was evidently limited), the basic outline of the set of beliefs and practices that came to be known as Hinduism is clearly visible. Since this is one of the earliest known extended European descriptions of Hinduism, it seems fair to claim that Hinduism, if it was in fact constructed by the Europeans, can be traced back to the very earliest European accounts. The fact that virtually all European accounts—whatever the language or period in which they were written, and whether or not they are likely to have mutually influenced each other—follow this same general outline suggests that the European writers were in fact "constructing" Hinduism directly on the basis of what they observed and what they were told by their native informants. These informants were in turn simply summarizing a construction of

Hinduism that already existed in their own collective consciousness. This does not mean that Hinduism was unchanged during this period, nor that the European and colonial presence did not foster important changes in the way Hinduism was conceptualized by the Hindus themselves, but it does clearly show that the idea that Hinduism was constructed or invented by nineteenth-century Europeans is mistaken.

Hindu Identity Before 1800

A large part of the claim that Hinduism did not exist before it was invented by the British in the early 1800s depends on the belief that before this date the Hindus themselves lacked a self-conscious religious identity, as opposed to a diffuse ethno-geographical identity. The textual evidence against this claim is so overwhelming that I am frankly at a loss to explain why so many worthy scholars apparently accept it. I have only two tentative ideas to offer as at least partial explanations.

First, many liberal and left scholars have been reluctant to accept the idea that the often antagonistic modern Hindu and Muslim identities, both individual and communitarian, arose out of political and religious conflicts during the historical periods of the Delhi Sultanate, the Mughal Empire, and the regional Sultanates. These scholars tend to attribute the invention, construction, or imagining of the modern form of all major Indian institutions to the influence of the colonial state in particular, and the nineteenth-century imaginary in general. As the political scientist Paul Brass once said to me, only half joking: "Everything was invented in the nineteenth century." When it comes to communalism *per se*, as opposed to the wider concept of Hindu identity, most liberal and left scholars—from Bipan Chandra (1984) to Gyanendra Pandey (1992) to Veena Das (1990) and beyond—insist that it was originally a product of the colonial period. The arguments of scholars such as Christopher Bayly and Sheldon Pollock that the roots of communalism lie deeper in the past have often met with open hostility.[22]

The second possible reason why many scholars have not acknowledged the existence of a conscious Hindu religious identity before 1800 is perhaps more interesting. My argument here starts from the fact that Sanskrit literature written before this date systematically ignores the Muslim presence. Muslims, when they appear, are mostly described simply as "foreigners." In his fascinating new book on references to Muslims in Sanskrit sources, mostly inscriptions, B. Chattopadhyaya (1998, 92–97) lists about seventy-five Sanskrit references to Muslims. Among the terms used are *tajika, turushka, mleccha, parasika, yavana, hammira,* and *shaka.* The term *musalamana* is listed only once, from an inscription of 1264 CE Although some of these terms are ethnic in origin, most had acquired the broad generic meaning of "foreigner" or "west Asian" by the time they were applied to Muslims.

In both Sanskrit and vernacular literature, Muslims were often portrayed in the implicit, coded form of demons, as evidently happened in several medieval renderings of the *Ramayana*. Most important in North India was, of course, Tulsidas's late sixteenth-century Hindi *Ramcaritmanas*, which soon achieved the status of a foundational text for the Hinduism of a broad range of castes, with the notable exception of the mostly low-caste followers of the Kabir Panth and related *nirguni* sects. Kampan's Tamil *Iramavataram* plays a somewhat analogous role in the South. Early Europeans and Christians were sometimes similarly coded as demons.

As far as I know, no premodern Sanskrit text includes anything approaching a systematic discussion of Muslim beliefs and practices. Similarly, the terms "Hindu" and "Hindu dharma" were never admitted to the premodern Sanskrit lexicon. The roughly equivalent term "sanatana-dharma" can, it is true, be traced back to the *Bhagavad Gita* and the Puranas, but, as Wilhelm Halbfass and other scholars have argued, its precise meaning has always been ambiguous.[23]

Why exactly Hindu Sanskrit literature written before 1800 treated foreigners and foreign religions, even indigenous Buddhism, in this Olympian fashion is not easy to understand, and would make an excellent topic for a separate essay, but here it is sufficient to note that this systematic ignoring of non-Hindu cultural traditions, whatever its cause, was a deeply embedded trait of premodern Hinduism. Halbfass's rather harsh judgment in this regard is, I think, inescapable:

> The Indocentrism developed in "orthodox" Hindu thought transcends by far what is ordinarily called "ethnocentrism." It is not simply an unquestioned perspective or bias, but a sophisticated theoretical structure of self-universalization and self-isolation. Seen from within this complex, highly differentiated structure, the *mlecchas* are nothing but a faint and distant phenomenon at the horizon of the indigenous tradition. They do not possess an "otherness" against which one's own identity could be asserted, or in which it could be reflected. They are neither targets of possible conversion, nor sources of potential inspiration (Halbfass 1988, 187).

What I am suggesting here is that many modern scholars, especially those who work principally with Sanskrit sources, may have unconsciously absorbed some of the self-imposed cultural isolation of premodern Sanskrit literature and then concluded that there was no Hindu awareness of the Muslim Other. As a consequence, they may also have assumed that the Hindus had no clear contrastive awareness of their own religious identity.

Whatever the reason for the scholarly acceptance of the idea that there was no religious Hindu self-identity before 1800, the evidence against this view in vernacular Hindu literature is clear and abundant. The bulk of this evidence takes the form of texts composed by the popular religious poet-singers of North India, most of them members of non-Brahman castes. This literature does precisely what Sanskrit literature refuses to do: it establishes a Hindu religious identity through a process of mutual self-definition with a contrasting Muslim Other. In practice, there can be no Hindu identity unless this is defined by contrast against such an Other. Without the Muslim (or some other non-Hindu), Hindus can only be Vaishnavas, Shaivas, Smartas or the like. The presence of the Other is a necessary prerequisite for an active recognition of what the different Hindu sects and schools hold in common.

To illustrate this process of mutual self-definition, I will use passages from the *nirguni* poet Kabir, the Ramanandi Anantadas, the Varakari Ekanath, and the Krishna devotee Vidyapati. Many more such passages can easily be cited, especially from the poets of the *nirguni* sant tradition such as Raidas, Nanak, Dadu, Rajjab, and Palatu Das, to name just a few. More orthodox vernacular poets such as Tulsi Das generally follow the evasive Sanskritic strategies of representing Muslims as ill-defined *mlecchas* or coded demons, but even in these writings such coded Muslims are often a palpable, and even necessary, presence.

Ekanath was a Brahman, a scholar and author, who spent most of his life at Paithan in Maharashtra. He was born there in 1533 and died there in 1599. Although he knew Sanskrit well, most of his numerous compositions were written in Marathi. Among them is a humorous poetic dialogue between a Hindu Brahman and a Muslim, the *Hindu-turka-samvada*. The term "Turk" (*turka*), like "Hindu," can be used in an ethno-geographical sense, but here—as in the texts of Anantadas, Kabir, and Vidyapati cited below, as well as in those of many other medieval poets—its primary meaning is clearly "Muslim."

In Ekanath's dialogue, cited here from Eleanor Zelliot's translation (1982), the Hindu and the Muslim mock the absurdities manifest in the popular rituals and myths of each other's faiths. Among the aspects of Hinduism attacked by the Muslim are the anthropomorphic forms of the Hindu gods ("God has hands and feet, you say / This is really impossible!"), the Hindus' ritual bathing ("You leap in the water like water ducks"), various improprieties committed by the gods in the myths of Hindu scripture ("It says God goes out to beg," "Your Brahma laid his daughter," "Thieves took away God's wife / So monkeys came to help him!," "Fool! Your God [Krishna] was imprisoned," "You call God a keeper of cows"), the general falsity of Hindu scripture ("The Vedas he preaches are all false / Your Sastras, your Vedas, your 'OM' / Are all evil tricks"), the Hindu practice of idolatry ("A stone statue rules over you / You give it the name of God / ... You bow and scrape in front of it"), the Hindu practices of ritual purity in cooking and eating ("If so much as a grain of his food falls on yours, / You catch him by the throat!"), and the Hindu male's hypocrisy in applying impurity rules to women ("That girl you have taken as mistress / You don't eat in the house of her people").

The Hindu's main attack and defense is that the Muslim refuses to admit that God is everywhere, rather than just at Mecca. If God is everywhere, why not in idols or the avatars of Hindu mythology? ("God is present in every place / Why not in prison?" "God is in water, in places, in wood, in stone"). The Brahman also attacks the Muslim's animal sacrifices ("When one creature gives pain to another, /How can he go to heaven?") and his efforts to convert Hindus to Islam ("He is supposed to catch a Hindu and make him a Muslim! / Did God make a mistake in making the Hindu?").

The dialogue concludes, in somewhat unlikely fashion, with a reconciliation between the two, on the basis that, for God, all are equal.

> The Brahman says, O yes, swami.
> As a matter of fact, you and I are one.
> This controversy grew over caste and *dharma*.
> When we go to God, there are no such things.
> The Turk says, that is the truth.
> For God there is no caste.
> There is no separation between devotee and God
> Even though the Prophet has said God is hidden.

The Ramanandi author Anantadas is the author of several verse biographies, or *paracais*, of Hindu saints and poets such as Namadev, Pipa, Kabir, and Raidas. He wrote his *Namadev paracai* in 1588 CE and is associated with the Raivasa ashram at Sikar in Rajasthan (Lorenzen 1991, 9–13, 75). A key passage that illustrates his view of the contents of Hindu is found in his *Kabir paracai*. According to Anantadas, when the Lodi sultan, Sikandar, came to Varanasi, a delegation of both Hindus and Muslims went to Sikandar to complain about Kabir's activities. When Sikandar asks what crime Kabir has committed, they reply that he has "done an unconventional thing."[24]

> He has abandoned the customs of the Muslims (*musalamamna*) and has broken the touchability rules of the Hindus. He has scorned the sacred bathing places (*tiratha*) and the Vedas. He has scorned the nine planets, the sun and the moon. He has scorned Shankara and the Mother. He has scorned the Sarada and Ganapati. He has scorned the rites of the eleventh day of the fortnight, the offerings to the sacred fire and the ceremonies for the dead. He has scorned the Brahmans, whom the whole world worships. He has scorned service to one's mother and father, sisters, nieces, and all the gods. He has scorned the hope of all religion [*dharma*], the six systems of metaphysics [*darashana*] and the rites of the twelve months.

He has scorned the [Hindu] rosary, forehead mark, sacred thread, the Salagram stone and the ten avatars. Kabir tells all these lies. He respects neither the Hindus nor the Turks. In this way he has corrupted everyone. He has put both the Hindus and the Turks in the same situation. As long as this low-caste weaver [*julaha*] stays in Varanasi, no one will respect us.

Here Anantadas is staking out a position for Kabir as separate from both the Muslims and Hindus. Almost all the objects of Kabir's scorn that Anantadas specifies, however, come directly from Hindu beliefs and practices, not Muslim ones. Including as they do the major gods, avatars and goddesses, the life-cycle rites, the six *darshanas*, the sacred bathing places, the Vedas, the touchability rules of caste, the sacred fire, and various seasonal observances, they comprise a substantial part of the standard model of Hinduism.

The songs and verses of Kabir himself display a similar rejection of the beliefs and practices of both Hinduism and Islam. Kabir lived in Varanasi between about 1450 and 1520 CE, and is said to have been raised in a Muslim family before becoming a follower of the Vaishnava guru Ramananda. The following song from the *Kabir-bijak* illustrates his often reiterated assertion that both Hinduism and Islam, as commonly practiced, had lost their grasp on spiritual truth:

Tell me, brother. How can there be
Not one Lord of the world but two?
Who has led you so astray?
God has taken many names:
Names like Allah, Ram, Karim,
Kesav, Hari, and Hajarat.
Gold may be shaped into rings and bangles.
Isn't it gold all the same?
Distinctions are only words we invent.
One does *namaz*, one does *puja*.
One has Siva, one Mohammed,
One has Adam, one Brahma.
Who is a Hindu, who a Turk?
Both must share a single world.
Koran or Vedas, both read their books.
One is a *panda*, one a mullah.
Each of them bears a separate name,
But every pot is made from clay.
Kabir says they are both mistaken.
Neither has found the only Ram.

One kills goats, the other cows.
They waste their lives in disputation.[25]

The most interesting evidence relating to the Hindus' religious identity in the period before 1800 comes from the historical romance called *Kirtilata*, a text written in a dialect of *Apabhransha* by the poet Vidyapati sometime early in the fifteenth century, roughly a hundred years before Kabir's songs.[26] The hero of the romance, Prince Kirtisimha, at one point passes through the city of Jonapur, identified with modern Jaunpur. Vidyapati's description of the Muslim quarter of this city is imbued with a sharp anti-Muslim bias. In it he sets out a series of contrasts between the religious customs of the Hindus and Muslims:

> The Hindus and the Turks live close together.
> Each makes fun of the other's religion (*dhamme*).
> One calls the faithful to prayer. The other recites the Vedas.
> One butchers animals by bleeding,
> The other cuts (off their heads).
> Some are called *ojhas*, others *khvajas*.
> Some (read) astrological signs, others fast in Ramadan.
> Some eat from copper plates, others from pottery.
> Some practice *namaz*, others *puja*.
> The Turks coerce passers by into doing forced labor.
> Grabbing hold of a Brahmin boy, they put a cow's vagina on his head.
> They rub out his *tilak* and break his sacred thread.
> They want to ride on horses. They use rice to make liquor.
> They destroy temples and construct mosques.[27]

One noteworthy aspect of this passage is the use of the word *dharma* (here *dhamme*)—coupled with the words *hindu* and *turake*—to apparently mean something quite close to "religion of the Hindus" and "religion of the Muslims." This clearly shows that this sense of *dharma* as "religion" (at the least "a set of religious customs") is not simply a modern usage for a borrowed European concept as Halbfass (1988, 310) and others have suggested.

One other point that can be made here is that the above-cited passages and others of this type generally emphasize the differences in religious customs and rituals, rather than in philosophy or theology, between Hindus and Muslims, although differences in religious texts and ideas are also noted. Customs and rituals are, after all, the primary practical means that ordinary people use to establish and mark off separate religious identities. In addition, we should remember that poets such as Kabir, Dadu, Palatu, and Nanak repeatedly insist on the one religious message that God and spiritual reality are the same no matter what names we give them, nor what ideas we have about them. In their view, the separate religious identities of Hindus and

Muslims are based on mostly worthless customs and ultimately false ideas. Only by seeing beyond such customs and ideas can one establish a true religious identity: an identity that their followers paradoxically define once again in sectarian terms.

Evidence of Hindus directly expressing consciousness of their identity as Hindus is more difficult to encounter in the period before 1400, at least in North Indian Hindu sources. One interesting earlier reference comes from Andhra Pradesh. Cynthia Talbot has analyzed how the military expansion of Muslim dynasties into the Andhra region in 1323 CE led to a sharper sense of regional, political, and religious identity among the Hindu population of the region. She notes that the title "Sultan among Hindu kings (*hindu-raya-suratrana*)," perhaps the earliest use of the term "Hindu" in an Indian language, "begins to figure in Andhra inscriptions from 1352 CE onward" (Talbot 1995, 700). She suggests that these references to Hindu kings likely implied more a geographical than a religious identity. Arguing against this, however, is the fact that Muslim dynasties had already been in control of most of the Ganges valley since the end of the twelfth century, that is, for about 150 years before the first appearance of the phrase "Sultan among Hindu kings" in the Andhra inscriptions. In the circumstances, how could the Andhra kings consider their Muslim opponents to be non-Hindu in a merely geographical sense, that is, non-Indians?

There is one other early Hindu source that should be mentioned here. This is the *Prithviraj raso*, a historical romance attributed to Canda Baradai. This text exists in several versions of quite different lengths, and its date has long been disputed. Traditionally it is said to have been composed not long after Muhammad Ghuri's 1192 CE defeat of the hero of the story, King Prithviraj. Most scholars have argued that all, or all but one, of the versions of the text are more recent, but they have not reached any consensus about which was written when. All versions are full of references to "Hindus" and "Turks" (sometimes "*mlecchas*"), but these references do not permit a clear distinction between the ethnic and religious senses of the words, with one interesting exception. In the Asiatic Society of Bengal's version, the text at one point states that "both religions have drawn their curved swords (*dou dina dinam kadhi bamki assim*)" (Canda Baradai 1992, 59). The Hindi word *din* is of Arabic rather than Sanskrit origin, but its meaning as "faith" or "religion" is not in doubt.

Muslim Sources

References to the Hindus and their religion in Muslim sources, mostly written in Persian, are of less direct relevance here since they cannot be used to directly prove or disprove the existence of the self-identity of Hindus as Hindus. These references also take the discussion into areas beyond my own linguistic competence. Nonetheless, these texts, like the early sources in European languages, are important for the evidence they offer about the existence of Hinduism from the point of view of outside observers. According to Richard Eaton, one of the earliest occurrences of the word "Hindu" in Islamic literature appears in 'Abd al-Malik 'Isami's Persian work, *Futuhu's-salatin*, composed in the Deccan in 1350. In this text 'Isami uses the word *hindi* to mean "Indian" in the ethno-geographical sense, and the word *Hindu* to mean "Hindu" in the sense of a follower of the Hindu religion.[28]

According to Carl Ernst, "the beginnings of the concept of 'Hindu' religion are to be sought in the Persian literature of the Ghaznavid period, beginning about 990," and its "more precise formulation" in the famous Arabic work of al-Biruni (d. 1048; see Ernst 1992). While Ernst curiously ignores the ample evidence for the Hindus' own conceptualization of their religion, his identification of al-Biruni as the first outside observer to formulate a clear and detailed representation of Hinduism is undoubtedly correct. Al-Biruni was attempting to write a general account of Indian religion, philosophy, literature, history, geography, manners and customs, and festivals, and especially of Indian cosmography, astrology, and astronomy. Although his emphases are different than those of the other authors we have been discussing, his account of Hinduism covers most of the topics of Monier-Williams's standard model.

Al-Biruni's text includes—roughly in order, and omitting secular topics—discussions of the Hindu concepts of God, the soul, transmigration, heaven and hell, morality and law, the three different paths to salvation, the pantheon of gods, idol worship, the four social classes (*varnas*), the four Vedas, the eighteen major Puranas, the law books (*smriti*), the *Mahabharata*, cosmogonic and cosmographic theories and myths, theories of time cycles including the four yugas, the mythology of Vishnu and his more important avatars, calendrical and astronomical rites, linga worship and its mythology, the four life stages (*ashramas*), the rites and customs of various castes, pilgrimages, life-cycle rites, dietary customs and fasting, and calendrical festivals. Al-Biruni knew Sanskrit and used various Sanskrit texts in his research, including the *Bhagavad Gita*, Patanjali's *Yoga Sutra*, a text on *Samkhya*, the *Vishnu Purana*, several other Puranas, and many texts on astronomy, astrology, geography, and chronology. Although the English translator liberally uses the word "Hindu," the original Arabic text appears to only use phrases literally equivalent to "[of] the people of India [*hind*]."[29] Nonetheless, al-Biruni clearly understood the difference between the people of India as a geographical or ethnic entity and as a religious group.

Conclusions

The main purpose of this essay has been to show that the claim of many scholars—that Hinduism was invented by the British in the early nineteenth century—is false. A larger issue, however, is also implicitly involved. This is the tendency of many historians of modern India—especially those associated with the subaltern school—to adopt a postcolonialist perspective that privileges the British colonial period as the period in which almost all the major institutions of Indian society and politics were invented or constructed. As Richard Eaton (1998) notes in a recent critique of these historians: "The notion of 'postcoloniality' situated *all* Indian time in reference to the British imperial period: time was either precolonial, colonial, or postcolonial" (Eaton 1998).

One postcolonialist historian, Nicholas Dirks, has claimed that even caste, that uniquely Indian institution, was in some sense invented by the British: "Colonialism seems to have created much of what is now accepted as Indian 'tradition,' including an autonomous caste structure with the Brahman clearly and unambiguously at the head" (Dirks 1989, 43). Although Dirks is using hyperbole to make his point, and he does include some important but easily overlooked qualifications, the argument seems to me to be grossly overstated.[30] As the Hindi critic Purushottom Agrawal recently quipped: "We Indians may well have been denied the capacity to solve our own problems, but are we so incapable that we could not even create them on our own?" Caste, like Hinduism, undoubtedly responded to the British conquest with significant changes, but neither institution was so radically transformed during the colonial period that it makes any sense, even in terms of a transformation of pre-existing institutions or concepts, to claim that the British invented them. Whatever cultural garments the British stitched together, caste and Hinduism weren't among them. At least in these respects, the Empire has no clothes.

If Hinduism is a construct or invention, then, it is not a colonial one, nor a European one, nor even an exclusively Indian one. It is a construct or invention only in the vague and commonsensical way that any large institution is, be it Christianity, Buddhism, Islam, communism, or parliamentary democracy. In other words, it is an institution created out of a long historical interaction between a set of basic ideas and the infinitely complex and variegated socio-religious beliefs and practices that structure the everyday life of individuals and small, local groups.

In this interaction, both the basic ideas and the everyday beliefs and practices are constantly changing—sometimes slowly, sometimes rapidly. Major historical changes in the economic and political institutions of India during the Turco-Afghan conquest, the Mughal invasion, the consolidation of the

Mughal polity, and the establishment of the British colonial regime undoubtedly effected important changes in the religious traditions of India, but the rapid changes of early colonial times never had such an overwhelming impact that they could have led to the invention of Hinduism. Hinduism wasn't invented sometime after 1800, or even around the time of the establishment of the Delhi Sultanate. What did happen during the centuries of rule by dynasties of Muslim sultans and emperors was that Hindus developed a consciousness of a shared religious identity based on the loose family resemblance among the variegated beliefs and practices of Hindus, whatever their sect, caste, chosen deity, or theological school.

From the point of view of a modern observer, one can see the family resemblance taking a recognizably Hindu shape in the early Puranas, roughly around the period 300–600 CE. Although the religion of these Puranas displays many continuities with the earlier Vedic religion, its principal features and emphases—particularly its greatly expanded mythology of the gods Vishnu, Shiva, and Devi—do, I think, justify marking this religion off as something new, as the beginning of medieval and modern Hinduism. This Hinduism wasn't invented by anyone, European or Indian. Like Topsy, it just grow'd.

Notes

1. Yule and Burnell's bibliography lists the book as being published in Portuguese at Goa in 1563, but the English translation they give seems to be an old one.
2. I thank many scholars for their comments on this and earlier versions of this essay, particularly Saurabh Dube and Sabyasachi Bhattacharya.
3. Somewhat different but compatible arguments can also be found in Bayly 1985, Pollock 1993b, and Rogers 1994 (this last reference on Sri Lanka).
4. This reference was brought to my attention by Patricio Nelson.
5. The derivation from *indu* was suggested by Alexander Dow in a text published in 1768: "The Hindoos are so called from Indoo or Hindoo, which, in the Shanscrita language, signifies the Moon; for from that luminary, and the sun, they deduce their fabulous origin" (Marshall 1970, 114). In the same text Dow also offers the biblical derivation, but Nathaniel Brassey Halhed, in a text published in 1776, suggests that the derivation from *sindhu* is probably the correct one. He also claims that the name Hindu was probably adopted by the Hindus to distinguish themselves from the Muslims:

> Hindostan is a Persian word, equally unknown to the old and modern Shanscrit, compounded of Stan, a region, and the word Hind or Hindoo: probably Colonel Dow's elegant translation of Ferishteh's History gives us the true derivation, in that author's conjecture, that it is taken from Hind, a supposed son of Ham, the son of Noah; and, whatever antiquity the Indians may assert for themselves (of which some notice will subsequently be taken) the Persians, we believe, will rest contented to allow, that the first intercourse between the two nations commenced in the third descent from the deluge. But, if this definition were rejected, the common opinion, that India was so

named by foreigners after the river Indus, is by no means repugnant to probability. ... Hindoo therefore is not the term by which the inhabitants originally
stiled themselves ... and it is only since the aera of the Tartar government that
they have assumed the name of Hindoos, to distinguish themselves from their
conquerors, the Mussulmen (Marshall 1970, 149–50).

6. See also W. C. Smith 1991, 256. I have criticized C. Fuller's similar resort to this
   etymology in Lorenzen 1995, 11–12.
7. It may be possible, as W. C. Smith (1991, 256) suggests, that examples of the term
   "Hindu Muslim" can be found in European languages. Even if such examples could be
   found, and Smith does not cite any, I doubt that the authors would have had any
   significant contact with or knowledge of India. Similarly, Dermot Killingley reports
   (1993, 61) that the term "Hindu Christian" has sometimes been used, again without
   citing examples. In Spanish the word *hindu* is still used in popular speech to mean
   "Indian," but news reports and educated speech now generally use *indio* or *de la India*
   for "Indian" and reserve *hindu* or *hinditsta* for "Hindu." In Latin America, the original
   motive for preferring *hindu* was probably to distinguish the South Asian Indians from
   the large population of Amerindians, normally called *indios*.
8. Good examples of the metaphysical approach include the texts of Zaehner (1966),
   Radhakrishnan (1968), and, in a somewhat different vein, Biardeau (1991). The
   historical and catalog approaches are discussed further below.
9. Representative texts by Halhed, Wilkins, and Jones are all conveniently collected in P.
   J. Marshall's *The British Discovery of Hinduism in the Eighteenth Century* (1970). See
   also Grant 1970.
10. See, for example, the texts in Wicki 1948–1972, vol. I, pp. 45 (*"moros, gentivos e maos
    christaos"*), 87 (*"mouros e jemtios"*), 629 (*"gentilidade"*). In early nineteenth-century
    English usage in South India, "Gentoo" signified "Telugu" (language or person) as
    opposed to "Malabar" or "Tamil" (language or person) (Trautmann 1998).
11. For Italian texts, see below. For Spanish, see the *Itinerario* of Sebastian Manrique
    (1946), written in 1649. N. B. Halhed, however, preferred a fanciful derivation of
    "Gentoo" from the Sanskrit *jantu*, meaning "animal" and also, he claims, "mankind"
    (Marshall 1970, 150).
12. See also the quote from Dr. Garcia de Orta, dated 1563, used as the epigraph to this
    essay.
13. A translation of this passage, minus Manrique's gloss, is quoted at greater length in
    Eaton 1996, 181. Baton's note (182) on the use of the word *indus* in this passage is not
    completely convincing. In the passage Eaton quotes, the original has *indus* not once but
    twice. The incident referred to took place in 1640.
14. One quite mundane reason why European states supported missionary endeavors in
    such remote and exotic locations was undoubtedly the usefulness of the monks' reports
    as military, political, and economic intelligence. The monks themselves, on the other
    hand, were certainly more intent on saving souls than on gathering intelligence for
    European rulers. The essential point for present purposes is that the monks were
    observing Hinduism in societies in which the influence of European imperial expansion
    was still negligible.
15. See also Halbfass 1988, 38–43 and Neill 1984, 279–300. Halbfass and Neill give
    references to several other texts by and about de Nobili in their notes.
16. On Ziegenbalg and Stephens, see also Halbfass 1988 and Neill 1984. Other general
    works useful for a study of these and other early missionaries include Lach 1965, Murr
    1983, Petech 1952–1956; and Wicki 1948–1972. None of these works have much to
    say about Fernandes Trancoso or Marco della Tomba.

Marco della Tomba was part of a large Italian Franciscan mission to Tibet, Nepal, and North India that was active throughout the eighteenth century. An important seven-volume collection of some of the writings of those of these Italian Franciscans— and one important Jesuit, Ippolito Desideri—who worked in Nepal and Tibet has been published by Luciano Petech (1952–56). Unfortunately, no comparable collection of writings by the Franciscans of this mission who worked in North India has been published apart from the single volume of selected texts by Marco della Tomba.

17. The Hindi dialogue by Giuseppe Maria da Gargnano (1709–1761) is entitled "*Jababas-vala aik Kristian aur aik Hindu ke bic mo iman ke upar*" (A dialogue about religion between a Christian and a Hindu). Another work by this same title has been attributed to Costanzo da Borgo San Sepolcro (in India and Tibet from about 1775 to 1787), but this is in fact a slightly modified version of Giuseppe Maria's text together with Costanzo's line-by-line Italian translation. A few facsimile pages of the manuscripts of both versions have been published in an article by Umberto Nardella (1989, 57–63, 67–68). Both manuscripts are now in the Vatican Library. I am currently working on a study of the texts by Giuseppe Maria, Costanzo, Marco della Tomba and other Franciscans of this mission.

18. I discussed Marco's translation of this text and its misidentification by several scholars in a paper presented at a June 1999 Heidelberg conference held to celebrate six hundred years of Kabir. A revised version of the paper will appear in a book being edited for Manohar by Monika Boehm-Tettelbach.

19. Giuseppe Felice da Morro was in Kathmandu from the beginning of 1715 to about 1719, then in Dvags-po, returning to Kathmandu in 1721. He died there the following year, at about forty years of age.

20. As the editor, Petech, notes, this goddess apparently has nothing to do with the serpent goddess Manasa of Nepal. Rather, she seems to be equivalent to God's power or *Shakti*. There does not seem to be any identifiable textual source for this story.

21. Lord arrived in Surat in 1624. It is curious that John Zephaniah Holwell claims that during the capture of Calcutta in 1756, he "lost many curious Gentoo manuscripts, and among them two very correct and valuable copies of the Gentoo *Shastah*" as well as "a translation I made of a considerable part of the *Shastah*, which had cost me eighteen months hard labour" (Marshall 1970, 46). *Shaster* and *Shastah* are of course equivalent to *shastra*, a general type of text and not a specific title. I suspect that Holwell may have Lord's *Shaster* in mind.

22. See Pandey's (1992, 15) hostile reaction to Bayly's 1985 article about the "pre-history" of communalism and B. Chattopadhyaya's (1998, 98–115) extended criticism of Pollock's 1993 article, "Ramayana and Political Imagination in India." Chattopadhyaya's most palpable hit is that Pollock has made a very selective reading of the evidence when he associates the reaction by Hindus against Islam and Turko-Afghan or Mughal conquest exclusively with the rise of the devotional cult to Rama. The Hindus undoubtedly conceptualized and mythologically represented the conflict between Hindu kings and Turko-Afghans or Mughals with figures other than just Rama and Ravana, but this, I think, only puts an interesting qualification to Pollock's basic argument.

23. See the discussion and references in Halbfass 1988, 310–48. I suspect that the term "eternal dharma" may have been used in part to distinguish Brahmanical and Hindu religion from the more historical religions of Buddhism and Jainism, but Buddhist scholars have told me that Buddhism itself is sometimes called the "eternal dharma."

24. The preceding phrase and the first paragraph of the quote are from my published translation of the Niranjani recension. The second paragraph is from the text in the oldest manuscript of 1636 (Lorenzen 1991, 107, 230).

25. *Kabir-bijak* (Kabir 1982), *shabda* 30. The *Bijak*, associated with the Kabir Panth, is one of three old collections of his compositions. The others are the Dadu Panthi *Kabir-granthavali* and the Sikh *Adi-grantha*. Not all the compositions attributed to Kabir in these collections are necessarily his, but all date from the sixteenth century. Many other songs with a similar message can be quoted from all collections. See, for instance, *Kabir-bijak*, *Shabdas* 4 (anti-idolatry), 8 (anti-avatars), 10 (anti-sacrifice), 61 (cremation/burial), 75 (Hindu/Turk bodies the same); *Adi-grantha*, *asa* 5 (anti-yoga, anti-*shastras*), *bhairo* 20 (God is above Puranic gods), *vibhasa-prabhati* 2 (anti-ritual). Translations can be found in Hess and Singh 1983, and Dass 1991, respectively.

26. This difficult text has been well edited, analyzed and translated into modern Hindi by Sivaprasad Simha (1988). The passages discussed here are also discussed by Gaeffke 1977 and Lutgendorf 1997, 31–35. I thank Lutgendorf for bringing this text to my attention.

27. Simha 1988, 269–70. I have followed Simha's interpretation throughout. *Ojhas* are a type of Hindu healer and *khvajas* a type of Muslim ascetic.

28. Personal communication from Richard Eaton citing 'Isami 1967–1977, texts 405 and 606, trans. 2:613 and 3:902.

29. This at least is the preliminary conclusion of Richard Eaton, who kindly looked through the Arabic text for the original equivalents at my request.

30. To this statement, from Dirks's 1989 essay can be added another ambitious claim he makes in a more recent text: "Even as much of what we now recognize as culture was produced by the colonial encounter, the concept itself was in part invented because of it" (Dirks 1992, 3). Both these passages are cited in Eaton 1998.

4

UNITY AND PLURALITY: HINDUISM AND THE RELIGIONS OF INDIA IN EARLY EUROPEAN SCHOLARSHIP

Will Sweetman

The term "Hinduism" is … a particularly false conception, one that is conspicuously incompatible with any adequate understanding of the religious outlook of Hindus. Even the term "Hindu" was unknown to the classical Hindus. "Hinduism" as a concept they certainly did not have. … There are Hindus, but there is no Hinduism (W. C. Smith 1991, 63, 65).

Hinduism does not merely fail to be religion; it is not even a meaningful unit of discourse (Staal 1989, 397).

The creation of Hinduism antedates that of Buddhism. By this, I do not imply that Hinduism existed in India before Buddhism came into being—this claim, after all, is a standard text-book trivium—but that the Europeans created Buddhism after they had created Hinduism (Balagangadhara 1994, 138).

[T]here has never been any one religion—nor even one system of religions—to which the term "Hindu" can accurately be applied. No one so-called religion, moreover, can lay exclusive claim to or be defined by the term "Hinduism." The very notion of the existence of any single religious community by this name one may further argue, has been falsely conceived (Frykenberg 1997, 82).

In recent scholarship on Indian religions there has emerged a consensus on the inadequacy of the concept "Hinduism."[1] "Hinduism" is assumed by contemporary scholars to be a western concept, one not found among those who are supposed to adhere to the religion it designates, which religion in fact does not exist, or at least did not exist prior to its invention by European scholars. None of these claims will be challenged here.[2] Rather, it will be accepted that, like the term "religion," Hinduism "is solely the creation of the scholar's study" (J. Z. Smith 1982, xi), "a conceptual tool ... not to be confused with an ontological category actually existing in reality" (McCutcheon 1997, viii). The scholarly consensus extends to the account given of the process by which this concept emerged. It is this account that will be challenged here, including the idea that it first emerged in the colonialist context of the late eighteenth or early nineteenth century and that Jewish and Christian preconceptions about the nature of religion resulted in a monolithic and distorting reification of Indian religious beliefs and practices.[3]

Richard King's recent account of what he calls "the modern myth of 'Hinduism'" (see King 1999, 96–117) is representative of the scholarly consensus identified here. King writes that "'Hindu' in fact only came into provenance among Westerners in the eighteenth century. Previously, the predominant Christian perspective amongst Europeans classified Indian religion under the all-inclusive rubric of Heathenism. On this view there were four major religious groups, Jews, Christians, Mahometans (i.e. Muslims) and Heathens" (King 1999, 99; cf. Balagangadhara 1994, 111). Although there were references in the eighteenth century to "the religion of the Gentoos," the term "Gentoo," like other terms, "functioned as an alternative to 'Heathen'" (King 1999, 100) and therefore did not depart from the prevailing classification of heathenism as one of the four religions of the world. It is not, King argues, "until the nineteenth century proper that the term 'Hinduism' became used as a signifier of a unified, all-embracing and independent religious entity in both Western and Indian circles" (King 1999, 100).[4] According to King, "the key to the West's *initial* postulation of the unity of 'Hinduism' derives from the Judaeo-Christian presuppositions of the Orientalists and missionaries" and especially their conviction "that distinctive religions could not coexist without frequent antagonism" and that the "relatively peaceful coexistence of the various Hindu movements [could not] be explained without some sense of religious unity" (King 1999, 105 [italics added]).

King "highlights two ways in which Western colonisation has contributed to the modern construction of 'Hinduism': first by locating the core of Indian religiosity in certain Sanskrit texts (the textualisation of Indian religion), and second by an implicit (and sometimes explicit) tendency to define Indian religion in terms of a normative paradigm of religion based upon contemporary Western understandings of the Judaeo-Christian traditions" (King 1999, 101). While both of these factors influenced the later development of the concept of Hinduism, their role in the first emergence of the concept is less significant. For European writers from the sixteenth to the mid-seventeenth century, the paradigm of religion identified by King had yet to become normative, and we ought not to assume that it constrained their understanding of Hinduism.[5] Rather, the earliest modern European writers on Hinduism were fully cognizant of religious diversity in India, and the idea of Hinduism as a pan-Indian religion—an idea that does not begin to emerge until the early eighteenth century—owes more to Indian self-representations and the evolving European conceptual grasp of India as a coherent geographical entity than to the imposition of Jewish or Christian presuppositions about the nature of religion.

For these reasons it is significant that most other accounts of the European invention of Hinduism begin, as King's does, in the late eighteenth century, making only passing references to what went before. Brian K. Smith writes that "As a discrete Indic religion among others ... 'Hinduism' was probably first imagined by the British in the early part of the nineteenth century to describe (and create and control) an enormously complex configuration of people and their traditions found in the South Asian subcontinent" (B. K. Smith 1987, 35). Robert Frykenberg attributes the "newly-coined concept of Hinduism" to "scholars in the Enlightenment from Nathaniel Brassey Halhed and William Jones ... to Max Muller" (Frykenberg 1997, 86). Ronald Inden locates the invention of Hinduism in nineteenth-century European works (see Inden 1990, 86), and his account makes no reference to earlier sources. Inden spells out what Smith alludes to in saying that "Hinduism" was imagined in part in order to control South Asians: "the formation of Indological discourse made it possible" for "European scholars, traders, and administrators to appropriate the power of Indians (not only the 'masses,' but also the 'elite') to act for themselves" (Inden 1986, 403). Although P. J. Marshall notes that "English writers in the second half of the eighteenth century were heirs to over two hundred years of attempts by Europeans to interpret Hinduism" (Marshall 1970, 29), he tends to project eighteenth-century views of Hinduism onto earlier accounts. For example, of the authors[6] of the texts he excerpts, he states that "As Europeans have always tended to do, they created Hinduism in their own image" (Marshall 1970, 43). He does not attend to the earlier works, noting that "published accounts of India [which] appeared in Europe during the sixteenth and seventeenth centuries ... do not seem to have received very much public notice" (Marshall 1970, 2). Likewise, of the twenty-one essays in a recent collection entitled *Representing Hinduism* (Dalmia and von Stietencron 1995), only three discuss representations prior to the nineteenth century, only two of those are concerned with European representations, and one of these two is primarily concerned with representations of caste rather than of Hinduism as such (see Dharampal-Frick 1995). The remaining essay is by Heinrich von Stietencron (1995), one of several in which he has outlined the origin of the concept of "Hinduism."[7]

Stietencron departs somewhat from the scholarly consensus which locates the emergence of the idea of Hinduism as a unitary religion in the late eighteenth or early nineteenth century, for he stresses the dependence of the concept on earlier European visions of the religions of humanity. He is right to consider these earlier works. I will argue that it is in these works, particularly those from the first decades of the eighteenth century, that something like the modern concept of Hinduism first emerges. However, while Inden, Marshall and others tend, by ignoring them, to assimilate seventeenth- and early eighteenth-century European accounts of Hinduism to later works, and hence also to the colonial context in which those later works were produced, Stietencron comprehensively assimilates the concept of Hinduism in seventeenth- and eighteenth-century writers to the theological concept of heathenism of earlier centuries. He argues that "although the term 'Hinduism' came into common use as late as the nineteenth century, the underlying concept of a unity of Indian religion was already in existence in the West before that religion was actually encountered by European missionaries and traders. ... The concept ... was present in Europe throughout the Middle Ages and it was totally independent of any concrete knowledge about India" (Stietencron 1995, 72). The concept to which Stietencron refers is "heathenism" in the fourfold classification which King mentions: "European missionaries and traders who settled down on the shores of India from 1598 [*sic*] onwards ... knew for certain that the entire population of the world was divided into four major religious systems or laws, namely, *lex christiana, les iudaica, lex mahometana* and *lex gentillium*, i.e. the religious norms and doctrines of the Christians, the Jews, the Moslem and the heathen" (Stietencron 1995, 73–74). From the early missionaries' view of the religion of Indian heathens came the idea that it was *one* single Hindu religion with which one had to do. The later provision of the name Hinduism, which first gave it a conceptual identity, merely cemented what had long been the most important premise of scholarly research on Indian religions (see Stietencron 1988, 149). Like King, Stietencron argues that since early European writers on Hinduism:

> were used to the Christian tradition of an absolute claim for only one truth, of a powerful church dominating society, and consequently of fierce religious and social confrontation with members of other creeds they were *unable* even to conceive of such religious liberality as would give members of the same society the freedom, by individual choice, to practice the religion they like (Stietencron 1997, 37 [italics added]).

The conviction of King and Stietencron that Christian presuppositions made it impossible for European writers to perceive religious plurality in India appears to blind them to the places where, as will be shown, they describe and analyze such plurality.

Stietencron argues that the dominance of the idea of a single unified heathen religion in India meant that "striking differences within this heathen religion had to be treated as sectarian differences. There was no other possibility. For that they could be treated as different 'religions' was precluded in advance by the general conception of the four religions of humankind" (Stietencron 1988, 127–28). Of course, there was in principle another possibility, namely, that the general conception of the four religions of humankind might be abandoned. Although Stietencron concedes that "[s]ome of the early missionaries, like Roberto Nobili, were interested in the language and culture of the Indian heathen," he insists that:

> they knew for certain that what they saw was one of the hitherto unknown sects of heathendom, and whatever differences they could gradually detect within this sect were attributed to further splitting up into subsects. It never occurred to them that they might have to do with different faiths because their conceptual framework regarding the religions of this world had no room for any new creed other than the superstitious creed of the followers of Satan; and the apparent contradictions within this world-wide system of the heathen only confirmed their belief that Satan had created the baffling variety of superstitious cults precisely in order to confuse and enslave these poor, ill-guided people in the snares of delusion. As late as the first quarter of the eighteenth century when Bartholomaus Ziegenbalg wrote his famous book on the Malabarian heathendom this was still the world view of European missionaries (Stietencron 1995, 74–75).

Stietencron's choice of Nobili and Ziegenbalg as exemplars of missionaries compelled by the fourfold classification to treat Hinduism as a single religion is particularly interesting. A close examination of Nobili's writings on Hinduism will demonstrate that not all early European missionaries treated Hinduism as a single religion. And it is in the works of Ziegenbalg that a sense of Hinduism as a single, pan-Indian religion begins to emerge—not on the basis of a preconceived idea of Indian heathenism but from attention to the ways in which Indians classified their own traditions. The idea of Hinduism as a unified tradition emerges not from the idea of heathenism within the fourfold classification but from engagement with Indians' own ideas of their religious adherence.

Roberto Nobili: *"hi populi unum habeant civilem cultum, religionem vero multiplicem"*

Nobili's works on Hinduism[8] were not written to inform Europe about the religions of India, except insofar as such knowledge served the real purpose of these works, which was to justify the practice of "accommodation" or "adaptation" in the Madurai mission which he had founded (or re-founded) in 1606. Nobili, following to some extent the principles of the Jesuit mission in China of Matteo Ricci, allowed Brahman converts to continue in certain practices which, he argued, were only signs of "a certain social and political rank" and were not implicated in "idolatry" (Rajamanickam 1971, 103).[9] The denunciation of these practices by his fellow Jesuit, Goncalo Fernandes Trancoso, provoked the so-called "Malabar rites" controversy.[10] Nobili's position in the controversy presupposed that "there is a norm by which we can distinguish between social actions and the purely religious" ("*quod regulam, qua dignosci debent, quae sint apud hos Indos politica et quae sacra*" [Rajamanickam 1971, 145–55]). Nobili was thus already concerned with questions of definition in regard to Indian or Hindu religious belief and practice. In the course of his argument in *Narratio Fundamentorem* (1619), his most important treatise in defense of his position, he develops an explicit account of three kinds of religious differences—itself enough to refute the view that all early European missionaries in India treated Hinduism as a single religion.

The context is Nobili's third reason (of twelve) for the proposition that "the thread and the tuft are social, not religious insignia" ("*Lineam et Curuminum non inter superstitiosa, sed inter politica esse*" [Rajamanickam 1971, 86–87]):

> There are among these gentiles, several sects, which entirely disagree with one another in the question of religion and adoration of the divinity. Now when these sects are so antagonistic to one another they cannot possibly have one common religious emblem. Therefore the string and tuft, which are used by all these sects in common, cannot be the emblem of any of those sects in particular (Rajamanickam 1971, 93).

Nobili considers an objection of "a certain genteman," Fr. Andrea Buccerio, who had criticized an earlier treatise of Nobili on this subject. Buccerio "tried to upset this argument, saying: these gentile sects, although contrary to one another, agree in one thing, and thus may have a common sign. If you ask: in what do they agree? He answers: in that they all worship, not the true God, but the idols; hence, the string is the badge of idols in common" (Rajamanickam 1971, 93). Nobili states that "this way of arguing is no answer" to his initial claim, giving four reasons, the last of which is that:

> an emblem which various sects use to signify their religious tenets serve also, morally speaking, to distinguish these sects from one another. I say morally speaking, because, though it is physically possible, it is not actually done. To take an example: will the Christians, the Jews and the Turks ever choose a common emblem to signify that they all believe in

one God? But whatever it will be elsewhere, among our gentiles, it is inconceivable; for their sects are so opposed to one another, that one sect will refuse to use a word, which perfectly applies to its divinity, if it is already used by another sect. ... These gentile sects are so opposed to one another that it is impossible for them to agree together even in matters so light as words, even though these words are applicable to this or that god. If so, what reason have you to believe that these sects will agree in having one common emblem? The conclusion is inevitable, that the string is not a religious emblem, for if it were, it would not be worn by sects so opposed to one another (Rajamanickam 1971, 95).

In expounding this point, Nobili sets out an explicit account of three kinds of religious differences, identifying the kind of differences found among religions in India as the most fundamental of these:

In this connection let me call to mind what doctors are wont to teach. Three kinds of differences exist. The first is when, in one and the same sect, various modes of life may be found. Thus we have in the Christian religion various Religious families [*in una Christiana religione variae Religiosorum virorum familiae*]; of course these can use a common symbol of their faith, because they are of one faith [*protestativum propter unitatem fidei*]. The second is when a sect differs from another in such a way that, although they differ in some essential point, they can still use the same denomination. Thus heretics differ from Catholics, yet they are called by the same name Christian [*huiusmodi est oppugnantia haereticorum cum Christiana et catholica religione, quibus tamen remanet commune nomen Christianum*] and use the same Christian symbols, as baptism, the cross, etc. The third is when each sect adores a god peculiar to itself. Now, it is concerning this last case that I said: it is morally impossible that these sects agree in a common religious symbol. For every act of worship is addressed to a determinate god [*nam cum religionis actus versetur circa Deum determinatum*]; but if the god is indeterminate, that is, if it is not this or that god in particular, the act of worship will also be indeterminate, and consequently there cannot be any one definite religious emblem. *Now, it is this last kind of difference which is to found among the sects of the people here* [*Atque haec contrarietas in sectis huius gentis reperitur*—i.e. not like Christian religious families or even heretical sects]. Therefore the string cannot possibly be a symbol of divinity common to all (Rajamanickam 1971, 95–97 [italics added]).

When Nobili writes that "these people follow one common way of life, but many religions,"[11] it is thus clear that he means that among Hindus who use the thread and tuft there are religious differences which go beyond the religious differences between Catholics and other Christians, and even beyond that between "the Christians, the Jews and the Turks [who] ... all believe in one God" (Rajamanickam 1971, 95).[12] Nobili certainly perceives similarities among the Hindus,[13] but the requirements of his theological argument on the Malabar rites lead him to insist on the fundamental nature of their religious differences.[14] Ironically, then, insofar as his theological preconceptions influenced his view of Hinduism, they, far from leading him to conceive of Hinduism as a single religion divided into different sects, had in his case precisely the opposite effect. Of course, his view of the Hindus as adhering to a number of different religions emerges not only from his theological preconceptions but also from his direct engagement with members of the religions he identified.

Although Nobili continues to use the term "sect" to refer to different religious groups, it is clear that for him this term does not indicate their participation in a single overarching religion which can be signified by a single common emblem. Rather, he does not appear to have drawn the rigid distinction between religion and sect implied in Stietencron's account of his work. The same is true of other writers of this period who, like Nobili, refer to a plurality of religions in India. The Chaplain to the English East India Company at Surat in the 1620s, Henry Lord, refers both to "the sect of the Banians" and to "the Banian religion," as well as to the "sect" and "the religion of the Parsses." Far from treating Indian heathenism as a single monolithic religion, Lord distinguishes different religions and groups within religions at every level.[15] In general, European authors prior to the eighteenth century treat Indian religion on a regional basis—either, within the sequential narrative of travel accounts in which the author proceeds from place to place, describing religious beliefs and practices along with other noteworthy features of the physical and cultural landscape, or, as in the works of writers such as Lord and the Dutch Chaplain Abraham Roger, describing the religion of a particular region in which they spent an extended period of time. Thus the subtitle of Roger's 1651 work, *De Open-Deure tot het Verborgen Heydendom*, offers a description of "the life and manners, the religion and divine service, of the Bramins who dwell on the Coromandel coast and the surrounding country," that is, the area in which he lived from 1632 to 1642.[16] Although the term "religion" (*Religie*) appears in the subtitle of the posthumously published work, Roger rarely uses this term or its derivative *religieus*. Instead, he uses *Gods-dienst* and *Godsdienstigh*."[17] In the first half of the seventeenth century *Gods-dienst* was to some extent synonymous with *Religie*, but *Religie* itself had not yet fully acquired the meaning that "religion" and its equivalents have today. While the *De Veritate Religionis Christianae* (1627) of Hugo de Groot (Grotius) had appeared in an earlier, poetic form as *Bewys van den Waren Godsdienst is ses Boecken gestelt* (1622), Wilfred Cantwell Smith comments that even in the prose, Latin version, the transition to the modern sense of religion "is not yet complete: [de Groot's] position set forth under that title is about three-quarters of the way or more along a road leading from 'the genuineness of Christian religiousness' to 'the truth of the Christian religion'" (W. C. Smith 1991, 39). There is therefore reason to believe that when Roger, who left Holland in 1630, speaks of "den Gods-dienst der Bramines," we should not read into his work a more reified sense of "religion."[18] Roger's work demonstrates that, far from the religious beliefs and practices of India being forced into a preconceived mould of an objectified heathen "religion," the concept "religion," and the concept which will later be named "Hinduism," were developing in tandem in the seventeenth century.

A further reason that we find no real conceptual grasp of Hinduism as a single, pan-Indian religion prior to the eighteenth century is that writers on Hinduism in this period have no concept of India in anything like its modern sense. Of the European conception of India as a geographical entity, Matthew Edney notes that prior to the eighteenth century European maps framed India in three distinct ways:

> Beginning in the early 1500s, general maps showed the traditional region of the Indies, from the Indus to Indochina. The subcontinent was, of course, a prominent feature of those maps, but it was not their focus. Later, in the sixteenth century, Europeans began to produce maps that framed only the peninsula south of the river Krishna, the area of their principal involvement. The third framing developed early in the seventeenth century and focused on the polity of the Mughal empire. These maps emphasised the seat of Mughal power in the northern plains. They also included the Mughal territories west of the Indus: the Punjab, the Hindu Kush, and on occasion Afghanistan. They omitted the peninsula (Edney 1997, 4–5).

Maps which merged the latter two regional framings to produce a map of "the entire region usually considered to be India *per se*" began to appear in the first decades of the eighteenth century. Edney reproduces "one of the first maps to show all of South Asia in its modern conception," published in 1717 (Edney 1997, 7–8). He argues, however, that it was only "during the 1760s and the 1770s that the two regional framings completely merged to create a conception of India as a region. ... It is in [James Rennell's] highly influential maps that we find the establishment of India as a meaningful, if still ambiguous, geographical entity" (Edney 1997, 9).[19] Likewise it was not until the first decades of the eighteenth century that the idea of a Hinduism as a pan-Indian religion began to emerge in the works of Ziegenbalg and other European authors.[20] As the European conceptual grasp of India as a geographical entity consolidated, so too did the concept of Hinduism. Thus William Robertson, in his account of "the religious tenets and practices of the Indians" which appears as the appendix to his last work, *An Historical Disquisition concerning the Knowledge which the Ancients had of India* (1791)[21]—itself inspired by his reading of James Rennell's *Memoir*—presents Hinduism as "the national religion" of India, "publicly established in all the extensive countries stretching from the Banks of the Indus to Cape Comorin" (Robertson 1791, 321, 302).

Bartholomaus Ziegenbalg: *"Denn es sind unter diesen Heiden zwei Hauptreligionen, namlich Tschiwens Religion und Wischtnus Religion: Diese aber sind in viele Religionen zertheilet"*

At first sight Ziegenbalg appears to conform to the conventional fourfold classification of the religions of the world. His first major work on Hinduism, the *Malabarisches Heidenthum*, begins with the assertion that "all the inhabitants of the whole Earth are divided into four main religions [*Hauptreligionen*], thus there are Jews, Christians, Mahometans and heathens" (Caland 1926, 9).[22] The heathens make up the largest of these four main religions, but they "are however not uniform, rather although they all have one father, namely the Devil, they have nevertheless divided themselves into many different sects. For different gods are worshipped by the African heathens, others by the American heathens, and yet others by the East Indian heathens, [they] are also very much different from one another in their teachings." Furthermore, the East Indian heathens "are once again divided into different sects, among which [the sect of] those who are called Malabarians by the Europeans is one of the largest" (Caland 1926, 10). This Malabarian heathenism, the subject of Ziegenbalg's book, "is spread far and wide in India" stretching from Ceylon to Bengal and "deep within the Mogul realm" (Caland 1926, 23). Ziegenbalg's sense of the geographical spread of "Malabarian heathenism" is clearly a step in the direction of the conception of Hinduism as what King calls "a unified, all-embracing and independent religious entity" (King 1999, 100). When Ziegenbalg adds that "this whole extensive heathenism is divided into two primary main sects [*Hauptsecten*]," which he identifies as Shaivism and Vaishnavism ("Tschiwasameiam" and "Wischtnusameiam," i.e. *civacamayam* [Skt. *Shivasamaya*] and *vishnucamayam* [Skt. *Vishnusamaya*]), he appears to conform precisely to Stietencron's claim that the early missionaries deduced a single heathen religion from the fourfold classification and were unable to conceive of difference within that religion in other than sectarian terms.

The true picture, however, is more complex. Later in *Malabarisches Heidenthum*, Ziegenbalg uses the term *Hauptreligion* to refer to Shaivism and to Vaishnavism (see Caland 1926, 26), and in his other major work on Hinduism, the *Genealogie der Malabarischen Gotter*, he writes that the Malabarians "have forged many different *religions*, among which there are in particular, two main *religions*: the Sivamatha of the Sivabhaktas and the Vischnumatha of the Vischnubhaktas" (Germann 1867, 34–35 [italics added]). Among the other religions of the Indians, he refers to Jainism and to Buddhism as separate religions. Commenting on a reference to *camaners* in a letter from a Shaivite correspondent, the missionary writes that the "Schammaner were a nation who, apart from the two main religions mentioned so far, had a separate religion."[23] In the *Genealogie* Ziegenbalg quotes at length from another of his correspondents, who writes that "[t]here were formerly two nations called Buddhists and Samaners. These had a pernicious religion and were purely evil sects. They blasphemed Visnu's and Siva's religion and compelled all Malabars to adopt their religion." The followers of these religions are said by the Vaishnavite author of this letter to have rejected caste and to have blasphemed books on theology. He concludes that "their religion had no similarity either to our Malabarian, or to the Moorish, or to the Christian religion, but rather was a destruction of all religions."[24] Elsewhere Ziegenbalg lists Buddhists and Jains along with Mimansakas, mlecchas and two other groups difficult to identify as the six "other religious sects" regarded as heterodox by the Shaivas and Vaishnavas (see Caland 1926, 29). Other letters to the missionaries cited in the *Genealogie* or published in the *Halle Berichte*, a series of reports from the mission, confirm the impression that while Shaivas and Vaishnavas extend some degree of mutual recognition, they regard Buddhists and Jains as belonging to entirely separate religions. This, then, is the basis for Ziegenbalg's claim that among the many religions of the Indians, the two *Hauptreligionen* are Shaivism and Vaishnavism, while the degree of similarity and mutual recognition between them allows him to treat them as "sects" of a wider religious entity when he is considering "Malabarian heathenism" as a whole.

Ziegenbalg's concern in the *Genealogie* is with the relation of the gods, and not of their devotees, to one another. Nevertheless, his analysis of religious adherence is consistent with that of *Malabarisches Heidenthum*, although the focus on the gods in the *Genealogie* leads him to prefer the term "religion" for Shaivism and Vaishnavism and to reserve the term "sect" for their subdivisions. Thus he remarks of Shaivism that "[t]his religion is divided into different sects" (Germann 1867, 35). In one of the annotations to the "Correspondentz," we find the term religion extended still further and applied to the subsects of Shaivism and Vaishnavism: "There are among these heathens two main-religions [*Hauptreligionen*], namely Siva's religion and Visnu's religion. These, however, are divided into many *religions*" (Liebau 1998, 90 [italics added]). The context here is an equivocal answer to the missionary's question, "Whether the Malabarian Law constitutes only *one* Religion, or is divided into many sects?" (Liebau 1998, 89f.), examination of which will demonstrate the extent to which Ziegenbalg's reduction of these "many religions" to two *Hauptreligionen* is based on the perceptions of his Tamil correspondents. Although the writer begins by stating that "our religion is sub-divided into different sects," of which he enumerates seven, he concludes with the claim that "the law is not more than one law, but the sects are manifold" (Liebau 1998, 90, 94). Moreover, while seven sects are listed, according to the author of the letter, the first three sects (the *civavetam, viracaivam* and *cilamatakarer*) may all be "named with one word, *Tschaivamadam* [*caivamatam*, Skt. *Shaivamata*] or *Tschaivakalam* [*caivakulam*]" (Liebau 1998, 93). Likewise the other four (the *visnuvetam, tattuvatikaran, namaperumalvetam* and the "Tschainermadam"[25]) "all belong to Vishnu's religion and are different only in their way of worship" (Liebau 1998, 94). Thus the seven mentioned sects[26] are reduced to two main groupings, Shaivite and Vaishnavite. The reduction of the manifold sects to two main religions is also set out explicitly by the missionary annotator of the "Correspondentz." Commenting on the first of the seven sects, the missionary writes:

> *Civavetem* is the religion of those who honor Siva and all the gods who are of Isvara's family, as the highest gods, in which religion there exist yet many other sects, which the correspondent does not touch upon here. There are among these heathens two main-religions [*Hauptreligionen*], namely Siva's religion and Visnu's religion. These, however, are divided into many religions (Liebau 1998, 90).

Thus the annotator of the "Correspondentz" employs the categorial framework of *Heidenthum* and the *Genealogie*: the two main religions [*Hauptreligionen*] recognized by the Malabarians are subdivided into groups which may be described either as "religions" in their own right or as "sects" of the particular *Hauptreligion* of which they are a part. The "Malabarische Correspondentz" and the letters from Hindus quoted in the *Genealogie* demonstrate the degree to which Ziegenbalg has derived that framework from his Tamil informants.[27] Not only are Tamils enabled to speak for themselves in print in Europe for the first time,[28] but they also are able to dictate to some extent the terms on which they are represented. The publication of their letters, together with the annotations to them, allows us to observe how the missionary worked with his sources to build up a picture of Indian religions.

Gita Dharampal-Frick characterizes Ziegenbalg's "interchangeable use of the terms 'religion' and 'sect'" as "unsystematic" (Dharampal-Frick 1994, 359). While it is clear that, like Nobili, Ziegenbalg does not draw a rigid distinction between the terms, nevertheless, when seen in the appropriate context, his use of these terms is to some degree consistent. The object of *Malabarisches Heidenthum*, Ziegenbalg's first major work, is the "Malabarian heathenism" and in the title and introductory passages of the work Ziegen-balg treats it as a single religion, divided into two great sects ("Vomehme haupt Secten"). These sects are distinguished from each other by, above all, the gods that are the focus of their worship. When discussing these gods in the *Genealogie*, Ziegenbalg makes his primary unit of analysis the group that takes each god as "the highest being," i.e., Vaishnavites and Shaivites. While he usually refers to them as "religions" in their own right, he notes that they are also subdivisions of a larger entity and are themselves divided into groups which he describes as "sects." When discussing the subgroups listed by his Tamil correspondent, he acknowledges that in relation to each other the sects of Shaivism and Vaishnavism may be treated as religions. Just as writers at this time in Europe might speak of both "the Catholic religion" or "the Protestant religion" and "the Christian religion" (cf. W. C. Smith 1991, 41), so Ziegenbalg speaks of both "Vishnu's religion" or "Shiva's religion" and "Malabarian heathenism." Dharampal-Frick concludes that Ziegenbalg's "view of things is not very far from Stietencron's view of the different religious groupings of the sub-continent" (Dharampal-Frick 1994, 359–60). But it is in fact very far indeed from Stietencron's account of early European constructions of Hinduism as emerging from "the westerners' preconceived notion that it was *one* religion they were dealing with" (Stietencron 1997, 37).

Conclusion

The use of the terms "religion" and "sect" in Ziegenbalg and other early European writers indicates that we should be wary of reading a highly reified concept of "religion" into their works. The concept of religion was itself still developing in this period, and not least as a result of the study of Indian religions and the challenges of definition that they posed.[29] It is pre-cisely this process of development in the conception of religion that is ignored by writers such as King, who decry the "tendency to define Indian religion in terms of a normative paradigm of religion based upon contempo-rary Western understandings of the Judaeo-Christian traditions" (King 1999, 101). For King, this normative paradigm includes such familiar elements of western religions as authoritative texts, an ecclesiastical hierarchy, doctrinal uniformity and above all an exclusivist claim to truth (see King 1999, 105). But King and Stietencron deny that Hinduism is a religion in terms of the same normative paradigm that they detect in the writers they criticize. Hindu-ism fails to be a religion for Stietencron because:

> There is hardly a single important teaching in "Hinduism" which can be shown to be valid for all Hindus, much less a comprehensive set of

teachings. ... Most important: the god whom one Hindu adores with full devotion as the supreme deity and as the only Lord of the universe— that same god may be considered inferior or even totally insignificant in the eyes of another Hindu. ... Moreover the different religious groups use entirely different sets of holy scriptures said to be revealed by their highest god. They worship with different rituals and with different prayers, and they have, in some essential points, different views of cosmogony, anthropology and of the nature of salvation (Stietencron 1997, 36–37).

At the same time Stietencron is prepared to identify Vaishnavism, Shaivism and Shaktism as religions because "there would be essential common features in each of these religions. Founders of Hindu religions could, in some cases, be traced. Krsna could be regarded as such, Kakulisa maybe. ... For each of the literate religions there would exist a corpus of recognized holy scriptures. ... Members of each religion would adore the same deity as the Highest Being and Lord of the universe" (Stietencron 1997, 47). Thus von Stietencron's proposed definition of religions as "*corporately shared systems of world explanation and values*" based on "a belief in the existence of superhuman beings or powers" and including "human actions directly related to these systems" (1997, 45) appears in practice to amount to religions sharing a founder, a body of texts and a deity. By contrast, King considers some more sophisticated defenses of the unified nature of Hinduism—for example, Julius Lipner's attempt to define Hinduism in a non-essentialist manner as "an open construct. ... an intrinsically plural phenomenon" (ch. 2 in *Defining Hinduism*) and Wilhelm Halbfass's identification of "the elusive yet undeniable coherence of Hinduism ... its peculiar unity-in-diversity" in the term "dharma" (Halbfass 1988, 333; see King 1999, 108–10). Nevertheless, King concludes that "Hinduism" is "inappropriate as a term denoting the heterogeneity of 'Hindu' religiosity in the precolonial era," finding evidence of heterogeneity in "the lack of an orthodoxy, of an ecclesiastical structure, or indeed of any distinctive feature that might point to the postulation of a single Hindu religion" (King 1999, 111, 105).

Thus the argument put forward by King and Stietencron for denying that Hinduism may appropriately be called a religion depends upon a particular monothetic definition of a religion, a definition that requires elements such as doctrinal orthodoxy and a common deity. The terms "Hinduism" and "religion" do not, however, require monothetic definition in order to be useful analytic tools. Moreover, the conception of Hinduism in the minds of early European writers on Indian religions did not result from their slavishly and unconsciously applying this kind of definition to an Indian religiosity which their theological preconceptions forced them to perceive as unified. Rather, Indian religiosity was initially conceived, as in the work of Nobili, as consisting of a plurality of religions. Somewhat later writers such as Ziegenbalg formed a view of Indian religion as a collection of different religious groupings characterized by a range of degrees of affinity with one another. For Ziegenbalg, at least, it is possible to demonstrate that he arrived at this conclusion in part on the basis of what Indians themselves reported about their religious affiliation.

Notes

1. See also Fitzgerald 1990; King 1999; Larson 1995; and Stietencron 1988, 1995 and 1997. Lorenzen (ch. 3 in *Defining Hinduism*) and Smith (ch. 5 in *Defining Hinduism*) have offered a contrary view.
2. Both the factual basis and the significance of some of these claims can be challenged. For example, regarding the absence of the term among those supposed to adhere to the religion it designates, O'Connell (1973), Wagle (1997) and Lorenzen (ch. 3 in *Defining Hinduism*) provide some evidence of an emergent Hindu identity in the context of strained relations with Muslims. Ninian Smart has questioned the relevance of such absences: "The non-traditional nature of western terms does not *by itself* mean that there is a distorting reification. 'Gamesmanship' is of fairly recent coinage, but games-manship preceded the coinage (hence the success of the coinage)" (Smart 1974, 46).
3. I am grateful to Julius Lipner, Robert Segal, and an anonymous referee for *Religion* for their comments on earlier drafts of this article.
4. The term "Hindooism" in fact appears in the late eighteenth century. It is used by Charles Grant in a letter to John Thomas written in the early months of 1787: "In case of converting any of the Natives, as soon as they renounce Hindooism, they must suffer a dreadful excommunication in civil life, unless they are under the immediate protection of the English" (quoted in Morris 1904, 105). Grant also uses the term in his "Observations on the State of Society among the Asiatic Subjects of Great Britain, particularly with respect to Morals, and on the means of Improving It. Written chiefly in the year 1792" (first published in 1797, republished in *Parliamentary Papers*, 1812–1813, X, Paper 282, pp. 1–112). I am grateful to Geoffrey Oddie for drawing my attention to Grant's use of the term.
5. Likewise, although an interest in Indian religious texts is evident in the earliest of European writings on Hinduism, the emphasis laid upon them there is less than it was to be from the late eighteenth century on, when the number of Europeans able to read Sanskrit and other Indian languages began to increase.
6. John Zephaniah Holwell, Alexander Dow, Nathaniel Brassey Halhed, William Hastings, Charles Wilkins and William Jones.
7. For others, see Stietencron 1988 and 1997. In her essay on representations of caste, Dharampal-Frick notes that "Since scientific theories and scholarly interpretations from the late eighteenth century onwards were highly coloured by intellectual preconcep-tions, determined to a large extent by the colonialist framework ... by referring to the historical period prior to the establishment of British rule (i.e., pre-1757) a differently oriented representation of Indian reality may be gained" (Dharampal-Frick 1995, 85).
8. The most important of Nobili's works on Hinduism are his *Narratio Fundamentorum quibis Madurensis Missionis Institutum caeptum est et hueusque consisit [An exposition of the basic principles which inspired the founding of the Madurai Mission and continue*

to guide it, 1619, ed. S. Rajamanickam, trans. J. Pujo, *Adaptation*, Palayamkottai: De Nobili Research Institute, 1971] and *Informatio de quibusdam moribus nationis indicae [Information concerning certain Indian customs*, 1613, ed. S. Rajamanickam, trans. Peter Leonard, *Roberto de Nobili on Indian Customs*, Palayamkottai: De Nobili Research Institute, 1972]. All quotations in English from these works are from the translations of J. Pujo and Peter Leonard in Rajamanickam's bilingual editions.

9. The practices included wearing the Brahmanic thread, the *kudumi* or tuft of hair; the use of sandal paste; ablutions; and the use by Hindu women of the *tali*, a necklace, instead of a ring as a sign of marriage. The issue was initially resolved in favor of Nobili by the 1623 Bull of Gregory XV, *Romanae Sedis Antistes*, but the debate was revived in the first part of the next century and finally went against the Jesuits.

10. On the dispute between Nobili and Fernandes, see Zupanov 1999.

11. "*hi populi unum habeant civilem cultum, religionem vero multiplicem*" (Rajamanickam 1971, 112–13). Although the phrase translated by Pujo as "one common way of life, but many religions" can also be translated as "one common way of life, but a [single] manifold religion," it is clear from Nobili's discussion of religious difference among the Hindus that Pujo's interpretation of this sentence is to be preferred.

12. By contrast, among the Hindus "each sect adores a god peculiar to itself" (Rajamanickam 1971, 97).

13. Zupanov argues that Nobili saw more uniformity than his opponent Goncalo Fernandes Trancoso, who, Zupanov writes, "saw a classifiable diversity where Nobili saw basic uniformity" (Zupanov 1999, 116). Although this statement must be qualified in the light of the sections from the *Narratio Fundamentorum* cited, it does indicate that Nobili was aware of some degree of similarity among the people he described, even if it was limited to the realm of the social.

14. Cf. Nobili's *Informatio de quibusdam moribus nationis indicae*: "the sect of the Atheists cannot be said to be an unorthodox offspring of the sects of the idolaters. ... [T]hose sects do not agree in any of their tenets, just as the sects of the Gnanis have nothing in common with these same idolaters" (Rajamanickam 1972b, 36–37). The "Atheists" are Buddhists ("Bauddha matam or Nasticam"). In the *Narratio Fundamentorum* Nobili identifies the "Gnani" as "the Vedantam sect called Gnani or Spiritual men" (Rajamanickam 1971, 117). However, he places the "Mayavadis," the "Tadvavadis" and the "Visnuvas"—the followers of "Ciancaraciarier" (Shankaracarya), "Madhuva" (Madhva) and Ramanuja—among the idolaters.

15. For details, see my edition of Lord's work (Sweetman 1999).

16. This pattern of geographical classification is reflected in seventeenth-century compilations of reports of religions such as Alexander Ross's *Pansebeia: or, A View of All Religions in the World*, first published in 1653. Following his section on the "religion of the ancient Indians," derived from classical sources, Ross discusses separately the religions of Siam, Pegu [Burma], Bengala, Magor, Cambaia [Gujarat], Goa, Malabar, Narsingar and Bisnagar [Vijayanagara], Japon, the Philippiana Islands, Sumatra and Zeilan [Ceylon] before proceeding to the religion of the ancient Egyptians and then that of the modern Egyptians. For Ross, there are only three basic religions: Judaism, Christianity, and Heathenism. All others are made up from these three. Of all the religions, some "are meerly Heathenish, some Jewish, some meerly Christian, some mixed, either of all, or some of these; Mahometanism is mixed of Judaism, Gentilism, and Arrianism: the Muscovite Religion is, partly Christian, partly Heathenish" (Ross 1696, 363). It is no surprise, then, that he reports that the religion professed in Japan is "the same Gentilism that is professed in the rest of the Indies, with some variation of ceremonies" (Ross 1696, 63).

17. *Religie* appears four times in the body of Roger's work. By contrast, *Gods-dienst* appears twenty-three times. *Gods-dienst* is used of both the "Bramines" and the Eleusians. By contrast, for Christianity we have "het Christelijcke gheloove" (Caland 1915, 14). In chapter V of part one, the phrase "de Leere der Bramines" is used twice (see Caland 1915, 23). Those who edited Roger's work for publication after his death in 1649, especially Andreas Wissowatius in his preface, use *Religie* much more frequently than Roger himself, and may be responsible for its appearance in the title of his work.

18. Thus S. N. Balagangadhara translates Roger's statement "Ende Overmits daer een Godt is, oock een God-dienst *moet zijn*; soo sullen wy ons gaen begheven tot het ondersoeck" (Caland 1915, 112) as follows: "Because where there is a God, a religion *must exist* too; it is thus that we shall approach our investigation" (Balagangadhara's emphasis). Balagangadhara suggests that this is how "this missionary [found] out whether religion existed among the Brahmins of Coromandel" and suggests that rather than being based upon empirical research, the conclusion of Roger and those who followed him "was based upon non-empirical considerations in Augustine and Calvin," that is, on their certainty that there was no nation without a religion (Balagangadhara 1994, 66–67). Roger's statement might better be translated as "Where there is a God, there must also be worship of God."

19. Rennell's first general map *Hindoostan* was first published in 1782. *Memoir of a Map of Hindoostan* appeared first in 1783, and in subsequent editions in 1785, 1788, 1792 and 1793. See Edney 1997, 99.

20. In addition to Ziegenbalg, who will be discussed, the concept was also developing at this time in the works of Nobili's successors in the Jesuit Indian missions. Their sense of the geographical spread of Hinduism, which they owed to their own geographical dispersion in India and to the "oral tradition and the notes, treatises, memoirs and other manuscript documents by means of which the missionaries transmitted and exchanged their knowledge of the 'terrain' " (Murr 1987, II, 70), was reinforced by their observations of pilgrimage sites of pan-Indian importance. For example, Guy Tachard noted the large numbers of "pilgrims who come to Jagrenath [i.e. Jagganatha in Puri] from throughout India" (*Lettres edifiantes et curieuses, ecrit des missions etrangeres par quelques missionaires de la Compagnie de Jesus*, 34 vols. Paris, 1702–1776, vol. XII, p. 433).

21. Geoffrey Carnall suggests that "[j]udging from the manuscript of the Disquisition, the appendix may have been written first, with the narrative as an afterthought" (Carnall 1997, 211).

22. Translations into English from Ziegenbalg's works are my own. Although the term *malabarische* suggests the western coast of India, for Ziegenbalg the term does not refer only to this region. In many cases he uses it where we would use Tamil, for example when mentioning his translation of the New Testament into "die malabarische Sprache" (Caland 1926, 11). In others, the range of reference is much wider.

23. Ziegenbalg and Grundler 1714, 484. The letters from Hindus published in the seventh and eleventh parts of the *Halle Berichte* as the "Malabarischen Correspondentz" are often assumed to have been chosen, translated, and annotated by Ziegenbalg. In his recent edition of some of these letters, Kurt Liebau argues that in fact the translation and annotations are substantially the work of Grundler (see Liebau 1998, 26–27). However, as Liebau acknowledges, Grundler used Ziegenbalg's works on Hinduism for the annotations and would not have dispatched the letters for publication without Ziegenbalg's agreement. Grundler is co-signatory to the preface to the *Genealogie*, described in Metzger's translation as "Ziegenbalg's Preface." Even if, as Germann remarks, "Grundlers Name unter der Vorrede ist nur ein Zeichen collegialer Freundschaft" (Germann 1867, x) rather than a recognition of his contribution, his appearance in the

preface indicates the degree of co-operation between the authors. We can, therefore, assume that Ziegenbalg would have identified himself with the position of the annotations regarding Hinduism, although he might not have been responsible for the way in which that position was expressed. The position of the "Malabarischen Correspondentz" is in any case the same as that found in *Malabarisches Heidenthum* and *Genealogie*, which were written just prior to and just following, respectively, the annotation of the first batch of letters. I therefore do not attach importance to the question of which of the missionaries was responsible for the annotations and refer to the author of the annotations only as "the missionary," by which I intend to indicate their joint agency and to avoid the problem of distinguishing their precise contribution.

24. This passage is translated from a manuscript copy of the *Genealogie* (Royal Library, Copenhagen, Ledreborg 424, p. 88) which reads: "Es waren ehemals zweij *Nationen Buddhergol* und *Schamanergol* gennant. Diese hatten eine schadliche *Religion* und machten lauter bose Secten. Sie lasterten des *Wischtnums* und *Tschiwens Religion* und zwangen alle ubrige *Malabaren,* dass sie ihre *Religion* annehmen musten. ... Ihre Religion hatte keine Ahnlichkeit weder mit unserer Malabarischen, noch mit der Mohrischen, noch auch mir der Christlichen *Religion*; sondem sie war ein Verderb alter *Religionen*." A somewhat altered version appears in Germann's edition of the *Genealogie* (Germann 1867, 96).

25. Liebau suggests *cainamatam,* or Jainamata, for "*Tschaindermadam*." We have seen that the Jains are treated as a separate religion by both the missionaries and the authors of letters included in the *Correspondentz* and the *Genealogie.* The "*Tschaindermadam*" are here subsumed under Vaishnavism, both by the Tamil writer and also explicitly by the missionary annotator, who comments: "*Tschaindermadam* ist auch eine Sekte, so zu des *Wischtnums* Religion gehortet" (Liebau 1998, 90). The reason appears to be that, unlike the other writers, the author of this letter states his view that the Jains do use the *tirunamam,* or divine name, and worship Vishnu: "Die *Tschaier* aus der siebenten Sekte nehmen gleichfalls *Dirumanum* an sich und verehren den *Perumal*" (Liebau 1998, 94). Either the identification of the "*Tschaindermadam*" as Jains is incorrect, or Ziegenbalg was unaware that the "*Tschaindermadam*" and the "*Schammaner*" were one and the same.

26. Both the first and the last annotation to the question note that the writer of the letter could have mentioned many more sects: see Liebau 1998, 90, 94.

27. It is worth recalling that much of the *Genealogie* is based upon direct quotation from these and other letters. Moreover, comments in Ziegenbalg's catalog of his collection of more than a hundred Tamil works and the internal evidence of the work itself suggest that other sections of the *Genealogie* may represent a partial translation of a Tamil text in his collection. Of this text, which he calls *Dirigala Sakkaram* [Tirikilaccakkaram], Ziegenbalg writes, "This book shows the genealogy of their great gods. ... Once I had it in mind to translate this work into German but I could not help wondering whether this was really advisable. ... But I am still keeping my mind open whether or not I should do this translation, so far I am not sure about it myself (Gaur 1967, 88–89).

28. Albeit translated and edited by Europeans, and in response to questions set by Europeans.

29. For some examples, see Smith, ch. 5 in *Defining Hinduism*.

Part III

Hinduism in the Colonial Period and in Independent India

ORIENTATION

With "Questioning Authority: Constructions and Deconstructions of Hinduism," we move into colonial and independent India. Brian K. Smith, who earned a Ph.D. from the University of Chicago and who is a professor at the University of California, Riverside, has written two books about classical Indian culture (1989, 1994), and also several articles related to the problem of defining Hinduism (1987, 1992, 1996, 1999, 2000). Here Smith analyzes the arguments of contemporary scholars who would deconstruct Hinduism as a single, unified whole. The deconstructionists are not taking issue with the nineteenth-century Orientalists, Smith insists, though they may pretend that they are, because the Orientalists themselves had a notion of Hinduism that was pluralistic rather than unified. The deconstructionists are really attacking three sets of "native authorities": (1) Brahman pandits; (2) Neo-Hindus; and (3) Hindu nationalists. According to this essay neither the Neo-Hindus nor the Hindu nationalists actually advocated a fixed and bounded Hinduism. Smith's analysis of the latter is particularly interesting: "the Hindu nationalists do not seem to be constructing a new 'monolithic' form of the Hindu religion. ... Rather, driven by aspirations to spearhead a mass movement among India's diverse 'Hindu' population, the Hindutva leaders have been concerned to formulate a version of 'Hinduism' that is as inclusive, and vague, as possible." By the time Smith is finished deconstructing the deconstructionists, only the Brahman pandits are left standing to defend a bounded Hinduism.

Perhaps Smith himself should be counted as weighing in on the side of the Brahman pandits, because he concludes his essay by suggesting that "the time has finally come in Indological circles not to abandon the concept of 'Hinduism' but to refine and define it as a religion among and comparable to others and to do so in consort with selected traditions and authorities in Hinduism that have also represented it in such a manner." Yet there is an argument in "Questioning Authority" that would seem to disqualify Smith from making this move. Early in the essay, Smith quotes Jacob Neusner's opinion that the definition of any religion is a theological enterprise, beyond the competence of the scholar. Several times in this essay Smith takes scholars to task for attempting to impose their own views of Hinduism onto Hindus themselves, but I am not sure that he isn't doing the same thing himself in the end.

"Constructions of Hinduism at the Nexus of History and Religion" teases out the various strands that developed over the course of history that were woven together to form the contemporary notion of Hinduism, which Robert Eric Frykenberg insists is a "modern phenomenon," "different from anything that was previously known." Frykenberg earned his Ph.D. from the School of Oriental and African Studies at the University of London and is emeritus professor at the University of Wisconsin-Madison. He has written several articles relating to the themes of this essay (1987, 1989 [1997], 1993b, 1994), as well as other works on modern Indian history (1977, 1996, 2003; and Frykenberg and Brown 2002). The first strand of Hinduism according to Frykenberg is the caste system, which divided humankind into various groups "and then ranked these hierarchically according to innate (biological, cultural, and ritual) capacities and qualities." When imperial states developed in this social context, Frykenberg writes, they could only do so by forging "[b]onds of mutually beneficial relationships of loyalty and reciprocal obligations between client and patron" with various communities, especially with the Brahman overlords of caste society. Finally, in the colonial period, there emerged "a new kind of Hinduism and Hindu self-consciousness as strategies for the careful and deliberate integration of all of India into a single entity." British Orientalists and their Indian collaborators plumbed the depths of the history of South Asia to construct "a *single* and *ancient* religion," projecting something into the past that had not previously existed there.

Frykenberg's analysis acknowledges a profound tension in what is now known as Hinduism. It is famously "'inclusivistic,'" "epitomizing all that is eclectic, syncretistic, and tolerant." Yet earlier in the history of the religions of South Asia separate caste communities lived each in such isolation that "there could be no question of being syncretistic or tolerant." And, now, "chauvinistic, exclusivistic, fundamentalistic, and even imperialistic" forces have attacked that tolerance. Frykenberg presents Hindu revivalism as a response to the aggressive proselytizing of Christian missionary groups in British India in the nineteenth century. But on another level it can be seen as the ironic consequence of understanding Hinduism to be one thing, ironic because what first developed as a device to unite disparate groups in India is now being used to divide them. The broad umbrella which emperors used as a symbol of the expansiveness of their regimes has become a stick to beat those who do not belong under that umbrella.

It is important to note that caste is a crucial aspect of South Asian culture for both Smith and Frykenberg, but the reader must also see that what they make of caste is very different. In Smith's essay, it is the Brahmans who have defined a Hinduism that is similar to other world religions, with a canonized body of sacred literature, a more or less coherent system of religious beliefs, and a recognizable priestly elite, the Brahmans themselves. On the other hand, Frykenberg sees the various castes as fundamentally distinct, disagreeing not only on "practical policy" but also "cosmic principle" such that their religions themselves are different. About the Brahmanical religion Smith describes, Frykenberg would likely say that it is just that, the Brahmans' religion and only theirs.

5

QUESTIONING AUTHORITY: CONSTRUCTIONS AND DECONSTRUCTIONS OF HINDUISM

Brian K. Smith

Questioning Authority

The title of my essay is taken from a well-known bumper sticker, spotted on vehicles throughout North America. The sentiment expressed is one that I find admirable, although it is practiced by most of us mainly in the breach. As scholars, however, questioning authority is one of the principal features of our professional enterprise; and for those of us who are scholars of religion, it is, in my opinion, the *sine qua non* of the discipline.[1]

First and foremost, it is necessary for each generation to re-evaluate the authoritative pronouncements of our intellectual ancestors. The self-evident truths of the past are perpetually contested and replaced by new "facts" and "better" interpretations and theories. This need not be postivistically envisioned as "progress" but as an opportunity to reflect upon historical relativity and the interestedness of all knowledge. Our new truths, produced out of the nexus of current assumptions, interests, and concerns, will also inevitably be subjected to the same interrogation, criticism, and overturning by future scholars.

For those of us in the academy who assume personae as nontheological scholars of religion, the mandate to question authority pertains additionally to other sets of discourses. Joined to the work of critically examining the assumptions and conclusions of our intellectual forebears, students of religious traditions are also faced with the task of questioning the bases of authoritative claims put forward by the religious themselves. For religions are characterized—and possibly defined—by the particular kind of authoritative truth claims they make. The sources of authority that religions rely upon are not those of the merely human, the subjective, or the historically and culturally conditioned. Rather, the appeal is to the supernatural and transcendent, the objectively and absolutely true, the timeless and universal.

Questioning, and indeed countering, such claims to ultimate authority is not only desirable but also inevitable in an academic discipline that regards religion as a product of human beings, adopts the historical method, and recognizes the cultural conditioning and relativity of all religious claims and authorities.[2] These very methodological principles will entail a description of the object of study at odds with the self-description of religion put forward by the religious. I agree with Claude Lévi-Strauss when he writes that "No common analysis of religion can be given by a believer and a non-believer" (1972, 188), although I also believe it is possible for a "believer" to analyze religion from the perspective of a "non-believer" as part of his or her professional stance.

Things are complicated, however, when scholars of religion ignore or simply dismiss certain claims issuing forth from the religious. It is indeed the case that the bases upon which religions make their authoritative claims to truth—having been acknowledged and described—may and must be challenged by those of us in the academy who make claims to a different sort of truth based on different epistemological grounds. On the other hand, it seems problematic when scholars of religion arrogate to themselves the authority to decide for religions what does and does not count as orthodoxy and religious identity.

The picture is further muddied by the fact that within any religion there will be competing voices, each appealing to supernatural and transcendent sources for its authority, and each with varying notions about what is orthodox and who is "in" and who is "out." Religions are neither monolithic entities, nor are they unchanging over time, despite the claims often made for them by their theologians. They are rather historically variable, culturally figured and reconfigured, and often encompass within themselves a bewildering variety of diverse and divergent doctrines, practices, texts, and leaders. Thus, within any religious tradition, among different sectarian wings, and even within those sectarian wings at any given historical moment, there will be different voices claiming to speak authoritatively for (and to) that religion.

How the scholar of these traditions adjudicates competing claims to authority within what is ostensibly a single religion can be vexing. The scholar of religion, here again, will necessarily oppose some of the religious authorities he or she studies. By privileging one kind of articulation of the religion over others, one will inevitably end up opposing and delegitimating other authorities.

Such complex issues of authority and the relations between scholars, their discipline, and their objects of study have taken center stage in the contemporary study of Hinduism. The issues raised here have important implications for the present and future directions of the general field of religious studies. The study of Hinduism has been making significant contributions to the study of religion since at least the nineteenth century, when Friedrich Max Muller and others used Indian data extensively in their formulations of the new disciplines of comparative mythology and comparative religion (*Religionswissenschaft*). Recent trends, both in the academy and in India, make it possible that this subfield will have continuing impact on the larger discipline, if, and only if, both the data of Hinduism and the interpretive thinking issuing forth from Indology can be set in a comparative framework.

In what follows I will attempt to review and evaluate some of the issues surrounding one feature of the contemporary study of Hinduism. I concentrate here on the conflicts in authority that characterize Indology at present and that center around the definitional problem: What is Hinduism? The controversy over the definitional contours of this variegated tradition is one that concerns conflicts (and alliances) between authorities of different sorts, varying interests (sometimes incompatible, sometimes overlapping) driving the different parties, and the different consequences (intellectual and political) each position entails. Most of all, it increasingly involves questions as to the role, if any, of indigenous (that is, "Hindu") authorities in the constitution of their own religion.

What is at stake in this issue has implications that spill over into the broader field of religious studies. How is a religion conceived and defined, and who is legitimately responsible for doing so? Is the case of the study of that complex entity known as "Hinduism" unique, or is it comparable to issues in the study of other "religions"?

Western Constructions and Deconstructions of Hinduism

Many works have recently been published which are designed to contest, reevaluate, and deny the legitimacy of categories generated by scholars of the past to interpret India. One thinks especially of Ronald Inden's (1990) analysis of various Indological received truths; the rise of "subaltern studies" and their challenges to histories written by and for the elites; critiques like Gyanendra Pandey's (1992), which argues that communal identities are constructs of British colonialism, or Partha Chatterjee's (1986), which similarly posits that nineteenth- and twentieth-century conceptions of Indian national and cultural identity were foreign in origin and largely imposed on the colonized.

It is in this genre that one can assign a whole spate of recent works contending that modern articulations of a unified "world religion" called "Hinduism" are nothing more than imaginary representations issuing forth, originally, from western intellectual imperialism (for example, Dalmia and Stietencron 1995; Sontheimer and Kulke 1989; cf. Doniger 1991; Duara 1991; Hawley 1991; Hiltebeitel 1991; Larson 1995). In recent years it has thus become an ironic, if not paradoxical, truism among many professional western experts of Hinduism that the object of their expertise does not really exist. This misleading category of "Hinduism," it is argued, must be deconstructed in the interests of truth in advertising and atonement for the sins of our Orientalist forebears. The Indological authorities of the past created "Hinduism," and the Indological authorities of the present are now busy disestablishing its conceptual existence.

It is now averred that, in reality, Hinduism is not one religion but many, and always has been, as this enunciation of the position forcefully argues:

> There has never been any such a thing as a single "Hinduism" or any single "Hindu community" for all of India. Nor, for that matter, can one find any such thing as a single "Hinduism" or "Hindu community" even for any one socio-cultural region of the continent. Furthermore, there has never been any one religion—nor even one system of religions—to which the term "Hindu" can accurately be applied. No one so-called religion, moreover, can lay exclusive claim to or be defined by the term "Hinduism." The very notion of the existence of any single religious community by this name has been falsely conceived (Frykenberg 1989, 29).

The contention here is that "Hinduism," as a singular term depicting a monolithic religion, is a false category that elides the many and variegated differences "on the ground" in South Asia. "Hinduism" should be pluralized—or even abandoned altogether—as a term with no real referent:

> More a vehicle for conveying abstract ideas about institutions than for describing concrete elements or hard objects, Hindu came to be the concept used by people who have tried to give greater unity to the extreme cultural diversities which are native to the continent (Frykenberg 1993a, 526).

Others have taken this line of thought even further. Frits Staal has suggested that employing the label "religion" to describe Asian traditions such as "Hinduism" is also a category mistake—the result of a misguided and hegemonic move to import another western classificatory rubric to eastern data. There are, Staal argues, no "religions" in Asia, but only Asian ritual traditions. While the term "religion" might be appropriate when discussing western traditions (where orthodoxy is emphasized), it is illegitimate to apply the term to Asian "orthopraxic" traditions:

> The inapplicability of Western notions of religion to the traditions of Asia has not only led to piecemeal errors of labeling, identification and classification, to conceptual confusion and to some name-calling. It is also responsible for something more extraordinary: the *creation* of so-called religions. ... Thus there arises a host of religions: Vedic, Brahmanical, Hindu, Buddhist, Bonpo, Tantric, Taoist, Confucian, Shinto, etc. In Asia, such groupings are not only uninteresting and uninformative, but tinged with the unreal. What counts instead are ancestors and teachers—hence lineages, traditions, affiliations, cults, eligibility, and initiation—concepts with ritual rather than truth-functional overtones (Staal 1989, 393; emphasis in original).

Staal therefore concludes, "The concept of religion is not a coherent concept ... and should either be abandoned or confined to Western traditions" (1989, 415).

Thus, according to some scholars, neither a unified religion called "Hinduism" nor any traditions we can call "religions" exist in South Asia. Both "Hinduism" and the notion of a "Hindu religion" are the category mistakes of western intellectual imperialism. Questioning the authority of these categories, it is claimed, will retrieve a more authentic view of Hinduism(s) while rectifying the Orientalist errors of the past.

There is certainly a case to be made for this position. As is well known, "religion" is a term that nonwestern traditions did not have before contact with the west. This point is directed not only to state the obvious but also to argue that there are no indigenous terms that can properly be *translated* by the term "religion."

This line of argumentation was first taken by Wilfred Cantwell Smith, who demonstrated several decades ago that the names for particular "religions"—"Buddhism," "Hinduism," "Taoism"—are, like "religion," of foreign origin. "Hinduism" in particular, argues Smith, "is a concept certainly [Hindus] did not have before the encounter with the West" (1963, 63). More recently, Heinrich von Stietencron has stated that "Not only is the term modern[,] ... but also the whole concept of the oneness of Hindu religion was introduced by missionaries and scholars from the West" (1995, 51; cf. Frykenberg 1993a, 523).

Most nonwestern "religions" such as "Hinduism"—at least as they are usually understood today—are the conceptual and discursive products of the historical western encounter with nonwestern traditions. As comparative categorical frameworks emerged in the late seventeenth and eighteenth centuries, what Peter Marshall and Glyndwr Williams call "systems of belief" were designated "religions"—analogous to the known "religion" of Christianity:

When studying other systems of belief eighteenth-century Englishmen applied to them assumptions which they held about Christianity. They believed that Asia was clearly divided between adherents of distinct "religions," which in time they were to classify as "Hinduism," "Buddhism," "Taoism," or under some other name. Each "religion" had, as Christianity was thought to have, a fixed body of doctrine stated in sacred writings. ... Assumptions that Asian religions had distinct identities, formal structures and historical traditions akin to Christianity, even if there was a huge gulf between them and it in all matters of substance, provided a framework for comparisons. From the sixteenth century more and more books appeared in Europe describing "new" religions and comparing them with one another and ultimately with Christianity (Marshall and Williams 1982, 98).

The "religion" dubbed "Hinduism" was a product of this time. The very name "Hindu" was invented by outsiders, a label conceived and deployed to classify (and conceptually unify) a wide variety of inhabitants of the Indian subcontinent. The use of the term "Hinduism" to depict the religion of some of those inhabitants is of more recent vintage and is now said to be the direct product of the Orientalist intellectuals working in the colonial period of British rule.[3] Under this reading of recent history, scholars from the west created a religion comparable to the religions of the west—with canonical sacred books (principally the Vedas, but also the *Bhagavad Gita* and other texts that attracted western attention), a priesthood (the Brahmans), a body of orthodox teachings and practices (centering around *varnashramadharma*)—and called it "Hinduism."

Given this reconstruction of history, one of the major impulses guiding the move to deconstruct the category of "Hinduism" comes from the current critique of past wrongs perpetrated by western colonialism and its intellectual arm ("Orientalism"). From this vantage point, contesting and deconstructing (or at the very least pluralizing) the concept and label "Hinduism" can be understood as an attempt to right injustices inflicted on India and Indians as well as an intellectual move designed to return a recognition of pluralism and diversity to a tradition (or set of traditions) inaccurately portrayed as unified and monolithic.

It is, from this point of view, an *intracultural* debate, with the western Indological authorities of the present challenging a category generated by the western authorities of the past. Furthermore, the deconstructive move can also be represented as restoring to indigenous India a truer and more authentic version of its own pluralistic and variegated history. Thus the deconstruction of a monolithic category like "Hinduism" can be portrayed as in the interests not only of "truth" but also of "authenticity." For if "Hinduism" is a category imposed on India from the outside, deconstructing it can be represented as a restorative move to resurrect indigenous (and multiple) notions of tradition, community, and systems of belief and/or practice.

Western Definitions of Hinduism

One problem with this depiction of western understandings of "Hinduism" is that it is difficult to find in the annals of scholarship many conceptualizations of Hinduism that conform to the supposed monolithic and essentialist position being opposed.[4] Some Orientalists and later Indologists have indeed argued for a definition of Hinduism centering around caste, the *varnashramadharma* system, and the primacy of the Brahmans[5] or have identified a set of defining "orthodox" doctrines;[6] while others have seen "Hinduism" as defined, in one way or another, as centering around the authority of the Vedas.[7] The vast majority of western experts, however, have envisioned Hinduism in precisely the very fluid, pluralistic terms that contemporary deconstructionists favor.

Indological authorities have not usually, *contra* depictions otherwise, constructed a "monolithic" Hinduism with clear definitional boundaries. Rather, statements put forward about Hinduism by western scholars have most often been vague in the extreme. Usually arguing that Hinduism, unlike other world religions, has no founder, no centralized authority, no "church," no agreed-upon canon comparable to the Bible, Quran, Torah, and no doctrinal unity, scholars have found it difficult to compare such an amorphous entity to the more discriminating and bounded religions of the west. "Hinduism" has most often been represented *not* as a religion comparable to other religions but as a peculiarly unbounded and nondescript entity that resists definition altogether.

The assumed indefiniteness of Hinduism has, in the past, often meant conceiving of the religion in metaphorical terms. Hinduism, as Inden has noted, has been constituted by westerners as "a *female* presence who is able, through her very amorphousness and absorptive powers, to baffle and perhaps even threaten western rationality, clearly a male in this encounter" (1990, 86; emphasis in original). Hinduism, according to the great nineteenth-century Indologist Monier Monier-Williams, is like an Indian banyan tree whose "single stem sends out numerous branches destined to send roots to the ground and become trees themselves, till the parent stock is lost in a dense forest of its own offshoots" (1877, 11; cited in Hawley 1991, 22). Alternatively, Hinduism is likened to an excessively fecund and chaotic jungle:

> Hinduism has often and justly been compared to a jungle. As in the jungle every particle of soil seems to put forth its spirit in vegetable life and plants grown on plants, creepers and parasites on their more

stalwart brethren, so in India art, commerce, warfare and crime, every human interest and aspiration seek for a manifestation in religion, and since men and women of all classes and occupations, all stages of education and civilization, have contributed to Hinduism, much of it seems low, foolish and even immoral. The jungle is not a park or garden. Whatever can grow in it, does grow. The Brahmans are not gardeners but forest officers. ... Here and there in a tropical forest some well-grown tree or brilliant flower attracts attention, but the general impression left on the traveller by the vegetation as he passes through it mile after mile is infinite repetition as well as infinite luxuriance. And so it is in Hinduism (Eliot 1954, II, 166–67; cited in Inden 1990, 86–87).

"Hinduism" by definition, these scholars claim, cannot be defined. It is too fluid, too all-encompassing, and, most of all, too "tolerant" to be subjected to a concept like "orthodoxy" or even "orthopraxy," let alone "monolithic." An articulation like the following, written by J. A. B. van Buitenen (in the *Encyclopaedia Britannica*'s entry on "Hinduism," no less), is not atypical:

As a religion, Hinduism is an utterly diverse conglomerate of doctrines, cults, and ways of life. ... In principle, Hinduism incorporates all forms of belief and worship without necessitating the selection or elimination of any. ... A Hindu may embrace a non-Hindu religion without ceasing to be a Hindu (1974, 519).

Note that in this articulation one does not even have to be a "Hindu" to be a "Hindu"! Confronted with "Hinduism," western scholars of the nineteenth and twentieth centuries have tended to retreat from, rather than insist upon, categorization. It is the other side of the Orientalist heritage—the Romantic vision of the "mysterious East"—that has been dominant as Indologists describe "Hinduism." As one scholar put it, "Even a superficial acquaintance leaves one with the impression that the religious life of India is fascinating, complex, and mysterious, but, above all, different from the religious traditions of the West" (Younger 1972, 9). Or again, "An approach to Hinduism provides a first lesson in the 'otherness' of Hindu ideas from those of Europe. The western love of definition and neat pigeon-holing receives its first shock" (Spear 1949, 57).

Thus, despite the revisionist history of modern deconstructionists, most Indologists of the nineteenth and twentieth centuries have declared Hinduism either too disorganized and exotically other or too complex and recondite to be subjected to the definitional strictures applicable to other religions and cultures. "Hinduism," we have been informed by the experts in the west, can mean practically anything. Indeed it appears difficult *not* to be a Hindu (see B. K. Smith 1993); "Hinduism" is an entity so fluid and "tolerant" as to encompass a variety of religions and communities under the shade of its ever-spreading banyan tree.

It turns out that the contemporary deconstructionist model of plural Hinduisms (or no "Hinduism" at all) is not that far removed from what appears to be the standard received wisdom of Indology. If virtually everything counts as "Hinduism" (and this, it would seem, is the dominant Indological model), then the term "Hinduism" means nothing at all (as some of the deconstructionists would have it). Many of the western authorities of the past and the western authorities of the postmodern present thus agree: There really is no such thing as *a* Hinduism, with clearly defined boundaries and definitional strictures. "Hinduism" is constituted, in either case, as *different* from other, more circumscribed religions; it is thus incomparable because it is uniquely unsusceptible to definition. The much maligned Orientalists and their later Indological successors are, on this score at least, mostly straw dogs.

Questioning Indigenous Authorities: Hindus and Hinduism

The move to deconstruct "Hinduism" is not, it would seem, principally an intracultural debate between past and present Indological authorities. For these two sets of western experts tend to be in basic agreement about the entity. If the real target of the deconstructionist agenda to do away with the category of "Hinduism" is not the mainstream of western Indological thought, who are the authorities these contemporary scholars are really questioning?

What modern deconstructionists may really be objecting to is the self-identification of many Indians as "Hindus," adherents of a "religion" (comparable to Christianity, for example, and Islam) called "Hinduism." The notion that contemporary western scholars of India are restoring to Hindus some kind of precolonial authenticity that was lost as a result of western machinations is complicated by the fact that many "Hindus" now have adopted and utilized the very categories that certain modern Indologists wish to reason away. Challenging the constructions of Hinduism thus entails contesting the authority not only (or not even primarily) of the western Indological past but also of indigenous authorities who claim to speak for a unified "Hindu religion." It is, then, partly or even primarily an *intercultural* debate between the postmodern west (and some contemporary Indian intellectuals) and Indian religious authorities.

The Hindus who do claim and have claimed to speak for "Hinduism" are, need it be said, multiple and various; there are many different "Hindu" voices, with different and various conceptions of the "Hinduism" they claim to be speaking for. But in all cases, the postmodern critique of *any* monolithic conceptualization of "Hinduism" has as one of its ramifications to question the authority of anyone who claims to speak for a singular "Hinduism."

Who are these multiple indigenous authorities that modern western decon-structionists are also implicitly or explicitly contesting—and delegitimizing? One of the principal sets of religious experts that has, for millennia, claimed to speak for "Hinduism" or "the Hindu religion"[8] is the Brahman *pandits*, theologians, and philosophers. Members of this elite class have portrayed themselves as the spokespersons for truth and orthodoxy since at least the middle of the first millennium BCE (the time when competing, "heretical" traditions first arose).[9] These Brahmans, regardless of sectarian affinities, have tended to be fairly clear about what Hinduism is and what a proper Hindu should believe and practice. Their vision of Hindu orthodoxy is of course extremely self-serving: a Hindu is one who accepts the authority of the Vedas (texts composed, preserved, and interpreted by Brahmans), follows the particular prescriptions for him or her in the *varnashramadharma* scheme (in which the Brahman class has placed itself at the top of the hierarchy), and accepts the Brahman class as the supreme earthly authorities on "religion."[10] While "not a creedal religion in the same sense as Christianity," Brahman *pandits* for thousands of years have "nonetheless understood Hinduism to have a doctrinal core, deviation from which would mean ceasing, at least intellectually, to be a Hindu" (Young 1981, 140).

The authority of the Veda was particularly singled out as the hallmark of orthodoxy in Brahmanical formulations. In Dharma texts the Veda is declared "unquestionable" (*amimansa*; *Laws of Manu* 2.10-11), and those who deny its authority are reviled (12.95). Other authorities, from the Mimansakas to Shankara, have insisted upon acceptance of the authority of the Veda as the defining criterion of orthodoxy, and virtually all sects usually thought to be "Hindu" have, in one way or another, paid at least lip service to the notion that they are all somehow linked to the Veda and the Vedic past (B. K. Smith 1987; 1989, 13–29). Unqualified adherence to the authority of the Veda is "the thread" that has united Brahman polemics and apologetics "in spite of differences in space and time" (Young 1981, 135).

Insofar as western Orientalists and Indologists did conceive of *a* "Hindu religion" with real definitional contours, it was largely on the basis of what this class of learned Brahmans told them about the tradition and its unifying principles. Europeans did not invent the notion that the Veda was the "holy book" of Hindu India, or that caste was the defining religious and social institution, or that Brahmans were the authoritative leaders of the tradition. They were, at least in part, representing the Smarta Brahman view of things. While the exact configuration of "Hinduism" as a "religion" was certainly shaped (how could it be otherwise?) by the culturally and historically con-ditioned expectations of westerners of the nineteenth and early twentieth centuries, the raw materials for such a reshaping were readily supplied by traditional Brahman informants.

Conversely, when confronted with missionaries and Orientalists and made aware of the categorical expectations of these westerners, Brahman *pandits* had no difficulties in drawing upon traditional discourse and redeploying it in the terms of western debate (see Dalmia 1995; Young 1981). In this way, Brahman authorities, albeit now in a dialogical or dialectical relationship with westerners, continued to act as spokesmen for a unified "religion," now known by the term "Hinduism" (or its Sanskritized equivalents, for example, *hindu dharma*).

Deconstructing the concept of "Hinduism" is thus, in part, a move to delegitimate the authority of certain Brahman *pandits* and theologians to pronounce on what "Hinduism" is. I myself have argued (B. K. Smith 1994, 314–25) that certain claims Brahmans make for the Veda and for the constitution of the class and caste system in which they have given themselves a privileged position must be contested.[11] It is, however, another matter to deny the theologians of a tradition the legitimacy to pronounce on what constitutes "orthodoxy" and what exactly lends the tradition its conceptual unity.

In fact one could argue it is precisely the theologians of a tradition who construct (and continually reconstruct) the principles that allow for a category of self-identification like "Hindu." Jacob Neusner has recently argued that "the issue of theology bears consequence because upon the result, in the end, rests the question of whether we may speak of a religion, or only of various documents that intersect here and there" (1995, 239). The theologians of a tradition provide the "glue" to an otherwise disparate set of data, "facts," sectarian differences, and all other particularities:

> The conception of "Judaism," or "Christianity," or "Buddhism," serves the purpose of holding together in a coherent philosophically harmonious and proportionate construction diverse and otherwise inchoate facts, e.g., writings, artifacts of material culture, myths and rites, all of them, with distinction as to provenance or origin, deemed to contribute to an account of one and the same systematic composition, an -ity or -ism; and, further, all of them—beliefs, rites, attitudes and actions alike—are assumed to animate each (Neusner 1995, 239).

Questioning the authority of theologians to do what theologians do—create a doctrinal umbrella underneath which the particularities of any religious tradition are organized—seems a bit presumptuous. One may nevertheless wish to do so in order to decenter traditional sources of authority, to represent the interests of competing voices with the tradition that have been disregarded or silenced (discontents or "heretics"). But there is certainly no reason to single out the theologians of Hinduism. Such an enterprise, if set into motion, should be directed at *all* of the "religions." "Buddhism," "Christianity," "Islam," and "Judaism" are all, at least in part, the conceptual products of their theologians.[12] "Hinduism," from this point of view, is hardly a unique case, a point to which I will return below. For now I would argue, however, that if we as students of religion decide it is incumbent upon us to decenter the theological authorities of the religions we study, we should be mindful of the ethical and intellectual consequences of such interventions. We should carry out this self-appointed task in our study of all religions and not just a selected few.

Religions do of course change over time; and the conceptualizations of any particular religion will inevitably be altered by history. The contours of modern indigenous (that is, "Hindu") views of "Hinduism" have also undergone such change, especially in light of the interactions Hindus have had with the west. Traditional Brahmanical views of Hinduism have themselves been adapted to the new conditions of the nineteenth and twentieth centuries and, more importantly, have been joined by other modernized (and, to some extent, "westernized") indigenous visions. It is with two other sets of Hindu authorities that have arisen in the wake of this intercultural encounter over the past two centuries where this kind of adaptation to modernity is most visible: the so-called "Neo-Hindu" reformers, and the Hindu nationalists.

Scholars who contest the monolithic conceptualization of "Hinduism" regard the Neo-Hindu movement as something like the native shadow of the Orientalist project. For it is in the formulations of "Hinduism" issuing forth from such various nineteenth- and twentieth-century reformers like Aurobindo, Dayanand Saraswati, Sarvepalli Radhakrishnan, Rammohun Roy, and Vivekananda that the impact of the western ideas is most obvious.[13]

The Neo-Hindu indigenous authorities are often dismissed as "inauthentic," their claims to legitimacy compromised by their encounters with modernity and western social, political, and intellectual trends. Their representations of "Hinduism" are delegitimized as merely the native restatement of ideas originating in the west. As Paul Hacker writes:

> Neo-Hinduism is not a unified system of ideas. In fact it is chiefly because of one common trait that I classify religious thinkers as Neo-Hindus. Their intellectual formation is primarily or predominantly Western. It is European culture, and in several cases even the Christian religion, which has led them to embrace certain religious, ethical, social, and political values. But afterwards they connect these values with, and claim them as, part of the Hindu tradition (1978, 582).

More recently, Gerald Larson has listed the Neo-Hindus as the only indigenous source for contemporary Indian ideas about Hinduism and religion, but he also characterizes the movement they led as a "defensive reaction" to outside forces:

Modern Indian notions of religion derive from a mixture of Christian (and mainly Protestant) models, Orientalist and largely Western reconstructions of India's religious past, and nineteenth-century indigenous reform movements most of which were defensive reactions against the onslaught of Westernization and Christian missionizing (1995, 5).

Questioning the authority of the Neo-Hindu version(s) of "Hinduism" seems to presuppose precisely what it also wants to argue against: that there is indeed some kind of "authentic" or "genuine" tradition or group of traditions (called Hinduism?) that has been compromised by those who have adapted to new historical, cultural, social, and political circumstances. The "syncretism" attributed to Neo-Hindu formulations of "Hinduism" assumes its opposite—a "real" and "unadulterated" Hinduism (or a variety of "real Hinduisms") that existed before the encounter with the west and was previously unaffected by historical change and intercultural and interreligious forces.

All religions, at various points in recent history and under varying circumstances, have adapted to the modern world and the accompanying intellectual trends of modernity. "Hinduism" (or "Neo-Hinduism") is not unique in this regard either; the Neo-Hindu movement shares many commonalties with developments in other religious traditions around the world over the past several hundred years. The study of religion is the study of traditions in constant change. The reforms of the nineteenth and twentieth century in Indian religion are no different in principle than the transformations that have occurred throughout the history of "the tradition." While it is necessary to the scholarly task to attempt to track such historical change and also to contest the claims of ahistorical continuity put forward by the religious, another form of "essentialism" occurs when one period of change is somehow constituted as a deviation or inauthentic swerve from some supposedly more or less timeless norm.

The specific contours of the "Hinduism" put forward by the Neo-Hindu movement are indeed attributable to the historical, cultural, and political circumstances of nineteenth- and early twentieth-century India (including the presence of western colonialism and intellectual imperialism). And while one can argue that a "monolithic" vision of newly conceptualized "Hinduism" arose out of these circumstances, it is important to note that the Neo-Hindus, by and large,[14] constructed a vision of their religion no less open-ended than definitions put forth by the mainstream of Indology.

The "Hinduism" portrayed by Neo-Hindus—tolerant, universalistic, all-encompassing, and nonsectarian—was created in part to represent it as the unifying agent in the nationalistic struggle. Confronted with both the reality of diversity and the British political critique of Indians as hopelessly divided,[15] "Hinduism" (or its essential core, Vedanta) was conceived and put forward as an all-encompassing mechanism of spiritual, cultural, and national unity. In fact many Neo-Hindus went even further, declaring that Vedantic philosophy was not part of a religion or even a religion in and of itself but "religion" in general; all religions could be incorporated under the umbrella of Vedanta. Thus, Vivekananda would assert that:

> Ours is the universal religion. It is inclusive enough, it is broad enough to include all the ideals. All the ideals of religion that already exist in the world can be immediately included, and we can patiently wait for all the ideals that are to come in the future to be taken in the same fashion, embraced in the infinite arms of the religion of the Vedanta (1970–1973, III, 251; cited in Halbfass 1988, 238).

Somewhat later, Radhakrishnan would similarly write (again using the "Vedanta" for the essential heart of "pure religion"): "The Vedanta is not a religion, but religion itself in its most universal and deepest significances" (1968, 18; cited in Halbfass 1988, 409).

While traditional Brahman authorities were the sources for one kind of western definition of Hinduism, the Neo-Hindus—acting out of their own interests and propagating their own agenda—were dialectically creating another version of "Hinduism" with another, and much more dominant, branch of Indology. Neo-Hindu articulations of Hinduism provide us with the Indian side of the same coin, stamped with the mainstream of Indological views of the tradition. Hinduism, in both cases, is not a religion comparable to others. The all-encompassing, pluralistic nature of the beast defies definition—it either is incomparable to other religions or was "religion" itself, the summary and supersession of all "religions."

Hinduism, it is claimed by both Neo-Hindus and Indologists, can be and is virtually everything. But for the Neo-Hindus, this nondefinition of Hinduism has played a different role than it has for western scholars. The latter have, it would seem, resisted definition out of befuddlement, atavistic notions of a "mysterious East" that defies rational categories, or simply failure of will; the former have done so largely out of concerns revolving around cultural pride and nationalistic aspirations. And, in either case, the end result is not dissimilar to the recent deconstructionist critique: There really is no such thing as "Hinduism" if by that term we mean a tradition that is both unified and bounded.[16]

The third set of native authorities that is challenged by contemporary deconstructionists is comprised of the Hindu nationalists, commonly called the Hindutva movement. Originating at about the turn of the twentieth century, this movement has recently undergone quite a revival and has become a major factor in modern Indian politics. Perhaps even more than traditional Brahmans and Neo-Hindus, it is the Hindu nationalist authorities and their pronouncements about Hinduism that many contemporary scholars have challenged by denying the existence of either *a* "Hinduism" or *a* "Hindu community."

Romila Thapar, in a widely cited article (1985), has argued that the Hindutva movement is creating a new form of "Hinduism" out of the pluralistic and variegated realities of the Indic subcontinent. She has labeled this monolith "syndicated Hinduism," formulated in reaction to the historical encounter with Semitic religions:

> The new Hinduism which is being currently propagated by the Sanghs, Parishads and Samajs is an attempt to restructure the indigenous religions as a monolithic, uniform religion, rather paralleling some of the features of Semitic religions. This seems to be a fundamental departure from the essentials of what may be called the indigenous "Hindu" religions (Thapar 1985, 15).

Pointing to its modern origins in the Neo-Hindu movement and to the important contributions made to it by Indians of the Hindu diaspora, Thapar characterizes this new form of Semiticized and synthesized Hinduism as a movement that:

> draws largely on Brahmanical texts, the *Gita*, and Vedantic thought, accepts some aspects of the *Dharmashastras* and attempts to present a modern reformed religion. It ends up inevitably as a garbled form of Brahmanism with a motley of "values" drawn from other sources, such as bringing in elements of individual salvation from the Bhakti tradition, and some Puranic rituals. Its contradictions are many. The call to unite under Hinduism as a political entity is anachronistic (1985, 22).

Finally, concludes Thapar, this new "Hinduism" was created "for purposes more political than religious, and mainly supportive of the ambitions of a new social class" (1985, 22).

Others have also criticized the Hindu nationalist movement on both these scores; that it is replacing pluralism and diversity with a monolithic ("syndicated," "organized," "Semiticized") form of Hinduism, and that it is not really a religious movement at all but, in essence, a political one (see, for example, Duara 1991; Jaffrelot 1993; Lochtefeld 1996). The academic effort to deconstruct this monolithic and politicized version of Hinduism has often been portrayed as in the interests of protecting those who have been victimized by the Hindu nationalist movement:

> It appears to me that by rediscovering and accepting Hindu religious plurality as one of the characteristic features of Indian culture, the tensions which at present cause conflicts between the so-called Hindus and the so-called non-Hindus could be reduced considerably (Stietencron 1995, 79–80).

But, as with the early Neo-Hindu movement, the Hindu nationalists do not seem to be constructing a new "monolithic" form of the Hindu religion which is, as one critic puts it, "contrary to the pluralistic and hierarchical essence of Hinduism" (Jaffrelot 1993, 522). Rather, driven by aspirations to spearhead a mass movement among India's diverse "Hindu" population, the Hindutva leaders have been concerned to formulate a version of "Hinduism" that is as inclusive, and vague, as possible.

Hindutva authorities have studiously avoided definitional statements about what "Hinduism" *qua* a "religion" really is. "Hindutva" itself is an intentionally ambiguous term, implicitly referring to the religion of Hinduism while explicitly constituted as having only a "cultural" referent. This ambiguity is obviously a strategic political move. For by actually defining Hinduism in terms of, for instance, allegiance to the authority of a "canon," the authority of the Brahman class, or the doctrines and practices associated with *varnashramadharma*, Hindu nationalists would lose elements of the mass movement they wish to lead. Many "Hindus" do not actually pay much attention to the Vedas; southerners resent the imposition from the north of Sanskrit and texts written in that language as definitive of "Hindu" identity; and the vast numbers of those historically persecuted by the religiously sanctified caste system will balk at any definition of "Hindu" that relies on Brahman privilege or its ideological underpinnings, *varnashramadharma*. Both "Hindutva" and "Hinduism" have been deployed by Hindu nationalists as mobilizing slogans (and have been effective as such) and not as clearly defined religious terms.

While the movement has certainly drawn upon the religious sentiments and resentments of many sectors of the "Hindu" populace, their definitional statements have thus tended to be as religiously vague as they are politically charged. "A Hindu," proclaimed Hindu nationalist Vinayak Damodar Savarkar in the 1920s, "means a person who regards this land of Bharat Varsha [that is, India], from the Indus to the Seas, as his Father-Land as well as his Holy-Land, that is the cradle of his religion" (1942, 1). Those who do not consider India as their "Holy-Land" (for example, Muslims and Christians) are regarded as "guests" by some Hindu nationalists. "The non-Hindu people in Hindustan," wrote Rashtriya Svayamsevak Sangh leader Madhavrao Golwalkar:

> must learn to respect and revere Hindu religion, must entertain no idea but that they must cease to be foreigners, or may stay in the country wholly subordinated to the Hindu nation, claiming nothing, deserving no privileges, far less any preferential treatment, not even citizens' rights (1939, 47–48).

The Hindutva movement is not so much constructing a new "syndicated Hinduism" as it is drawing upon and exploiting old notions of Hinduism as indefinable *qua* a religion and redeploying such notions to reposition Hinduism as the defining cultural and political ideology of India. It is, arguably, the *absence* of clear scholarly definitions of what constitutes Hinduism—as one religion among others in the subcontinent—that has made possible the discourse of Hindutva. Both Neo-Hindu and Indological traditions that have represented Hinduism as fundamentally *different from* other religions—in its infinite capacity to subsume all other religions within it—have left a legacy with new and perhaps unexpected consequences in the rise of Hindu nationalism.

The Hindu nationalist movement has also been criticized for being not "religious" at all but a purely political movement that merely exploits religious sentiment for political ends. Delegitimizing Hindutva authorities thus also entails representing them not as religious leaders but as misguided and dangerous politicos. The assumption here seems to be that there is an essential "religious" or "spiritual" dimension of religions like Hinduism and that introducing a political dimension somehow sullies that essence. This portrait ignores the fact that religion *has always* had a political dimension. While the nationalistic form this political element within religions has taken in recent times is, of course, historically and culturally conditioned, challenging the Hindutva authorities because their version of Hinduism has a political component is not persuasive. Criticizing the Hindutva movement for being "too political," and therefore not inclusive of genuine "religious" spokespersons, can carry with it assumptions about religion that are idealized and decontextualized from the historical and cultural realities in which religions always function. It may also have unfortunate resonances with Orientalist presuppositions regarding a "spiritual India" that is, in essence, apolitical and ahistorical.

Scholars have obligations, in my opinion, to contest some of the claims put forward by the Hindutva movement, especially when such claims appropriate the language of science, archeology, and history (B. K. Smith 1996). Scholars of Hinduism might also object to the kind of representations Hindutva authorities are putting forward as to what constitutes "Hinduism." Doing so effectively, however, will involve providing alternative definitions of Hinduism as a religion that cease to imagine it as uniquely incapable of definition and then incomparable to religions elsewhere.

The history of modern "constructions" (and "deconstructions") of Hinduism, both in India and in the West, seems to demonstrate that all such representations have had a stake in portraying this religion as more or less indeterminant, unbounded, pluralistic to the point of all-embracing—as, in other words, distinct and different from other religions. The indigenous authorities who have been seriously challenged are not the Neo-Hindus or even the Hindu nationalists, both of whom tend to rework basic Indological assumptions about Hinduism. Rather, it has been the traditional Brahmans and their authoritative pronouncements—in which one finds clear statements of definition regarding Hinduism as a religion, which also provide the means for constituting Hinduism in a way comparable to other religions—who have been the losers over the past several centuries of western and Indian inter-action.

The Study of "Hinduism" and the Study of Religion

The issues surrounding the current debate over the definitional contours of Hinduism could have important ramifications for the study of religion in general. But if they are to do so, scholars of Hinduism must relinquish the time-honored notion in this field that our subject matter is, for whatever reason, exceptional. The definitional problem in the study of Hinduism is, I would argue, comparable to similar problems confronted by scholars of other religions.

The set of concerns I have concentrated upon here—those surrounding "Hinduism" as a descriptive and/or interpretive term, competing sources of authority for depicting this religion, and the relationship of religious self-identification to categories used in the academic study of religion—is by no means confined to the Indian situation. While there are obviously specific circumstances that surround these problems in terms of the study of Hinduism, the issues are similar to those faced elsewhere.

That "Hinduism" was "constructed"—by Orientalists, Neo-Hindus, Hindu nationalists, separately or in concert—is not some kind of epistemological revelation, nor is it a historical anomaly, nor is it a feature common only to this entity. One might equally, and with as much validity, argue that *all* such designations for world religions are "constructs." As Larson notes, "These designations are for the most part little more than conventional labels. ... Each is a singular label disguising what is in reality a pluralist array of cultural traditions" (1995, 31).

The postmodern effort to destabilize the essentialistic dimensions of various terms and concepts (for example, "Hinduism") can easily end up in a logical regress *ad infinitum*, ending in pure atomism. Swamped by the recognition of historical, cultural, social, and even individual particularities, one can eschew general categories, throw up one's hands, and declare that a label like "Hinduism" is nothing more than an artificial construct with no referent and no "hard" or "concrete" reality. Other traditions too—even those with more obvious traditional authoritative sources of self-definition than in the case of Hinduism—are, as Larson points out, "pluralistic arrays of cultural traditions"; and concepts like "Hinduism" are after all concepts.

Recognizing such pluralism and the conceptual nature of such labels, how-ever, does not necessitate the abandonment of scholarly general categories that lend meaning to "naturally" disparate data. Other scholars of other traditions have also faced this problem; one of them concludes, after consideration of whether one can speak of "Judaism" or only of "Judaisms," that the road to unbridled pluralism leads to a philosophical dead end:

> So there is no possibility of claiming there never was, nor is there now, such a thing as "Judaism," but only "Judaisms." For once we take that route, there will be no "Judaisms" either, but only this one and that one, and how we feel from day to day, and this morning's immutable truth and newly fabricated four-thousand-year-old tradition (Neusner 1983, 235).

Description of particularities logically entails and is followed by acts of interpretation, of "making sense" of the data; and this latter inevitably involves comparison, that is, the deployment of general categories and classificatory schemes of similarities and differences. General categories provide, as Marshall and Williams noted for previous constructions in the age of "discovery" (and colonialism), a "framework for comparisons." Such classifications that are "constructed" and used by scholars, like "Hinduism," are themselves comparable to the genus of which they are species. "Religion," as Jonathan Smith has noted, is a category produced by an "act of second-order reflexive imagination which must be the central preoccupation of religious studies" (1983, 217). What Smith writes about "religion" can easily be applied to the even more specific category of "Hindu" and "Hinduism":

> That is to say, while there is a staggering amount of data, of phenomena, of human experiences and expressions that might be characterized, by one criterion or another, as religious—*there are no data for religion*. Religion is a creation of the scholar's study. It is created by the scholar's imaginative acts of comparison and generalization. *Religion has no independent existence apart from the academy* (1983, 217; emphasis in original).

It is important—and in the nature of things—for scholars to continually debate, challenge, and revise the "imaginative acts of comparison and generalization" that spring forth from our studies; it is crucial that we continually question the authority of our predecessors in the effort to refine our categories. In the Indian case we may well decide that, upon reflection, "Hinduism" is a category in need of revision, replacement, or dispersion into other categories. But if the study of Hinduism is to contribute to the study of religion, the grounds on which we make such determinations should be applicable elsewhere; and if we abandon the category of "Hinduism," on what new grounds can we compare that which was formerly known as Hinduism to other "religions"?

As the material presented above demonstrates quite clearly, however, scholars of religion do not exercise their authority to write about religion(s) in a vacuum. Indeed, the case of Hinduism points to the quandaries we face as scholars when confronted with the claims of those who act as representatives of the religion we are describing, interpreting, and comparing. While it is certainly not appropriate simply to reproduce the religious discourse of religious people, can the authorities and adherents of a religion be disregarded in the scholarly enterprise of description, interpretation, comparison, and generalization?

One of the principal ramifications of the trend in Indology to deny the existence of a unified religion called "Hinduism" is to delegitimize those in India who, in varying ways, have represented themselves as "Hindus" and their religion as "Hinduism." Such indigenous representations are, in the extreme forms the deconstructionist effort has sometimes taken, cavalierly dismissed out of hand. Stietencron, for example, has recently declared that it really does not matter if "Hindus" today claim to be followers of a "religion" called "Hinduism": "The Indian acceptance of the term 'Hinduism' cannot serve to prove the existence of a 'religion' called Hinduism" (1989, 15).

This kind of indifference to indigenous conceptualizations of self-identity is one unfortunate end result of the argument that Indology and Orientalist concerns singlehandedly "constructed," "invented," or "imagined" a unified religion called Hinduism. This position is especially problematic in an age where western scholars often claim to be concerned to allow the "natives to speak" and "assume agency" over representational discourse. Since the publication of Edward Said's *Orientalism* (1979), it is usually not regarded as advisable to blithely ignore or overrule the self-portraits of those "others" under study. In a post-Saidian era, we claim to take seriously native voices and thus counter Karl Marx's pronouncement (reproduced as one of the epigrams of *Orientalism*): "They cannot represent themselves; they must be represented."

Excluding indigenous representations of Hinduism is, ironically enough, one implication to be drawn from Said's postmodern master narrative itself. For, in that work, Said overstated the hegemonic power attributed to the discourse of Orientalism: "Knowledge of the Orient, because generated out of strength, in a sense *creates* the Orient, the Oriental, and his world" (1979, 40; emphasis in original). The overweening power and dominance granted to the west and its discourses reappear in many critiques of Indian nationalism, communalism, and religion (for criticisms of this tendency and alternative views, see Irschick 1994; van der Veer 1994). Here, as in the prototype, the argument fundamentally comes down to this: The west invented such notions as "the Orient," "India" *qua* modern nation-state,

"Hindus" *qua* a communal group, and "Hinduism" *qua* world religion; the east subsequently passively accepted these false notions; and now we (often, but not always) westerners need to deconstruct them for you easterners (and for ourselves). This vision of the relationship between west and east, and between modern scholarship and its object of study, is unfortunately reduplicative of such relations in the past.

Denying the legitimacy of any and all "Hindu" representations of Hinduism can easily crossover into a Neo-Orientalism, whereby indigenous discourse is once again silenced or ignored as the product of a false consciousness delivered to it by outside forces or as simply irrelevant to the authoritative deliberations of western Indologists. While there are many reasons for scholars to feel uncomfortable with the claims some Indians have and are making regarding "Hinduism," it is perhaps equally dangerous to deny them the legitimacy to declare what, for them, is "Hinduism."

Hinduism, construct or no, does indeed exist now, if not in the "scholar's study" then certainly in India and elsewhere where "Hindus" reside, albeit in varying configurations. Trying to deconstruct it in learned books and articles is very likely a rear-guard activity, with little chance of success and questionable purpose (compare the conclusions of Hiltebeitel 1991). We ignore the "Hinduisms" that do now exist at our own peril; in the absence of scholarly definitions and constructs, members of the real world will and have filled the vacuum. Perhaps the time has finally come in Indological circles not to abandon the concept of "Hinduism" but to refine and define it as a religion among and comparable to others and to do so in consort with selected traditions and authorities within Hinduism that have also represented it in such a manner.

Notes

1. I am indebted to Bruce Lincoln for his helpful comments on an earlier draft of this article.
2. For a concise statement of method in the study of religion, see Lincoln 1996.
3. "Hinduism" is also the byproduct of a British colonial administrative decision to divide up the populace into various "communities" defined by religion—Christian, Hindu, Muslim, and so on (see Frykenberg 1987; Pandey 1992; Thapar 1989).
4. I leave aside consideration of early missionary accounts of "Hinduism" that often did indeed tend to portray it as a "religion," albeit a "false" one. The general category, "heathen," for all "false religions" was eventually specified to "Brahmanism" or "Hinduism" to depict the principal "false religion" of the Indic subcontinent (see Stietencron 1995, 73–77). For a survey of the definitional problem, see Sharma 1986.
5. For example, "The acceptance of the caste system was considered by the orthodox to be the sole effective criterion of whether one was or was not a Hindu" (Zaehner 1966, 8; cf. Dharampal-Frick 1995; Inden 1990, 49–84).

6. For example, *sansara, karma, moksha*.

7. See, for example, Renou's declaration that the Veda "is precisely the sign, perhaps the only one, of Indian orthodoxy" (1965, 2). I have also argued for such a definition of "Hinduism," although the definition put forward is relational rather than essentialistic: "Hinduism is the religion of those humans who create, perpetuate, and transform traditions with legitimizing reference to the authority of the Veda" (B. K. Smith 1989, 13–14; see also 1987). For the importance of the Veda in self-definitions of Hinduism among Brahman apologists of the early nineteenth century (and the traditions they stood on), consult Young 1981, 131–35, 140, 152.

8. It may be granted that in traditional and largely Sanskritic texts these are not the terms used. It is, however, debatable at the very least as to whether Sanskritic terms like "*sanatana dharma*" and "*vaidika dharma*" cannot, with the proper concessions to historical, cultural, and ideological specificity, be comparable to and translated as "Hinduism" or "the Hindu religion." Conversely, terms like "*bauddha dharma*," found already in "Hindu" texts dating from before the Common Era, might very well be adequately translated as "the Buddhist religion."

9. As noted above, many modern scholars of "Hinduism" deny that the tradition has, or ever had, a sense of either "orthodoxy" or "heresy" (see also Rudolph and Rudolph 1987, 37). For medieval material concerning one sect's distinctions between itself as "Hindu" and others who were not in the fold, see O'Connell 1973.

10. Such definitional criteria have also entered into modern Indian law, where many cases have arisen that require the court to make judgments about who is and is not a member of "Hinduism" (see Baird 1993; B. K. Smith 1993).

11. On the grounds that such claims, like others made in religious discourse, depend on acceptance of superhuman, transhistorical, and universalist arguments that contravene the methodological principles we must follow as nontheological scholars of religion.

12. They are also, of course, the conceptual and discursive products of outsiders who have (as in the case of Hinduism) likewise constructed a unity out of religious diversity and given it a unified label. These two types of unifying projects—theologians working from within; and scholars, administrators, missionaries, and other agents working from without—often have significant overlaps. In the Indian case, as we have seen above, Orientalist scholars and others built their constructions largely following the same lines used for millennia by the "orthodox" Brahman *pandits*.

13. Their emphasis on a "golden age" of the Vedic past and the degenerate state of the Hindu present; a "return to the Vedas" movement, accompanied by a shift from traditional notions of what Daniel Gold (1991) has called "scriptural authority" to a more circumscribed vision of "scriptural canon" as a way to recover pristine "Hinduism"; the abolition of image worship and various socioreligious practices (caste abuses, child marriage, *sati*) as "non-Vedic"; the reinterpretation of traditional concepts and practices to accommodate modern, western notions of individualism and social service; the organization of the group along western lines; and, most of all, the nationalistically driven agenda to unite "Hindus" under the banner (usually) of Neo-Vedantic philosophy—all of these reforms, innovations, and adjustments are seen as driven by and derivative of the West.

14. Exceptions can be made for groups such as the Arya Samaj who tended to eschew the all-inclusive universalism of other Neo-Hindu groups and can be seen as the direct precursors to the Hindu nationalist movement of the twentieth century. For a comparison of Dayanand Saraswati and the Arya Samaj, on the one hand, and the Rashtriya Svayamsevak Sangh, on the other, consult Gold 1991.

15. And therefore not a "nation" and in need of foreign rule.
16. Neo-Hindu nationalistically driven universalistic claims for "Hinduism" (as all religions in one) have had interesting reflexes among modern Indologists. Critical of attempts, indigenous or foreign, to conceptualize Hinduism as a religion with clear boundaries (that is, as exclusive), some of the latter have found themselves saying things like "There is no religion in South Asia which is not, in some sense Hindu" (Frykenberg 1993a, 549) or "The alternative to Hindu nationalism is the peculiar mix of classical and folk Hinduism and the unselfconscious Hinduism by which most Indians, Hindus as well as non-Hindus, live" (Nandy 1983, 104).

6

CONSTRUCTIONS OF HINDUISM AT THE NEXUS OF HISTORY AND RELIGION

Robert Eric Frykenberg

The term "religion," with all its variety of meanings, has no exact equivalent in India (South Asia). Moreover, the roles of religion and history in India are almost impossible to disaggregate. Nevertheless, at the heart of virtually all interactions between history and religion during the past century has been one overarching conceptualization. However casually and carelessly used, it has come to dominate discourse, contributing more than any other term to misunderstandings about the nature of important events. As a consequence, claims in its name can also be credited with having added, in some measure, to human misery. This soft concept, this jumble of inner contradictions which has existed at the nexus of history and religion for hardly two hundred years, is "Hinduism."

Hinduism lies at the center of any attempt to understand India today. It not only provided the eventual excuse (if not foundation) for the creation of Pakistan, but has also played a pivotal role within and around all that India has become since the eighteenth century. Yet, all of the elements in that loose and undefined complex of ideologies and institutions, which have been brought together under this name, together with all of the aggregate collage of what has also been "organized" and "syndicated" under its banner, did not just gradually (or naturally) evolve. Nor did Hinduism simply spring, full-blown, into being. Rather, it was constructed, piece by piece. At times, and in part, this was done inadvertently; and at times, or in part, deliberately; out of materials and precedents which had already existed for a long time. As a concept, it is India's twin.

In other words, the label *Hinduism* has come to represent, all too simplistically, hosts of phenomena in contexts which often seem either incomprehensible or contradictory. It has been used to refer to structural features which, over the past few centuries, have characterized various cultural, social, political, and religious systems. By focusing attention upon actual events intimately connected to the origins and rise of this term, and upon institutional and ideological components and contexts surrounding those events and their trajectory, one can understand the interaction of history and religion in South Asia in a way that no other heuristic device can match.

For any number of reasons, the concept Hinduism, so bandied about throughout the world in popular parlance, has long suffered from what can only be described as multiple definitions. This multiplicity is itself a consequence of the historical circumstances in which the concept first arose and of the ways in which it has been shaped by historical events. At the very least, the distinction needs to be made between Hindu as a geographical concept designating anything and everything native to India, and Hindu as a category of ideas and phenomena more specifically cultural, social, and religious.

The first definition of this concept—anything native to the entire region of South Asia (or India)—can be characterized as comprehensively describing and encompassing phenomena of extreme complexity, multiplicity, and variety. This usage, begun by the ancient Persians and Greeks, if not earlier, ascribed no necessarily particular cultural, social, political, or other unity to the geographical area whereas, at the same time and in seeming contradiction to this perspective, it ascribed certain common peculiarities to all who lived within the geographical regions beyond the Indus. It is this paradoxically "nativistic" sense of the term which the Muslims acquired (or brought with them) and then applied to peoples whom they found within the continent. They used this term to distinguish between themselves as believers (or "holders of the faith") and Native (or *Hindavi*) unbelievers (*kafirs*). This term, both in Arabic and in Persian, was also used to distinguish Muslims from India—those who were called *Hindavi*—from Muslims who came from other parts of the Islamic world. Still later, native non-Muslims of India used a similar term, *Hindutva*, to distinguish between themselves and Muslim peoples or overlords. The regime (and rulers) of Vijayanagara is actually described in Sanskrit inscriptions as *hindurajasuratrana* (or *hindutva sultanat*). When early Europeans came into India—or South Asia—and described what they saw or experienced, they distinguished between peoples and things that were indigenous—labeled *Gentoo* and, later, *Hindoo*—and peoples or things that were not. In the early nineteenth century, long after the East India Company's Raj had established its paramountcy over India, it was still not uncommon for references to be made to "Hindoo Christians" and "Hindoo

Muslims" as distinct from those who were not native-born or culturally indigenous to the subcontinent.[1]

Even so, if one were to focus attention on separate human (anthropological or sociopolitical) elements alone, the number of distinct and separate ethnic entities—each with its own culture if not language—is enough to baffle and perplex. No one knows exactly how many distinct communities India as a continent contains: there could be two thousand, three thousand, or more separate peoples. Strictly speaking, no two of these groups, on grounds of practical policy, cosmic principle, or ritual purity were ever supposed to intermarry or interdine with each other. Deep convictions about purity of birth (*jat*) and blood, and about preserving each birth-group or caste (*jati*) from pollution, have helped to make this so. Possible dire consequences to security, well-being, wealth, or welfare, as reflected in countless anecdotal narratives about immediate actions of social, political, and ritual stigmatization which have resulted from violation of norms relating to exclusivity of birth, have served to drive home hard lessons about maintaining biological apartheid. The rules of separate genetic identity, on the whole, became a fundamental so stark and so important to life that all other fundamentals paled in significance. Determinants of birth and earth, and of sacred blood and sacred soil, are still so important that no attempts to eradicate or reform caste (or birth-groups) have ever succeeded.[2]

A second, and much more recent, meaning of Hindu has increasingly come into use, especially during the last one hundred years. This definition, no less complex, difficult to define, or more elusive, has become dominant. More a vehicle for conveying abstract ideas about institutions than for describing concrete elements or hard objects, Hindu came to be the concept used by people who have tried to give greater unity to the extreme cultural diversities which are native to the continent. Such efforts, even when they have involved only one way of looking at different kinds of cultural phenomena in India, have almost invariably been part of some institutional, ideological, or political agenda. As instruments for drawing all of India together, the program behind each effort has sometimes been overt and explicit; at other times, covert and hidden; or even, albeit rarely, simultaneously conscious and unconscious (or inadvertent).

Under this second definition, one can identify three main kinds of construction. These separate but interlocking kinds of structuring defy easy or simple labels. Yet, for convenience, I call them: (1) the Logic of Brahmanical, or Bio-Social (Purity/Pollution) Separation; (2) the Logic of Regal/Imperial (Non-Brahmanical), or Contractural Integration; and (3) the Logic of Constitutional, or Indo-European (Orientalist) Synthesis. The logic of each structural system can also be seen as a process, sometimes congruent or partially overlapping the others. Separate sequences of events led to the formation of each of these kinds of structural systems. Together, or cumulatively arising from all three, they produced what we now call Hinduism. They, along with their metaphorical representations, serve to help locate and define those often countervailing centripetal and centrifugal forces within the continent which have radically changed social and political realities: they epitomize the interactions of history and religion in India (South Asia).

The first structure was Brahmanical in origin. A highly sophisticated system for categorizing all life; it lumped all mankind into a single category and then subdivided this category into a color-coded system of separate species and subspecies, genuses and subgenuses; and then ranked these hierarchically according to innate (biological, cultural, and ritual) capacities and qualities. The Brahmanical (Sanskritic) name for this ranked ordering, *varnashramadharma*, was devised so long ago that its roots go back to the *Manu Smriti* (*Dharma Shastra*) if not to the *Rig Veda* itself. This term described a single and ordered, albeit highly stratified, hierarchical system that genetically accounted for inherent differences within all forms of life. It was an intellectual rationale for explaining inherently different properties (colors: *varnas*), or in-qualities. This system of arranging and ranking different birth communities eventually became so dominant, so deeply entrenched, and so pervasive that no force has ever been able to break it. It became so dominant, philosophically and politically, that its rationale and its epistemology came to be regarded as virtually synonymous with Cosmic Law (*Dharma*).[3]

Exactly how far this rationale for structuring all of society evolved and how it then came to be spread beyond the Brahmans themselves has been debated over the centuries. By virtue of extremely attractive, influential, and powerful abilities—clerical, cultural, intellectual, rhetorical, ritual, and political—Brahmans succeeded, long before the coming of Islam into India (c. 711 CE), in so asserting themselves and insinuating their influence among important communities that their views were, in varying degrees, accepted.

Those whom they influenced (and those who patronized them), conveniently or opportunistically, they obligingly placed within the upper, or "twice-born," stratas (*varnas*) of their epistemic model, just below themselves. These communities were those deemed as born, destined, and worthy to be rulers and warriors (*Kshatriya*); or communities born with entrepreneurial skills in banking, commerce, and industry (*Vaishya*). Especially important was the dual role of the Brahman in relation to any ruler, whether that ruler was a mighty monarch or a petty lord over a tiny village: first, as the ritualist who could certify the legitimacy of rulership and noble status by reference to purity of birth and unbroken descent from either of two hallowed lineages, that of the sun (*suryavansha*) or that of the moon (*chandrvansha*); and second, as the clerical administrator-bureaucrat whose advice and service, record-keeping, and meticulous management of details were deemed to be essential for assuring the security and permanence of any domain.[4] In short, much of the higher civilization, which had slowly emerged over several millennia (roughly between 3000 BCE and 1000 CE), became the special preserve of Brahmanical influence, definition, and censorship. "Brahmans" became dominant in many royal courts and in courts aspiring to royalty.

The second structure, which served to define what it meant to be Hindu, arose from political logic (and necessity). It drew upon political theory, from misty antiquity and from Indo-Islamic or Indo-Mughal, and finally from Indo-British precedents. Due to their limited numbers, when compared to the vast domains which they conquered, Muslims, like all of their predecessors, turned to locally indigenous elites for support. The support that was essential for the stabilization and expansion of their respective regimes required much more skilled manpower than any single alien ethnic community or group—whether Turk, Persian, Arab, or whatever—possessed. Many of those to whom alien rulers turned for assistance, and upon whom they relied for support, came either from indigenous (Brahman and Brahmanized) administrative elites or from local warrior elites (for example, Rajputs of Rajasthan, Marathas of Maharashtra, Telega, Velama, Kamma, and Reddi nayakas of Telengana, or Vellalar lords of Tamilaham). These elites, especially those who were bureaucrats and bankers, came from scores of separate castes in various parts of the continent. They provided alien rulers with many age-old secrets of statecraft, secrets especially appropriate to local conditions. Such secrets were essential if any single small community or coalition of small communities were to preside, much less rule, over such vast numbers of culturally and ethnically separate peoples: peoples whose basic, if not primary, loyalties were defined by purity of birth. Borrowed from statecraft going all the way back to Chandragupta Maurya (c. 300 BCE) came the essentially imperial (Kautiliyan) axiom of the Great (Many-Spoked) Wheel (*Mahachakra*), or Great Umbrella (*Mahachatra*).[5]

Expressed also in the Persianized idiom of the Mughals, leaders of each important Hindu (meaning Native and/or non-Muslim) elite community entered into a personal bond or familial contract with the ruler, Sultan or *Padshah*. Bonds of mutually beneficial relationships of loyalty and reciprocal obligations between client and patron were forged. Expressed in metaphors of shared salt: one was either salt-worthy (*namak-hallal*: salt-true and trustworthy), or salt-unworthy (*namak-haram*: salt-false and disloyal). By a delicate balancing of support from each and every important caste or community within each locality and within the larger realm—like the balancing of many spokes which rightly bound the elements of a distantly surrounding rim to a central hub—an intricate framework of personal bonds and contracts held together the many distant and far-flung elements of a Mughal emperor's realm. By such metaphors was an imperial edifice constructed. This system, however Islamic the exalted throne (*masnad mu'alla*) upon which its high rulers sat and however Islamic their own personal and household institutions, had to be Hindu in the political structuring of the bondings of loyalty.

Bonds had, of necessity, to be developed between alien rulers and scores of indigenous communities over whom (and with whom) they ruled. To be Hindu, *Hindavi* or *Hindutva*, in this sense, was to be part of an eclectic, syncretistic, and tolerant regime. Each elite community's separate identity, as manifested in its own ethnic purity and its own special rituals or symbols, had to be respected. Each group, however high or low, remained confined to its own family/community cantonment. If any regime were to survive and remain strong, given the highly segmented moral, social, and ritual structures which separated peoples from each other, no other political logic would work.[6]

Hindu, in this sense, did not refer to any one particular religion, certainly not to a single Hindu religion. Hindu as part of a political logic required a supporting ideology which attempted to provide an overarching and legitimizing authority for an imperial (or state) structure within which all communities and religions could coexist. Thus, a devout Muslim could be a reasonably good Hindu (Native, that is, Indian) without ever being obliged to set foot inside a temple or to worship the gods of *kafirs*. By this reckoning, each family/community, whether Muslim or non-Muslim, was Hindu—meaning that it was not only native to some locality within the continent but was subject to some regime within India, or what we now call South Asia.[7] Each high, or important, family kept its own household religion and household gods—the higher and purer a family, the more it would insist upon having its own household gods and its own household places of worship. Temples, by this reckoning, were essentially the palaces of divine kings (who were, ipso facto, royal gods); and palaces were the temples of royal deities. What was Hindu about them was the fact that they existed within the continent or some region thereof (for example, Hindustan, Assam, Bengal, Gujarat, and Punjab).

But efforts to construct this kind of Hindu identity (or Hinduism), with its political logic, was the antithesis of doctrinal/ideological exclusivism, or of any textual fundamentalism as we know it. Its purpose was not to *exclude* peoples within the bounds or under the authority of any integrating system; but, rather, to *include* as many peoples as possible. It could not and did not dare to become doctrinaire, in an ideological or religious sense, without running the risk of alienating people and, thereby, of threatening or undermining the structures of the system which it was trying to strengthen.

Thus when the "exclusivistic," to coin a term, and fundamentalistic *ulama* expressed outrage at Emperor Akbar's *Din Il-Illahi*—the synthetically fabricated ideology that he invented in order to integrate (and include) all his subjects within one huge "state religion" (if one may dare to employ such a composite metaphor)—they were also resisting an ideology specifically designed to strengthen the logic and authority of Mughal imperialism. Likewise, when the Marathas strove against the logic of Mughal imperialism and/or, conversely, when, as some historiography has continually claimed, they resisted the Emperor Aurangzeb's centralizing policy with its ostensibly Islamic (or fundamentalistic) features—resorting to *fitva* (or *fitna*: resistance) in order to establish their own *Hindutva* (Maratha-native) realm (*svarajya*), they were not doing so in the name of Hinduism as we know it today (Wink 1986). The nativistic revivalism of Ram Das notwithstanding, no "Hindu Nation" (*Hindu Rashtra*) of the kind now so militantly espoused by the Rashtriya Swayamsevak Sangh (RSS), Vishwa Hindu Parishad (VHP), or Shiv Sena then existed. Maratha princes, from the Chitpavan (*Konkaneshtha*) Peshwas of Pune to the Chatrapatis of Satara and the royal families (*rajavanshas*) of Baroda, Gwalior, Indore, and Nagpur, bowed before their own household, local, and native gods and would have fulfilled their own duties (*rajadharma*). But, except for resisting imperial designs upon their own customs, domains, and traditions, their resistance against Islam would not have been in the name of some vast and all-inclusive Hinduism. Maratha *svarajya*? Certainly! But Hindu Nation in the sense now used? Almost as certainly not.

From another perspective, there *is* no single or *proper* sense of the term Hindu. On one hand, each community's religion was its "own": it was "Hindu" in the sense that it was confined to its own people; and each people's particular religion (its own household gods and secrets) could belong to no other people without being polluted and devalued.[8] Thus, what one worshiped or did not worship was one's own or one's family's affair. If Muslims, Christians, and Jews, not to mention Buddhists, Jains, Sikhs, and others worshiped within their own mosques, churches, synagogues, or temples, so also Brahmans of highest status, not to mention Kayasthas, Rajputs, and Baniyas (Sheths, Komartis, and Chettiars) worshiped in their own family shrines, temples, and puja rooms. In every hamlet and quarter, meanwhile, local goddesses required blood, and poorer, more lowly or backward peoples rendered it. In any case, what one worshiped or how one worshiped, or did not worship, did not make one more or less Hindu. In a communal or doctrinal sense, with each religion confined to its own people, there could be no question of being syncretistic or tolerant of the religions of others, especially since one had nothing to do with their religions. Hinduism was merely a case of mutual coexistence.

The term "Hindu," in this sense, is confusing. Even more so is the phrase "Hindu religion." Such confusions have become wonderfully convenient in serving the many kinds of interests and purposes of chauvinisms which have arisen in this century. As a case of synecdoche, such obfuscation, sometimes crude and sometimes insidious and subtle, has been made to serve an imperialistic ideal—giving a common name to everything that exists within *ritual* and *sacred* boundaries of "the Motherland" or "the Nation." The fact that there is no clear marker between what is religious and what is political (that is, national) has been kept deliberately vague. Present-day movements such as the VHP, RSS, and Shiv Sena could hardly ask for anything better or more convenient.

The third structure that is indicative of what is now meant by the term Hindu is Indo-European. More precisely, it is Orientalist (the old term for structures of knowledge manufactured in India). In its origin, it also is truly Indian in the sense of being an amalgam of Indo-British (Anglo-Indian), Anglo-Brahman, and Anglo-Islamic elements. Both Indian (*Hindu*: indigenous) and European (*Farangi*) in its making, it was never exclusively British. Nor was it colonial, or even "Orientalist" in the dismissive and pejorative sense now in vogue.[9]

This construction, resting directly upon the foundations of the earlier two structures, saw the erection of a new kind of Hinduism and of Hindu self-consciousness as strategies for the careful and deliberate integration of all of India into a single entity. As with all previous regimes, indigenous resources—material, cultural, and intellectual—provided the means. Without Hindu (native Indian) manpower, money, and ideas, the Raj could never have come into existence; nor could it have been so firmly established and maintained. Madras, the first Anglo-Indian city-state, was inspired and supported by the Velugoti lords of Kalahasti and Venkatagiri, sanctioned by a contract (*sasanam*) of Sri Ranga Ray III, the last scion of Vijayanagar reigning at Vellore. Its gold coin (*hun*) was ritually minted within the sacred precincts of the Sri Venkateshwara temple-palace at Tirupati; its investments came from Komarti and Chettiar merchant-bankers; its armed forces were professional soldiers recruited from among local Baliga, Kamma, Kapu, and other martial peoples; and its administrative and diplomatic talent came from a mixture of local clerical and literate communities in and around Mylapore, Nungambakkam, and Triplicane. Local peoples, together with their local deities, benefited most from the new wealth that was generated. Such elites filled the armies and the bureaucracies of the East India Company as it constructed a new imperial system. The Raj, in other words, forged its grand all-embracing imperium out of earlier imperial institutions and ideologies that were appropriated and superimposed upon ideological, institutional, and material elements of the still earlier Hindu structures described above. The earlier epistemic, ontological, and ritual traditions of *varnashramadharma*, the color-coded and segmented system constructed by Brahmans, and the earlier structural features of *mahachakra* (and contractual *sanads* idealized in bonds of *namakhallal*) as epitomized in various durbars, provide the cultural and imperial (and later, national) foundations for the Raj.

Denigrators of Orientalism give too much credit to Europeans and too little to hosts of Native Indians (mainly Brahmans and others imbued with Brahmanical world views; but also Muslims imbued with Islamic world views) for the cultural constructions (and reconstructions) of India. These Indian elites did as much to inculcate their own views into the administrative

machinery and into the cultural framework of the Indian Empire as anything done by the Europeans whom they so outnumbered and with whom
they worked so closely. To Europeans they imparted not only their practical
experience and political savvy, but also their prejudices about purity of
birth. For this same reason other terms currently in vogue for purposes of
denigratory epithet and scorn, like *colonial* or *colonialism*—used simplistically in many anticolonialist theories as pejorative and reductionist synonyms
for *alien* (meaning European/western/racist) *domination* and *exploitation* of
benighted and hapless peoples—tend to give off more heat than light. What
went into the making of modern religions in India (South Asia) was much
more complicated than the fashionable nostrums that are now so often constructed in the name of supposedly "disinterested" scholars.[10]

The Indian Empire had already become a de facto Hindu Raj long before
the rule by the East India Company ended. It became increasingly more so
under the British Crown (Frykenberg 1989). This development arose from
two parallel and intermingling processes of further construction. Both, officially supported, established the substructures of modern Hinduism and provoked sharply religious, if not fundamentalistic, reactions (both in Britain and
in India) from communities that felt threatened by the newly rising Hindu
Establishment. Together, these official developments—one *institutional* and
the other *ideological*—brought into being elements that produced what is
now known as "Organized," or "Syndicated" Hinduism.

The first substructure was institutional, consisting of administrative and
political actions or policies. It involved a gradual takeover by the new Imperial State of all religious property, together with a systematic extension of
State supervision and fiscal management of all charitable and religious institutions. The Company's Raj, through local governments known as presiden-
cies and through a rationalizing system of laws and bureaucratic machinery,
gradually established its sway. This sway, rising under the shadow of Mughal
legitimacy, grew and spread, first in the Carnatic south and Bengal, and then
over the whole continent, until the shadow of its own parasol (*mahachatra*)
covered all of India. The Raj had become *the* paramount power. Yet, the
East India Company was aware of the fragility of its manpower resources
and of the structures of loyalty undergirding its regimes. Through partner-
ships with local bankers, merchants, landed magnates, and temples, its city-
states of Madras, Calcutta, and Bombay generated great wealth. Indigenous
manpower and money provided the means for gradually building a professional army of *sepoys* and *sardars*; they, in turn, helped to conquer the country and to set up governments. Such resources also enabled the employment
of an equally large professional service to carry on day-to-day administration under those governments.

Across the length and breadth of the empire were many tens of thousands
of temples (as well as mosques, even some churches and synagogues in the

south). Each of these temples was the royal palace of a local deity; each was supported by its own domains and endowments. Some of these were tiny, local god-houses; others were palace-temples. Some temple endowments and estates were so enormous that they constituted states or standing dominions in their own right. Revenues generated by endowments for such places— *inams* for temples, shrines, schools, and places of pilgrimage—were "alienated," or tax-exempt. Such tax-exemption removed as much as 10 to 15 percent of all potential land revenues from the imperial treasuries. Yet, at an early stage of its rule, the Company's governments cemented the local loyalties of their imperial servants, soldiers, and supporters by confirming the tax-exempt status of most such endowments, especially those supporting religious establishments.[11]

Not surprisingly, where amounts of wealth generated by religious institutions were substantial, struggles for control ensued. Such struggles, sometimes erupting into violence, but more often resulting in protracted litigation and controversy, brought pleas for State (imperial) intervention. As early as 1810, Hindu temple properties began to come under the management of local governments. Native (Hindu or Indian) officials took over the day-to-day control of religious and charitable endowments, managing them on behalf of the institutions which they were meant to support, sometimes even supervising daily rituals and calendar ceremonies. In Madras, for example, this process of gradually consolidating State control over Hindu institutions took more than a century (and is still going on). By decisions made in 1817, 1863, 1926, and 1952, for example, the Government of Madras set up its own system of controls: eventuating into the Hindu Religious (and Charitable) Endowments Board. At each stage, whether in courts of law or in legislative chambers, hosts of local functionaries and officials (*pujaris*, *stanikars*, pandits, vakils, judges, scholars, and others) became involved in day-to-day decision-making. In the process, the Government itself constructed a huge informational, institutional, and intellectual infrastructure for an officially supported reification of religion. In institutional terms, a modern and organized Hinduism, intermingling all sorts of previously unconnected elements, became part of the imperial establishment—something which had never before existed.[12]

Parallel to this institutional integration and consolidation within the imperial establishment ran a second process that contributed to the *ideological* and *intellectual* structures of this official kind of Hinduism. Hosts of Native and European scholars (pandits, mullahs, and others collaborating together in Oriental studies) worked for the East India Company from the late eighteenth century onward. Initially patronized privately by Warren Hastings, the first governor-general (1772–1786), and his successors, but later sponsored by private scholars and scholarly institutions throughout the world, detailed information from India's Brahmanical and classical (Hindu or pre-Muslim) past came to light.[13] These scholars collected, integrated, preserved, publicized, and continuously, with each successive generation, reconstructed an enormous structure of knowledge. This dynamic and ever-expanding structure conveyed, sometimes with romantic and fanciful embellishment, an image of the past such that had never been so fully known.

The "official" (or establishment) structure, in summary, consisted of at least five elements: (1) Hinduism as a nativistic synonym for all things Indian (or pertaining to India); (2) Hinduism as an ancient civilization, something clearly identifiable before 1800 and going back five thousand years; (3) Hinduism as a loosely defined label describing all socioreligious phenomena found or originating in India (comparable to, but less pejorative than, paganism as a label for nonmonotheistic religions in the ancient Greco-Roman world); (4) Hinduism as an institutional/ideological instrument for the sociocultural and sociopolitical integration of an all-India (imperial or national) sway; and (5) Hinduism as a single religion which, with the coming of Swami Narendranath Datta Vivekananda to the First World Parliament of Religions at Chicago in 1893, was gradually recognized and then elevated by liberally minded and eclectic western clerics into the rank of a world religion. A pragmatic and sometimes romantic blending of these five representations, as Hawley has argued, helped to reify Hinduism in popular imaginations. With western impetus, this blending was then projected onto the world.[14]

This codification of an "official" or establishment Hinduism as a conceptual framework is one of the most remarkable legacies of the Old Raj. The idea that "Hinduism" was a *single* and *ancient* religion gradually spread and solidified, becoming dominant and pervasive. In so doing, it created and perpetuated two accompanying myths. Both of these myths were expedient, if not essential, to the continued political integration of India (under the Raj); and both are no less expedient for the same political ends today. First, and above all else, was the belief that Hinduism is a benign, "inclusivistic," and singular religion, epitomizing all that is eclectic, syncretistic, and tolerant in human behavior, doctrine, and ritual; second was the belief that Hinduism, as *the* religion of India, represents (and hence should command allegiance from) *the* majority of India's (if not all of South Asia's) peoples. Together, these two corollary subconstructions served to enfold or incorporate all indigenous peoples of the continent as being elemental parts of Hinduism. Through a process of incorporation by definition, they were implicitly codified and reinforced by a host of homogenizing and synthesizing all-India fiats. These fiats, in one I way or another, *marked* the ethnic, linguistic, and religious identity of every person. The most important of these occurred with the Census of India (every decade from 1871); another occurred within the formal reports of the Linguistic Survey of India (from 1902). The detailed implementation of these registration measures was left to a predominantly Brahman and Brahmanized (or Hindu) bureaucracy. By the time that these events took place, and as a consequence of electoral impulses set in motion

after the great Reform Bills of Britain (1830 and 1870), this same bureaucracy had acquired a vested interest in defining an "organized" Hinduism as
India's "majority community" and majority religion, something quite distinct from various minority communities.[15]

This process of "inclusion by definition" embraced all life. As such, it
allowed for the inclusion of all of India's inhabitants, whatever their forms
of worship, however crude or sublime, however monotheistic, polytheistic,
or nontheistic. At the least, this action included as "Hindu" those who fell
outside the pale of purity, hundreds of millions who could never be allowed
to defile or pollute the sanctity of proper dwelling-places. These fiats became
devices for incorporating all aboriginals or tribals (*adivasis*) and *panchamas*
(fifths: so-called outcast or untouchable peoples outside the Four-Color-Code
or *Chatur-Varnya*)—peoples who currently account for some 20 percent of
India's population.[16] At the same time, however, by a contradiction of this
same logic, only two-thirds of imperial India's population were defined as
Hindus. All other peoples—Jews, Christians, Muslims, and sometimes even
Sikhs—were excluded from this category. (Today, by this same logic, over
80 percent of India's current population, and all others seen as native to
India's pure and sacred soil, are defined as Hindu, however less than touch-
able some are deemed.)

In strictly utilitarian terms, any definition of Hinduism that allowed for the
representation of ideologies/institutions/rituals that were essentially agnostic,
benign, eclectic, and integrative of the whole continent and that drew all peoples toward each other or toward a central authority, served an "official"
and politically acceptable purpose. In a continent so highly pluralistic, such
Hinduism helped to reinforce the construction of any single huge overarching political order, an order possessing a single all-embracing ideology or
religion.

As noted earlier, a Hindu symbol for this all-embracing construction of a
Hindu Imperium was the Great Wheel (*Mahachakra*). It is re-emphasized
because it has served every astute ruler from Ashoka (c. 300 BCE) to the present. Akbar's *Din Il-Illahi* reconstituted the stone representation of the symbol (found in the temple at Konarak) at Fatehpur Sikri. He placed himself at
the wheel's hub, surrounded by spokes representing every important ethnic
or sectarian elite. By cementing personal, face-to-face bonds (*namak hallal*)
with each community in turn, he sought to make himself Lord of all. The
same special logic, with its essential blend of eclecticism, syncretism, and
tolerance, characterized the Indo-British constructions of Orientalism. No
ideology better served the structural strength and security of the Government of India. Later, when such Hindu norms were violated by arrivals from
Britain who were ignorant of Hindu customs and the foundations of imperial
rule, the Native Hindu gentry reminded them of such verities. In massive

petition drives—for example, thirty thousand signatures gathered in Calcutta (1827) to defend *Sati* (*Suttee*), seventy thousand (1839) and twelve thousand (1846) in Madras to demand better education and protection from unfair religious interference by missionaries—they vaunted their long proved attachment to the Raj and reminded British overlords that Hindoo blood freely flowed to establish an essentially Hindu (Indian) empire (Great Britain 1827 and 1846; Norton 1848).

The same kind of official orthodoxy was codified in scholarship from John Zephaniah Holwell and Nathaniel Brassey Halhed to Monier Monier-Williams and Max Muller. The fifty-volume *Sacred Books of the East* from its publication until now has also served as a textual foundation for the construction of Hindu Nationalism. This particular Hinduism, constructed by the Company's Orientalist pandits and read in English and Indian-English texts, which translated and interpreted India's hallowed past, instructed and inspired nationalist leaders from Mohandas K. Gandhi to Jawaharlal Nehru. This perspective found its nationalist apotheosis (and *avatar*), if not its ultimate ideological reaffirmation, in the life, scholarship, and political career of Sarvepalli Radhakrishnan (president of India from 1962 to 1967).[17]

A special kind of official Hinduism evolved: this development served, first, to integrate all Hindu (meaning, native Indian) agencies and institutions, most notably all temples, under the protective administration of one great single institutional umbrella (*mahachatra*) provided by the State; second, to provide an ideological cover for all Hindu (meaning, native Indian) religions, sects, and scholarly traditions under a benignly eclectic, syncretistic, and tolerant—officially neutral (under the British) and secular (under the Congress of Nehru)—umbrella. In other words, integrative doctrines, furnished by the axis of Brahmanical-European Orientalism, nourished and strengthened the foundations not only for the praxis of the empire but also for the nation which superseded it.

But circumstances arose whereby this officially supported Hinduism eventually aroused fires of opposition. More abrasive, more exclusivist, and less tolerant forces of religion arose that rubbed each other the wrong way and brought about violent conflict. This happened both within India and within Britain. Akbar and his successors had to face rebellion from Islamic extremists, insomuch that Mughals of Aurangzeb's regime have ever since remained infamous for anti-Hindu intolerance and repression (justifying reactions by Marathas, Sikhs, and others). Certain groups, by giving offense or perceiving offense, either could not or would not allow such policies to stand unchallenged. Similarly, under the Company, from the 1790s but especially from the 1830s onward, there were reactions to this Hinduism from Christians, Muslims, and Sikhs (and, in this century, from various sets of Untouchable communities).

Christian protests against "unfair" advantages accorded to institutional and ideological forces of "heathenism" arose both locally and from overseas. Christians in India (both Native and European), especially those who were of a more evangelical, exclusivistic, and, sometimes, even fundamentalistic outlook, became outraged at what they saw as favoritism. Word reached Christians in Britain that officials of the Indian Empire were actually administering temple endowments, making renovations, and overseeing rituals, receiving public recognition and titles for upholding order or proper religious homage of one deity or another; and some, even Europeans, were not only making personal endowments to temple deities but were contributing funds to support ritual observances, doing so with ostentatious munificence.[18]

Since, by decree, ceremonies conducted within temples had come, in one way or another, under either direct or indirect supervision of the Government, this involvement of officials was hardly surprising. Ceremonies in South Indian temples, from the largest and oldest temples of Kanchipuram, Madurai, Srirangam, and Tirupati to the smallest, meanest, and newest shrines springing up beside busy thoroughfares or in remote villages, involved participation by minions of the Madras Government. Officials of the government not only took control of temple revenues and repairs, but stood watch over its ritual practices. Sepoys and sawars, some of them Christian but many more Muslim (and, later, Sikh), were required to stand on parade and salute local deities, or to attend blood sacrifices, remaining prominently visible at important religious ceremonies. Company functionaries collected tolls from pilgrims and taxes at fairs and festivals. Government officials, both military and civilian, were required to attend celebrations (regardless of private convictions, or violations of private conscience among Christian or Muslim officers), and government officials commandeered huge drafts of involuntary labor from hundreds of thousands of menials who were annually required to pull enormous temple cars (*rathas*), many falling and being propitiously crushed under the giant wheels.[19] Even temple dancing, music, and prostitution, involving hundreds of thousands of *devadasis*, came under the tolerant jurisdiction of the State.

From one end of the Empire to the other, heaven-born and twice-born (*dvija*) officials of the Company sat like deities. Each district office (*kachari* or *cutcherry*) was itself like a temple—with circles within circles of functionaries, standing attention like priests to make sure that only the cleanest and worthiest could penetrate into the innermost sanctum. There, in dark and mysterious seclusion, like a graven image, sat the *Huzur* (or Divine Presence)—the term by which each such deity was actually addressed. Few could approach the hallowed presence, and then, only through ranks of properly qualified intermediaries. To make petitions or prayers without propitiatory offerings was futile: gatekeepers and doorkeepers had to be properly propitiated by agents or brokers (*vakils*) who were employed. These, like priests entering a temple, understood the proper protocol and the appropriate offerings. If petitioners were polluting, access could be all but impossible. Untouchables sometimes had to lie face down in the dirt, some thirty to fifty yards away, begging for someone to notice them and to take up their cases. Proper (*pukka*) buildings, rooms, bridges, and roads were too pure to be defiled by such creatures (Khan 1848; Frykenberg 1982).

Exactly how each separate religious or sectarian community in South Asia came to terms with this official kind of Hinduism and how each reacted to situations of momentous consequence for their future survival are questions having relevance for any consideration of later relationships between a recent, reified, communal Hinduism, which also emerged, and many communities in India.

Christian interactions with the new Hinduism were mixed. Initially, Christians in India received little help or comfort from the Company. Most of India's Christians, even those converted in late eighteenth- and early nineteenth-century mass movements, lived in areas far from the Company's direct control (Tanjore, 1731–1799; Tinnevelly, 1786–1801; and Travancore, 1799–1840). Long opposed to European missionaries within its domains, although occasionally exploiting a few who worked outside its own domains, the Company remained aloof to petitions. Native Christians begged in vain for redress from persecution. Only the gradual rise of an Evangelical lobby among the Company's European servants within the Court of Directors and their forging of a strong coalition of merchant and missionary interests in Parliament forced grudging concessions from the Company, in the Charter Renewal Act of 1813.[20]

Yet, even after English missionaries began to enter into Company territories, and bishops established ecclesiastical structures in India, they encountered increasing resistance. Hindu establishments—with State participation in Hindu ceremonials and rituals—were already too deeply entrenched. Despite all of their powers as Lords Spiritual in Parliament, the Church of England in India remained subject to the Company's governments. These could and did overrule decisions of Church clergy and prelates (and unhappy relations with the Government of India were to continue to 1947). In shock and consternation, as the full implications of the situation began to dawn upon them, European Christians in India tried to take action. Hundreds, official and nonofficial alike, instigated by the Bishop of Madras, signed petitions (in 1835). Their plea was for all official connections with "heathen" institutions and practices to cease. But hope for relief from governments in India was soon dissipated. Their "conspiracy" was not appreciated: many of the disillusioned, including the bishop, were sternly reprimanded; and not a few, including General Peregrine Maitland, were forced to resign. Those who left India joined the Anti-Idolatry Connexion League in Britain, launching a pamphlet campaign against policies of the Company's "Hindu" governments.[21] Yet, after all such efforts, despite years of lobbying by missionary societies against violations in India of self-proclaimed government neutrality in matters of religion, little of substance was altered. Concessions that were made turned out, in the long run, to be more cosmetic than real.

On another plane, intellectual and ideological encounters between persons of particular and different religious persuasions entered a new phase with the advent of modern scholarship and translation. European and Indian scholars, in collaboration with each other, translated biblical texts from Hebrew and Greek into Sanskrit and Arabic, and into the many regional and local languages, and translated classical Indian (Sanskrit, Tamil, Arabic, and Persian) texts into European languages. In the process of employing the classical and other languages of India for purposes of religious and philosophical discourse, European scholars also engaged pandits and mullahs in serious debate (without insult, invective, or slur) (Young 1981, 173).

Resistance to radical changes, especially to conversion, was another matter. Not surprisingly, cultural, institutional, religious, or social changes—especially radical conversion (to Christianity) or reform touching long-entrenched domestic customs—were profoundly disturbing. The roots of religious extremism and revivalism, if not of fundamentalisms, whether from Hindu (non-Muslim: Buddhist, Christian, Jain, Jewish, Sikh, or Parsee) or Muslim (Hindu-Muslim or native Muslim) communities, can be seen as coming out of reactions to radical changes and to perceived threats against basic elements of "the old order." Established customs and traditions which had long existed within each birth group (*jati*) or domestic or sectarian community, especially those held by families of the entrenched elites, were too sacred and too sensitive.

But here was an irony. Despite the many changes which had enhanced the influence of Brahman and other high-caste (Hindu) elites within governments of the Indian Empire and changes which had brought about, however implicitly to the rulers and ruled alike, a massive "Hinduization" of the continent—and, perhaps because of such changes—there never was a time, from the late eighteenth century onward, when nativist reactions to radical changes in matters of religious or social consequence did not occur somewhere. Sometimes these were fierce, sometimes massive, and sometimes both fierce and massive. Often these were provoked by some perceived violation of custom or some perceived threat to purity. Institutions such as birth, caste, custom, duty, place, rank, or status were matters so hallowed that they, in themselves, constituted the most sacred fundamentals of religion. Where threats against sacred institutions came from attacks against doctrines and ideologies underpinning those institutions, whether against scriptural sources of authority or against philosophical foundations of authority, reactions became intellectual or polemical. Whatever their character, whether institutional or ideological, such threats were seen as actions designed to undermine traditions, established order, and religion: the *dharm* and *sanatana dharm* of high-born non-Muslims (and the *Dar-ul-Islam* of Muslims).[22] As often as not, non-Muslim reactions also came from Brahman and Brahmanically cultured individuals and groups who were not officials employed within the Empire.

Thus, by the nineteenth century, even while a New (All-India) Hinduism was in the process of being formed within and around official establishments, there were those, both inside and outside these establishments, who somehow felt threatened by rapid changes and who reacted against these changes. Among such changes, perhaps none was more disrupting than that initiated outside official control or sanction by increasing numbers of Christians from Europe, especially newcomers fired by the revivalistic fires of Evangelicalism and Pietism. Some of these European Christians, officials and missionaries alike, directly challenged the old ways and the old religions. They did so by not only launching frontal attacks upon existing heathen beliefs, customs, and practices, but by also conducting massive conversion campaigns and by establishing attractive educational programs. Such attacks, especially when they were insensitive or insulting and, worse yet, if they were threatening or seemed threatening, triggered responses in defense of *Dar-ul-Islam* and *sanatana dharm*. The cumulative effects of such reactions, if and when they ever combined, could be deadly. Indeed, having already helped to provoke the Vellore Mutiny of 1806 in south India, the same kinds of cumulative reactions were eventually to spark that much more serious conflagration in north India commonly known as the Great Rebellion (or Great Mutiny) of 1857 (Frykenberg 1986).

On a more down-to-earth or popular level, incipient progenitors of modern movements also organized. As institutional efforts to defend the old order, or to reform it, albeit reluctantly when or where unavoidable, many of these movements became radically and self-consciously "Hindu." Defensive, exclusivist, fundamentalistic, militant, or revivalist, their purpose was to "purify" the "sacred soil" from pollution and to do so by means of radical "reconversion" (*shuddi*: purification). Attitudes toward any ethnic or religious community not deemed to be properly Hindu, meaning not legitimately indigenous or *native* to Mother India (*Bharat Mata*), became increasingly hostile and intolerant, if not violent. Radical conversion movements were, in effect, modeled after comparable movements coming out of the Abrahamic traditions. Quite explicitly labeling themselves Hindu, they saw themselves as defenders of Hinduism (*Hindutva Dharm*). These "Hindu" movements, in varying degrees, blended together nativist elements which are peculiar to many, if not all, radical conversion movements (especially those which are fundamentalistic); and they did this with a particular kind of nationalistic fervor.[23]

As seen in south India, for example, such movements made their initial appearance in reaction to earlier mass movements of conversion to Christianity (among Shanars and Vellalars, for example). The Vibuthi Sangam, the Dharma Sabha, and the Chatur Veda Siddhantha Sabha (known in Madras as the Salay Street Society) arose during the 1820s to the 1840s. In aggressive exclusiveness and fundamentalism, they were forerunners of the Arya Samaj, the Nagari Pracharini Sabha, the Hindu Mahasabha, and the RSS, which later grew up in the north and west of India. These movements, in turn, led to others even more extremist and revivalist. Chief among the most militantly revivalistic groups which, in this century, have recently followed paths begun by earlier movements are *jagarans* of the Dharma Sansad, the VHP, the Virat Hindu Sammelan, Hindu Samajotsav, Bajrang Dal, and the Shiv Sena.[24]

All such radical movements in the post-Independence period have either appropriated or absorbed the institutional trappings of the official Hinduism that developed under imperial auspices during the nineteenth century. What has been constructed out of this blending of earlier elements is a culminating manifestation of Hinduism which, whatever its historical roots, is different from anything India has previously known. Often referred to as "organized" or "syndicated" Hinduism, it now possesses a much more discrete and reified form, and has acquired a denominationalistic or world-religion character. A modern phenomena, this Hinduism is not only proselytizing in its aims, but chauvinistic, exclusivistic, fundamentalistic, and even imperialistic, in its demands. It aims, in its most extreme form, to represent *all* the pure peoples of India (and, by inference, claims authority also over *all* other peoples, if not over all life). Its protagonists insist that, as *"the majority community"* in and of India, they both represent and speak for all (perhaps by divine fiat). Hinduism thus claims rightful dominance as *the* religion (*dharma*) for all peoples in South Asia (Thapar 1985; Frykenberg 1987).

Constructions of Hinduism are related to all religions in South Asia, including those which deem themselves to be non-Hindu religions. There is no religion in South Asia which is not, in some sense, Hindu. All religions have had to come to grips, in one way or another, with the overwhelming presence of one or more of the many constructions of Hinduism. Without discussing how each particular religious system has been influenced by one feature of Hinduism or another and how deeply penetrating or widely pervasive that influence has been, it is possible to pinpoint the indicators that illustrate the incredibly pervasive strengths of Hindu structures.

First, there is no religious community in India which has not been profoundly influenced by Hindu notions of pollution/purity, insomuch that careful regard and scruples about birth and contact are ubiquitous, along with ideas about social ranking and cultural status. What and how one drinks, eats, avoids bodily products (fluids, excrement, and so forth), and mixes with other living beings (family, other people, and animals) are matters of no small concern. The range of sensitivities to slights is enormous. Second, arising from this fact, is the distinctive character of both the structures and strengths of families in South Asia. The sense that many institutions come and go but that families are forever is all pervasive. Third, as a further consequence, whether in ideas or customs and rituals, there are few in India (South Asia)—Muslims, Jews, Christians, as well as Sikhs, Buddhists, Jains, and Animists—who have escaped attitudes and notions which arise out of one or more of the constructions of Hinduism which we have examined. In some degree, all religious groups and communities in South Asia are Hindu or "Hinduized": even those which deny and negate their "Hindu-ness" tend, by such strivings, to demonstrate how profoundly they have been touched by the presence of Hinduism.

Notes

1. Kulke (1985, 125) refers to the Hejje inscription of Marappa (c. 1347 CE). O'Connell (1973, 340–43) also indicates that the word Hindu appeared in Gaudiya Vaishnava texts of the sixteenth century, but only in texts describing strained relationships between Hindus as natives and Muslims as foreigners (*yavanas* or *mlecchas*). The term was never used by Hindus to describe themselves. *Hindu dharma* occurs seven times—four in Bengali texts—without definition, distinguishing native from nonnative elements. This indigenous usage is the closest earlier approximation to the modern term Hinduism.

   Tatwa-Bhodachari (Roberto de Nobili) and Viramamuni (Joseph Constantius Beschi) did not write of Hindus; see details in Caldwell 1881, 232–44; Kaye 1859; Marshall 1970 is a reprinting of such perspectives. For *Gentoo*, see Yule and Burnell 1886, 367.

2. From the standpoint of defining fundamentalism as defending the inerrancy of a sacred or ultimate text as *the* ground of Truth, here is that kind of text printed in the genetic code (DNA or genome) of each genus, which cannot be altered and from which there can be no appeal. See Andersen and Damle 1987, 76. Efforts to remove this placing of primal and ultimate value in purity of birth ostensibly date back at least to the time of Gautama Siddhartha, the Buddha. Such efforts in this century include recent radical movements launched by non-Brahman or anti-Brahman Adi-Dravida, Adivasi ("Aboriginal People"), Buddhist, Christian, Islamic, Marxist, and tribal auspices under such leaders as "Thanthai Periyan" Erode Viramani Ramaswami Naicke, Bishop Vedanayagam Samuel Azariah, Bhimrao Ramji Ambedkar, Maulana Muhammad Ilyas, and Manabendra Samuel Roy. See Rudolph and Rudolph 1967, 36–64, 64–87, 132–54; Isaacs 1965; Mujahid 1989.

3. Monier Monier-Williams (1889) called this *Brahmanism*. His small book *Hinduism* (1877) first brought the term into general use in the west. The word *Brahman* is an Indo-European cousin of our term *breath*. The term stood both for the class of priests, ritualists, and scholars who came into India with the Aryans, c. 2000 to 1700 BCE, and for Universal Spirit or Principle (or Deity) which encompasses all existence. *Varnashramadharma* means color-class, -category, -code, -order, -place, -ranking, or -status. De Bary, *et al.* 1958, 218–28; Basham 1954, 137–50.

Dharma/Karma, the most important concept in India's entire high civilization, was developed within the Brahmanical/Sanskritic tradition. *Dharma* comprehends, at once, our words for religion, order, immutable law, duty, and proper conduct. Its twin, *Karma*, like the opposite side of a coin, stands for action and consequence which, when extended, becomes the immutable (cosmic) law of cause and effect.

4. Below these twice-born peoples, in every locality, were a fourth category of peoples (*Shudra*) whose "privilege" it was to serve the three categorical strata above them. A fifth stratum existed, below all else, but was not formally included. It was called *pan-chama*. People in this category were considered to be so menial and so polluting that they were beyond the pale and beneath notice: they were not only deemed untouch-able, but unseen.

   In many realms, prior to the Turkish conquests, Buddhist and Jain functionaries had been able to compete with Brahmans for influence in providing local rulers with these administrative skills. Thereafter, these groups, although still influential wherever they survived, dwindled in number and became increasingly marginalized.

5. Another concept, referring to the relations between unequal and equal entities, was the delicately balanced twin logics: logic of fish (*matsya-nyaya*) and logic of circles, or spheres (*mandala-nyaya*).

6. Allowing a certain license for rituals belonging to a royal family, common, public, or imperial ceremonies acquired a kind of eclectic secularity. The larger the regime was, the more ceremonies were required.

   This system of bonding does not mean that there were no tensions between the purely Islamic imperative of *Dar-ul-Islam* and the imperatives of *real politique*. Yet all great rulers in India, from Akbar to Nehru, have understood this tension and worked their magic within its constraints.

7. Hindu and India are twins. To be Hindu, in this sense, was comparable to being European (*Farangi*) or American. It was the same as Indian.

8. Even the term *private* is hardly appropriate, since distinctions between *private* and *public* as we think of them today (or as embodied in law) did not exist.

9. Oriental scholarship, contrary to impressions conveyed in Said 1978, was never merely, only, or even a purely European construction. Nor, as he suggested, did Orientalism begin in the Middle or Near East with Napoleon. Rather, its origin and its fullest sense was a collaborative enterprise. It began in Persia, Bactria, and Greece: the term and some stereotypes linked to it are found in the work of Herodotus. In India, both native Indians and European Indians (Europeans long resident in India) worked together in producing it. For every European involved, there were hosts of natives/Hindus (whether of Madras, Calcutta, Bombay, or anywhere else) who made some of the most crucial contributions to this scholarship.

   Like Hinduism, *India* and *Indian* are modern terms. Coined by the East India Company, they are the direct products of the process being described. Hawley (1991, 30–34) traces Orientalism from ancient Persians and Greeks, through Marco Polo and Roberto di Nobili, to John Zephaniah Holwell, Nathaniel Brassey Halhed, Horace Hayman Wilson, Rammohan Roy, Henry David Thoreau, Monier Monier-Williams, Max Muller, and Sarvepalli Radhakrishnan. See Frykenberg 1991.

10. The overall European-Indian ratio of officials in the civil services (not counting the military services) was over 1:1000. This disparity was greater in *mufassal* stations. Few, if any, European Orientalists or ICS officers in India doing oriental research were surrounded by less than a dozen to twenty high-caste and learned local assistants, consultants, informants, and investigators who did much, if not most, of the actual scholarly work (Schmitlhenwer 1991). That European servants of the Company gained fame from publishing their Orientalist findings without giving due credit to their

Hindu (Native) mentors, and that their mentors did not complain does not alter the evidence of what they did. Jeffrey Russell (1991, 13–19) decries what he calls "chrono-centrism—the assumption of the superiority of 'our' views to that of older cultures—[a]s the most stubborn remaining variety of ethnocentrism." Such contempt for the past in relation to the superiority of a "more progressive" present seems as pervasive and subtle today as ever.

11. Chandra Y. Mudaliar (1974) was among the first carefully to study the complexities and intricacies of this subject. Her treatment of this development and its consequences is invaluable. See also Trevelyan 1908, 552–94; Frykenberg 1977, 37–53.

12. State-supported Hinduism was designed to be balanced, impartial, and inclusive—not only of existing Buddhist and Jain institutions, but also of Indo-Islamic, Sikh, Christian, Jewish, Zoroastrian, and other establishments. Here was Akbar's *Din Il-Illahi*, a writ, yet undefined, in which the State's role was as neutral arbitrator and sustainer.

    Findings summarized here come out of my own previous research and from many with whom I have been associated over the years. Especially important: Presler 1987; works by Carol Breckenridge Appadurai including 1976; Arjun Appadurai 1981.

13. Publication and distribution of materials is still patronized by the Government of India and by scholarly institutions the world over.

14. I am grateful to Eric J. Ziolkowski (1990, 11–12) for documentation on this discovery and validation which, in fascinating detail, remains within the proceedings of that event: Barrows 1893; Hawley 1991, 30–34.

15. Earlier local census reports of the Company, called *dehezadia*, drew upon precedents going back at least to Mughal times. Over a century ago, Sayyid Ahmad Khan sounded the alarm on the implications for Muslims of the combination of the census and democratic reforms. This fact has been reasserted by Hawley (1991, 23), again showing how many communities tried to distance themselves from Hinduism for economic, occupational, and political reasons. See also Frykenberg 1987.

16. The Sanskritic concept of *Brahma/n,* the Supreme Divinity or Cosmic Principle, was a sublime synonym for All Existence and, in its Indo-European roots, for "all breath" or "all that breathed." It was by this fiat of "inclusion by definition" that Gandhi was able to incorporate all of these same "polluting" peoples into Hinduism: he simply called them *Harijans* or "Children of Hari," another name for Krishna, the avatar of the Vishnu. This ambiguity of definition resulted, in part, from questions of identity put into the Census of India and, in part, from such a large part of the population being deemed so polluting that they were denied access to proper or purified houses and temples. Much is known about Gandhi's historic encounter with Ambedkar and other Untouchable leaders on this issue. Less is known about Gandhi's encounter with Bishop Vedanayagam Samuel Azariah. See Harper 1991, 277–317.

17. See Gopal 1989. Sarvepalli Radhakrishnan and Charles A. Moore's *A Sourcebook of Indian Philosophy* is still *the* standard work for the "Establishment" or "Secular Nationalist" Hinduism of the ruling Indian National Congress (and its later incarnations), as also, in some measure, for some rank-and-file members of communist, socialist, and other movements in India.

18. Arjun Appadurai (1981) deals with the involvements of the Parthasarathi Svami Temple of Triplicane. I do not concur with many of its arguments or its perspectives, but it provides data that is useful to the argument here.

19. The term *juggernaut*, coming from Jagannath, Lord of the Universe and avatar of Vishnu, entered the English vocabulary with the meaning: any relentless destroying force or object that crushes whatever is in its path.

20. Embree 1962 remains the classic work on this issue.

21. For a good treatment of frictions between the Church of England and the governments of India, see Harper 1991. Among a dozen Anti-Idolatry Connexion League pamphlets in the British Library, see *No. VI: A View of the British Connexion with Idolatry in the Madras Presidency* (London, 1841). See, for context, Frykenberg 1979.
22. "Hinduization" means both a sociopolitical and a cultural-technical integration (especially in communication and transport) within the continent, and a religious-institutional and religious-ideological integration of many peoples throughout India—processes that, as shown here, intermingled in complex ways. Muslim heart-searchings and reactions to change were as traumatic as those suffered by Hindus. See Hardy 1972; Metcalf 1982; Lelyveld 1978.
23. One of the best overviews of these developments is Embree 1990.
24. Less strident and more open to others were some members of the Hindu Literary Society, the Madras Hindoo Association, the Madras Native Association, and even the Madras Mahajana Sabha. These groups can be compared with such Bengali institutions as the Hindu College or Brahmo Samaj.

    Christopher King (1974) showed how defensive many Hindus in north India were becoming by the end of the nineteenth century. See also *India Today*, May 11, 1986, 30–39.

Part IV

Hinduism and Caste

ORIENTATION

This part of the book includes essays by Mary Searle-Chatterjee, Gail Omvedt, and Timothy Fitzgerald. In each of them the problem of defining Hinduism is related to the problem of caste. Mary Searle-Chatterjee earned her Ph.D. from Banaras Hindu University and is a lecturer at the University of Manchester. She has written several other essays on the Hinduism problem (1990, 1993, 1994b), as well as works on caste (1981 and 1994a). In "'World Religions' and 'Ethnic Groups': Do These Paradigms Lend Themselves to the Cause of Hindu Nationalism?" her focus is on diaspora Hindus in Britain and the study of them. Searle-Chatterjee argues against a tendency in religious studies and some schools of sociology to treat religions "as relatively bounded unities," neglecting "division and conflict." This has led scholars to assume that Hinduism is a primary loyalty of their British research subjects. Yet this assumption would not be accurate for South Asia, where "it was not religion but caste, the network of related lineages to which one belonged, which more frequently provided a basis for identification." And it is not accurate for Britain, because there religion is "only a category, used contextually and intermittently."

To assume the cultural primacy of religion is bad ethnography that is bound to produce defective social analysis, by Searle-Chatterjee's lights, and it also has more sinister political implications. She points to a relatively naïve apolitical analysis of the Hindu Swayamsevak Sangh, an organization with ties to the very political Rashtriya Swayamsevak Sangh (RSS) in India. The RSS and other Hindu nationalist groups deny that they promote the Hindu religion. Rather, they claim they are concerned with a broader Hindu "way of life." Yet Searle-Chatterjee interprets this as a move that is designed to isolate those who do not share the ideology of the RSS. "Unification is a political project, enabling mobilization against low caste, or leftwing movements (in India) and differentiation from stigmatized or low-status Muslims (in Britain)." It may be that the scholars who abet this political project do so unintentionally. In their desire to portray immigrants in a positive light, working against a "ethnocentric and racist context" in Britain, researchers end up stereotyping Hinduism in a way that serves the interests of conservative political forces, or at least that is what Searle-Chatterjee argues here. Of course, fundamental to that argument is the assumption of shared political goals on the part of "liberal academics."

In her brief "Introduction to *Dalit Visions*," Gail Omvedt also takes on the Hindu nationalists. Omvedt is a freelance writer and consultant on sociology, with a Ph.D. from the University of California, Berkeley, who has written extensively on anti-caste, environmental, and farmers' movements and rural women (1976, 1980, 1991, 1993, 1994). The Hindu nationalists claim that a cruelly ironic consequence of their religion's fabled tolerance is that Hinduism is under attack, and now Hindus must fight back. Against this political position, Omvedt says two kinds of movements have emerged, some secularist, calling for unity despite religious difference, and others reformist, insisting that the religiopolitics of the right are not the "true Hinduism." One of the planks of the reformist platform is that "much of casteism is in fact a colonial heritage," so that it is also not really part of Hinduism proper. Omvedt articulates a third alternative to Hindu nationalism, which she particularly identifies as the position of the Dalits, members of the lower castes who are organized to fight oppression. "In contrast to the secularist opposition to Hindutva they proclaim a politics of identity, and in contrast to the reformist Hindu identities *they define 'Hinduism' itself as an oppressive class/caste/patriarchal force.*"

In "Problems with 'Religion' as a Category for Understanding Hinduism," Timothy Fitzgerald's concern is not so much with the word Hinduism as it is with religion, or at least with the application of religion to Hinduism. Fitzgerald is a reader at the University of Stirling, with a Ph.D. from King's College, London. The thesis of this essay, which is similar to an earlier article and the chapter of a book by Fitzgerald (1990, 2000), is based on his study of Ambedkar Buddhists (1996, 1997b). Fitzgerald divides works about Hinduism into two groups, "the religious studies genre" and "the anthropological genre." The problem with the religious studies texts is that, though they may admit that social life is important to Hindu practice, they still ignore social structures; instead treating Hinduism as a religion and therefore something that transcends society. For example, Fitzgerald complains that R. C. Zaehner's book *Hinduism* (1971) "contains virtually nothing on caste, focusing upon myths and doctrines and philosophies presented as though they did not exist in a social reality." Fitzgerald does find social analysis in the anthropological works that he critiques, but faults them for, among other things, mistakenly trying to separate out a religious dimension in Hindu life. An instance of this is Lawrence Babb's *The Divine Hierarchy* (1975). In Fitzgerald's reading, Babb finds in Hindu society a "a core ritual symbolic structure that expresses hierarchy in terms of purity and pollution," and this structure is manifest even in relationships between humans and gods. But then Babb "uses the words 'religion' or 'religious' in such a way as to indicate a distinction between religion and society, based on the distinction between the supernatural and human," even though this conflicts with his own analysis of Hinduism's core structure.

In Fitzgerald's analysis the religionists are faulted for being "theological" and "ideological" in attempting to protect their own discipline by an asocial analysis of Hinduism. On the other hand, the anthropologists are commended for having "no theological intention" or being "transparently concerned to give a nontheological, humanistic account." Yet their analysis of

South Asian society is still marred by an uncritical adoption of the religion-ists' notion of religion, particularly as concerned with gods and the super-natural. It is not that Fitzgerald argues that there are no ideas of gods or the supernatural operative in India. On the contrary, Fitzgerald himself allows that low-caste Buddhists sometimes look upon the Buddha and even Ambed-kar as "supernatural beings who can bring benefits," however much that notion may have been obnoxious to Ambedkar himself. In his own analysis of the Ambedkar Buddhists at the beginning of "Problems with 'Religion,'" it seems that Fitzgerald's contribution lies in emphasizing the continuity in social practice across the supposed divide that separates the religious and secular. But he admits that Babb and Fuller do the same thing, even though he critiques them. It is almost as if the very use of the word religion itself is the problem, and not any defect in their actual analysis of Hinduism.

Searle-Chatterjee implies that caste is more important than religion in Indian society, and she claims that religion is an aspect of identity that might be taken as critical in some contexts but insignificant in others. I believe that this formulation allows for shifting relationships between caste and Hindu identities. Omvedt's Dalits take a stand against this shiftiness. For them, Hinduism is not only the religion of the upper castes, it is the religion that they use to oppress their inferiors. So there is a Hinduism, and it has a fixed and bounded position on caste at least. But it is only the reli-gion of the upper castes—the Dalits are not Hindu. In Fitzgerald's case we have yet another solution to the problem of the relationship between caste and religion. For him there really is no religion at all in South Asia, there is only caste.

7

"WORLD RELIGIONS" AND "ETHNIC GROUPS": DO THESE PARADIGMS LEND THEMSELVES TO THE CAUSE OF HINDU NATIONALISM?

Mary Searle-Chatterjee

1. The Argument

In this article I argue that the assumptions underlying much academic usage of the terms "Hindu" and "Hinduism" in Britain are consonant with the radical claims of rightwing Hindu nationalists.[1] This usage both expresses and reinforces dominant British understandings already shaping the local and national state policies which feed into processes of identity development among British South Asians. A variety of other factors contribute to the emergence of a more homogenized Hindu identity in Britain, including the desire to be differentiated from stigmatized or low-income Muslims. Self-consciousness induced by racism and minority status encourages the reification of religion and culture. The claims of Hindu nationalists which have in the last fifteen years changed the nature of public debate in India are now, in the diaspora, also influencing identity development, class differentiation, and political mobilization. These claims are as follows:

(1) that a "Hindu" identity is an encompassing one to which other identities of class, caste, gender, and so forth, are subordinate;
(2) that bearers of that identity share a distinct culture, despite variation, and have common interests;

(3) that "Hinduism" is a *phenomenon* which can be understood largely *sui generis*, and in isolation from political and economic processes and conflicts (see section 9);

(4) that "Hinduism" is primarily a culture, associated with a particular group of people, Indians, and with a particular country, India. This is a claim of great political import to be discussed further (see section 9). It implies that Muslims and Christians cannot be true Indians and cannot therefore deserve the protections of full Indian citizenship.

The first two claims assume that being "Hindu" is a primordial identity, rooted in a homogeneous and continuing culture. This assumption may provide benefits for certain groups of actors but does, of course, contradict current sociological and anthropological understandings of the fluid and contextualized nature of identity formation.

I shall explore the issue of how, as liberal academics, many of us have come to work with what are, in practice, rightwing assumptions, associated with groups which in India have been implicated in extensive violence against Muslims and Christians. Before examining some aspects of the literature on Hindus in Britain, I shall refer briefly to the British use of "Hindu" as a classificatory category both in the past and present.

2. Religious Classification in British India

It is not new for British conceptual usage to be implicated in South Asian political practice. Many historians consider that the emergence of a Hindu *identity* (as opposed to Hindu *cultures*), was stimulated by the colonial British practice of classification of people, in censuses and gazeteers, in terms of collective identities, as if those were bounded, singular, and unchanging (Pandey 1990, 68; Said 1991, 32; Dirks 1996, 266; for a different view see Bayly 1988). Identities perceived as "religious," or primordial, were privileged over others. This process was also seen in the writing of Indian history (Pandey 1990). It was James Mill who set the pattern of periodizing Indian history prior to the coming of the British in terms of religion. Even today it is common to read of Hindu, Buddhist, Muslim, and *British* (not Christian) periods (see Dwyer 1994, 166–67). This can be viewed as an expression of western self-understanding as much as of Indian reality. The dominant ideology viewed post-feudal British culture as rational, dynamic, and knowledge-seeking. Indian culture was seen as the obverse: stagnant, superstitious, and steeped in traditionalism. These images are still fundamental to white western self-understanding, both on the political left and right, as witnessed in the Rushdie affair. The British assumed that people in India must belong to a named "religion," to something recognizable as a religion in British cultural terms, but, more importantly, that this must be what determined loyalties and conflicts. There were also, on occasion, political gains from working with this approach which facilitated a "divide and rule" policy, including, at some stages, separate electoral quotas, and in the army, even toilets. Struggles for power in the British period increasingly, though not always, made use of the idiom of religion to mobilize support or claim legitimacy. Political instability increased the likelihood of the use of this device (Frietag 1989).

3. Religious Classification in Contemporary Britain

Usage of the label "Hindu" continues in Britain in various official publications (for example, Social Trends reports). Statistical research relating to racialized minorities routinely asks about religion (as well as about "ethnicity") unlike research about the population in general. It is more likely to ask about religion than about the mother tongue. Until recently, the term "ethnic" was applied to groups differentiated on the basis of national, cultural, or linguistic origin, not religion. The 1976 Race Relations Act provides an example of this. Increasingly, the term "ethnic" is being used to refer to groups differentiated by "religion." In 1991 an "ethnic" question was introduced in the British census. This was based on nationality of origin, phenotype, or a mixture of both, with given options from which the informant had to choose. There was also an open "other" category. In effect, only racialized minorities are marked with ethnicity, since the category "white" is not differentiated by national origin. In the next census a question on religion may be introduced and it is likely that this too would present a range of predetermined options, thus obliging people to condense their practices and beliefs into a particular pigeonhole. This is based on the assumption that an individual has a religious identity which is superordinate over other identities, and which separates her/him from others. The very word "religion" signals a range of acceptable possibilities, as witnessed by the difficulties which Rastafarians have often faced. The respondent already knows that "Hindu" is an acceptable category, whereas "Vaishnavite" or "Balmiki" is not. That is part of what is involved in learning to use the English language "properly." A different question, more in tune with actual thinking and practice, such as to whom do you do *puja* (worship), or *seva* (service), or who is your guru, would produce a different answer.

In the subcontinent, it was not religion but caste, the network of related lineages to which one belonged, which more frequently provided a basis for identification, even though the institution of caste was, historically, more fluid and segmental than the British realized. It is not surprising that in Britain many Indian organizations, including "religious" ones, are caste-based, as is well-recognized in Roger Ballard's collection, *Desh Pardesh* (1994). In 1978, at least thirty-one out of fifty-six Leicester Gujarati Hindu organizations were *jati* (caste) specific. Many of those interviewed believed that an organization with a "religious" identity was more likely to attract external funding than one apparently more parochial, based on an exclusivistic *jati* group. Elements of the Srimali caste therefore decided to continue stressing a Jain religious identity (Banks 1994, 243 and 246). "Religion" is a sacred category, it appears, for local authorities who may inadvertently stimulate the development of religious identities among people who are far from wholly committed to such a world view (Baumann 1996).

Religious classification is enshrined, uncritically, in law relating to state institutionalization of religious education. The 1988 Education Reform Act refers to "religions," and the working parties interpreting the Act have written in terms of a "world religions" paradigm (see Fitzgerald 1990 for an extremely useful discussion). This assumes that religious activity and belief can be understood independently of the contexts in which it appears. Religion is taken to be a separable and definable phenomenon which has crystallized into six or so distinct major "faiths" with specific institutions and literature. This is based on a Christian theological model.

Several academic disciplines also use religious classifications, again often as taken for granted categories. A striking recent example of this in sociology is *Asian Self-Employment* (Metcalf, Modood, and Virdee 1996). The only variable in terms of which tabular correlations are made is national origin, taken to correspond (questionably) with religion. Indian is assumed to correspond with Hindu and Pakistani with Muslim. The material is presented in such a way that it is impossible to explore sociological questions about the generation of small-scale business. One can only draw the conclusion, already implicit in the design of the study, that religion is the key defining variable of culture and social practice.

4. "Ethnic" Group Paradigms and their Critics

Early critiques of research which assumes the existence of homogeneous and stable minority groups, defined in terms of ethnicity and religion, rather than contextually in relation to specific interests and issues, were associated with Marxism and 1980s "antiracism" (for example, Centre for Contemporary Cultural Studies 1982) as well as with black and Asian feminism (for example, Trivedi 1984). A different type of critique stems from the work of Edward Said. His powerful, if diffuse, assault on "orientalist" disciplines, focused on what he called the process of "essentializing," by which a vast array of diverse individuals, societies, and traditions are bracketed together as if they had a single unchanging essence. This process of stereotyping was said to facilitate exploitation (1991). Anthropologists, too, have for decades been pointing to the cross-cutting, multiple nature of identities (see Patterson 1974). More recently, Rattansi, among others, argues for a more postmodernist understanding of the fluidity of identities (1994). This approach is a rejection of the distortions involved in pigeonholing as such, rather than a demand for a different type of pigeonholing by race, class, or gender.

The counter response to these critiques was that "ethnic studies" could help in the provision of welfare needs particularly for the first generation. The collection of ethnic data in the 1991 Census was defended by Ratcliffe (1996) and Karn (1997) for its potential contribution to policy-making, to estimating needs, for example, for the ethnic elderly. Defense of ethnic studies approaches has also come from Modood (1992) and Ballard (1992) who have argued that an exclusively racial or class focus did not do justice to the way people experienced their lives, could not account for variation among "ethnic groups," or for some of the developments among the second generation. Conflicts arise over cultural recognition and esteem as well as over access to material goods.

In this article I do not dismiss "ethnic studies" out of hand, but simply point to the political implications in much of the literature on Hindus.

5. Academic Writing on Hindus in Britain:
Impact and Context

I shall develop my argument through discussion of selected influential texts, Kim Knott's study, *Hinduism in Leeds* (1986), the collection by Richard Burghart, *Hinduism in Great Britain* (1987), the work of Robert Jackson and Eleanor Nesbitt, particularly *Hindu Children in Britain* (1993), of Steve Vertovec (1992, 1995), and relevant contributions from Roger Ballard's collection, *Desh Pardesh* (1994). It is not surprising that work in Britain should have implications for struggles among Indians, since identities emerge in dialogue with others as a result of seeing oneself with their eyes, in contexts usually involving political and economic competition (Alavi 1987). Several of those who have written on the subject of Hinduism in Britain have recognized such effects (see Knott 1986, 83). "British Hinduism is being shaped by the kinds of questions which non-Hindus as much as Hindus ask of it" (Burghart 1987). "Teachers and other concerned adults may have a more significant role to play than they realize in the moulding of British Hindu traditions" (Jackson and Nesbitt 1993). Marcus Banks even attributes the resurgence of Jainism to the impact of British attitudes (1994, 240). Western educationists and academics may themselves be influenced by specific interest groups, particularly Hindu nationalists, who are widespread in Britain, and now producing teaching materials for schools (see Prinja 1996). The nostalgia of immigrants often has a role in furthering nationalist causes (van der Veer 1995). (Hindu nationalists in Britain may, in turn, exercise a cultural influence on the subcontinental nationalist political parties to which they send funds.) Romanticized and reified images of "true" Hinduism may have been reinforced recently by an American much admired and cited by Hindu nationalists, David Frawley, who lectures in Indian astrology and Vedic studies at the University of Santa Fe. He is President of the American Council of Vedic Astrology, and has been a guest lecturer in various British university departments (Frawley 1995; Rajarama and Frawley 1995). He maintains an active presence on the Internet where he attacks critics of Hindu nationalism as enemies of India, as godless communists, or proselytizing Muslims or Christians.

Academic writing is a product of various social influences. I now examine two academic influences particularly evident in writing on the lives of Hindus in Britain.

6. The "World Religions" Paradigm of Religious Studies and the Durkheimian Tradition

These two approaches share at least four features: (1) a focus on what are perceived as relatively bounded unities—in one case, religions, in the other, societies or cultures; (2) a focus on shared norms; (3) neglect of division and conflict; and (4) a normative assumption that the object of study is of positive value.

Religious Studies is a discipline whose very existence has been posited on the construction of a particular object for study, religion and, sometimes, even God too (see Taylor 1987, 101). This is a consequence of its roots in Theology and Comparative Religion. A disciplinary mode of organization obliges one to have a differentiated product but no other field involving the study of social action is so tied to the use of a particular concept and to the belief in the existence of a particular phenomenon. The "world religions" paradigm which is embedded in western culture still provides the framework for the discipline, despite having been abundantly critiqued from within (Waardenburg 1973). Hinduism is seen as one of those distinct "world religions" despite the inevitable disclaimers to the effect that it is an umbrella term and a different sort of phenomenon from Christianity or Islam. Yet it is difficult enough to define even "religion," a polysemic concept (Southwold 1978). Burghart, though clearly aware of the problem, fell into the "world religions" mode (1987, 224, 244, 246), as did Jackson and Nesbitt (1993, 2–3, 167–68, 171, 174, 182). Vertovec speaks of the issue of reification of culture and religion though he attributes that to social actors/Hindus, rather than to academics (1995, 148–50). While recognizing divisions and variations based on caste, sect, and region of origin (146–47), some of his work focuses on Hindus as if they are a transnational *grouping* of people, rather than on "Hindu" as a transnational *category* which may be used for particular purposes to provide a basis for group formation. It is one thing to discuss the problems of reification in an abstract sense and quite another to operationalize that insight.

Isolating out a Hindu sample, rather than studying an existing social matrix, is in itself problematic, since it involves starting with the conceptions both of religion and of Hinduism as separable phenomena, as well as with the conception of "Hindu" as a pre-existing identity. Examples of this are in Jackson and Nesbitt's schools' sample where the object of study has been constructed from categorizations only invoked contextually. They suggested that their decision to study a sample of Hindu school children was influenced by Geertzian renderings of the Durkheimian (1915)/Radcliffe-Brownian (1952) holistic conception of cultures. They refer favorably to Geertz's (1973) approach of "grasping another culture" (Jackson and Nesbitt 1993, 19) and write "like any living *organism* Hindu tradition is changing" (vii, emphasis added), though such an approach has been exhaustively critiqued over the years for its neglect of historical process. It also has to be said that even for Geertz, let alone Radcliffe-Brown, culture was embedded in society. A tradition or group was not detached from its social context. Religion was seen as a dimension of social life. It may have been taken for granted as a category but it was but one chapter in an ethnographic monograph.

The "world religions" paradigm often shapes the presentation of material. Much of what is described in *Hindu Children in Britain* (Jackson and Nesbitt 1993) would be equally true of Muslims and Sikhs of similar class backgrounds originating from the north and west of the subcontinent. Examples of this are in the account of family roles and gender distinctions (ch. 4) and in the sections on job aspirations, attitudes to marriage, and caste (33–37). The same can be said of ch. 9 (on "cultural transmission"), particularly of the sections on films, music, and radio cassettes. Much of ch. 5 on "Food and Fasts" would not be applicable to Muslims, but nor would it be applicable to Bengali Hindus who are hardly ever vegetarian.

The influence of the idea that religions are bounded unities can be seen in the common failure to distinguish between the actor's (emic) use of the word "Hindu" as an identity label and the analyst's (etic) use of it as a summative category pointing to association with traditions having some family resemblances (Stietencron 1997), or even constituting a unified system based on notions of social order, power, and hierarchy (Fuller 1992). Little attention is paid to the way in which informants use the word "Hindu" and in what context. These categorizations do not denote corporate groups, though whites and Hindu nationalists, among others, often use them as if they do.

Much writing has neglected the anthropological maxim that one should pay close ethnographic attention to "local" usage (which, of course, is always changing), in order to avoid imposing inappropriate categories. An exception is Jackson and Nesbitt (1993) and Nesbitt (1994). Nesbitt's careful attention to detail means that she is able to problematize the "world religions" assumption of clearly bounded distinctions between Hinduism and Sikhism and also to show how "lower" caste perceptions of religious identity diverge from those presumed in monolithic accounts of Hinduism. Many of her "lower" caste informants do not perceive themselves as Hindu, or at least not unequivocally. Jackson and Nesbitt also made efforts to consider "less practising families." In other contexts, however, they attempt to force their informants into the distorting pigeonholes of the "world religions" paradigm. Where children say "my religion is Punjabi," they comment "they have confused their categories." The implication is that the informant ought to share the same categories as the researcher. They include examples of dialogues in which the interviewer attempts, desperately and unsuccessfully, to get children to identify themselves in "religious" rather than linguistic or regional terms (1993, 29–31). The parallels between this and the endeavors of the nineteenth-century classifiers who struggled with the awkwardness of informants whose identities seemed to overlap, or be indistinct, is striking. It has to be said that it is the transparency of Jackson and Nesbitt's presentation which makes their relocation of religion so visible.

A great deal of other work on Hindus in Britain similarly gives the impression that informants are providing information in terms of the categories which the researcher has supplied rather than from listening to spontaneous usage outside the context of an interview. Few researchers have explored the ways in which people actually use and construct religious and other identity labels in daily social life. Labels are often simply taken to refer to fixed identities rather than to be aspects of constantly changing identification (see Hall 1996, for this distinction). If we study the context in which the word "Hindu" is used, we find, not surprisingly, that it functions in a way very different from the term "Christian" which may be used *within* the tradition to indicate degrees of spiritual or moral achievement—"He a true Christian was." One cannot imagine a similar construction for a Hindu, since the traditions did not emerge from the teachings of a single founder by whose standards a person could be judged. Indeed, the word "Hindu" is used with very different meanings at different levels of the caste system. Research in Varanasi (Banaras) in north India in the 1970s and 1980s showed that urban "lower" castes used the word "Hindu" primarily to refer to "upper" castes. This usage was found among the oldest and least politicized individuals, and there is no reason to see it as a recent development. The "high" castes often used the term "Hindu" to refer to those who were seen as truly Indian, that is, not having any religious link or allegiance to "foreign" traditions. The term "Muslim" was often counterposed to *regional* rather than *"religious"* identities (Searle-Chatterjee 1994a, 1994b). We need to study in what context the term "Hindu" is used, with what connotation, and for what purpose, realizing that like any other identity label its usage varies and is contested. Fuller goes so far as to say that in India the term "Hinduism" still does not correspond to any concept or category that belongs to the thinking of a large proportion of the ordinary rural people (1992, 10–11).

Though in Britain various factors combine to make the category "Hindu" more salient, this does not mean that religious identity may be taken for granted as a basis for behavior. Such an approach is reminiscent of the studies of "tribalism" which the 1960s Manchester school of anthropology fought so hard against in their studies of African towns, arguing that one must look at social behavior in its present form, without focusing on divergence from a presumed earlier culture. The subject of study was to be "situational selection" of behavior rather than "adaptation" to a new context. As Gerd Baumann points out, the situation of ethnic studies in Britain today recalls that current in African studies before then! Baumann's work on Southall provides an example of an alternative model for fieldwork (1996). Instead of presuming that people have given religious identities, and that these are superordinate, he pays attention to the way in which identity labels are used, and considers cross-cutting allegiances and contextual fluctuations. It is not anthropology itself which is problematic as a discipline so much as neglect of some major strands within that discipline and of some of the lessons that have been learnt.

7. Cultural Change: Modes of Description

The study of patterns of change and adaptation in the new environment provides the avowed *raison d'etre* of many studies of Hindus in Britain, and it is generally presumed that a given phenomenon, the same as that found in India, is being studied, ignoring the fact that similar actions, words, and claims may have totally different meanings and functions in different contexts: that was, indeed, an item of faith in the functionalist manifesto fundamental to much of the anthropological tradition. A very different "phenomenon" may be under scrutiny though caste-fellows may be able to draw from the same "pool of values, ideas and legitimating strategies ... available as an inspirational resource" (Banks 1994, 248). For example, actions that in India were a form of petitioning to superior power might in Britain function primarily to show continuity with the past as well as to create group bonds. What often happens is that "Hinduism," or some sectarian subdivision of it, tends to be regarded as a phenomenon on which change impinges from outside. Marcus Banks (1994, 250) challenges this approach. "The conventional view of

migrants implies that they are subject to a series of ... transformations as
they move from one fixed pole to another ... but transformations are a feature inherent in the cultural process itself." One might also add that "the
cultural process itself" always has political dimensions, as well as symbolic
and ritual ones.

Studying the development of a geographically given religious center is in
itself less problematic than abstracting out a sample defined in terms of religion. It *is* problematic if "religious" dimensions alone are isolated for examination. Such studies have been published by Knott (1986, 1987, 1994), Carey
(1987), Taylor (1987), Vertovec (1992), Nye (1993, 1995), and Barot (1987).
Migration history and changes over time are described but religious activities
are not generally placed in a larger social context. Some of these studies make
no reference to class. The fact that little cognizance can be taken of those
who do not visit the temple is problematic if the object of study is seen to be
"Hindus," or "Hinduism," but not if the object of study is seen as the processes which have led to the construction of a temple (see Nye 1995).

In so far as the focus of interest is the ways in which religious practice is
changing in the diaspora, it is significant that certain aspects of changing religious practice have passed completely unnoticed by researchers. In the subcontinent, most non-elite "Hindu" groups share much religious practice with
non-elite "Muslims." They worship at the same shrines and make offerings
to the same "pirs" and "babas" (Imam 1975; Streefland 1979; Mines 1981;
Searle-Chatterjee 1994a and 1994b), though this seems to be declining in
urban areas. It appears that this sharing has disappeared in Britain. If this is
so, it is a matter of some interest to establish why. Lack of interest in this
aspect of religious change may be due both to lack of awareness of *popular*
religious practice in the subcontinent as well as to the influence of the
"world religions" paradigm.

I have felt it appropriate to point to ways in which studies of Hindus in
Britain relate to particular strands of anthropological practice because the
Burghart collection is clearly perceived as anthropological rather than sociological and both Jackson/Nesbitt and Ballard make a point of insisting that
neither they nor their contributors are sociologists. The authors in question
are either anthropologists or Religious Studies specialists who have been
exposed to the discipline of anthropology. The insistence that they are not
sociologists is presumably to justify their focus on ritual, and to defend
themselves from the possible charge that they are not discussing an issue but
are simply describing a particular group and the changes affecting it. Such a
concern for description, unconnected with theoretical, policy, or political
issues, emerges from a combination of influences, the "descriptive," interpretive approach rooted in Durkheimian functionalism, the "culturalist" tendencies of American cultural anthropology, and Indology, by which Burghart
at least was affected, and finally the culture of the discipline of Religious
Studies.

A focus on description may also be partly a result of market demands for publications within the "world religions" paradigm and of expectations that researchers will provide packaged "information" about *groups* ("communities"), for health professionals and others, rather than about *processes*. Ethnic Studies are akin to travel guides to the unfamiliar at home, and anthropologists, by tradition, are more inclined to study groups of "foreign," especially "postcolonial," origin. A study of something apparently more familiar, like a Catholic or Methodist center, would probably only seem interesting if related to a sociological question.

8. "Positive Images" and the Survivalist Problematic

Ballard insists that because the contributors to his collection are mostly anthropologists they focus on family, kinship, morality and networks of obligation and reciprocity, and the resiliences generated within self-created worlds. The image is a positive one, deriving again from the Durkheimian tradition, a welcome counterbalance to older images of deprivation and victimhood. Larger religious solidarities are, as he rightly points out, short-lived. "The groups have all been following broadly parallel trajectories" (1994, 8), "all the new minorities are strongly committed to cultural and religious reconstruction" (1994, 2). This "all" refers not to individual agents but to *groups* defined ethnically. It is interesting to place alongside this the recent finding in a British sample survey that less than one-third of Indians and African Asians said that religion was very important in how they led their lives (Metcalf, Modood, and Virdee 1996, 133). Though such a finding must be tested on other samples, it is striking, given that all of Modood's work has been premised on the importance of religion as a social variable.

Many accounts of Hindus in Britain are suffused uncritically with *"positive images."* This is surprising, for theological accounts of church schisms in the history of the west generally have no hesitation in showing the role of conflicting interest groups in the writing of texts and in the struggle to control both religious institutions and the interpretation of cultural representations. The same is true of anthropological studies of Hindus in India. This difference must be partly due to awareness of the ethnocentric and racist context within which such work is produced. Regardless of the intention of the author, work relating to racialized minorities in Britain will be received by the reader in terms of his/her own, often negative, assumptions and prejudices. Where little other material exists, and where the reader has little relevant personal experience by which to assess what is written, a particularly heavy burden falls on the writer. S/he must attempt to control all possible readings of the work, knowing that it will be subject to particularly intense scrutiny. The result is that many kinds of social and cultural contradiction

161

disappear from the writing. The irony of this is that such work may end up by conveying the impression that there are bounded groups, with particular essences, in some way cut off from the normal political and economic struggles in which western individuals participate. The parallels to "orientalism" as described by Edward Said (1991) are easy enough to see.

Two main arguments are generally put forward in the literature to explain the emergence of religious institutions among British Hindus. One treats this as simply a process of naturalizing, transplanting a potential which was already present (indeed, Werbner 1987, 177–78 uses this particular phrase in relation to Sikhs and Muslims). The other refers to the mutual support or sense of identity and meaning provided in an alien context (see Nye's 1995 discussion of this). A Durkheimian account of the process is provided by Burghart who refers to the establishment of a sect or temple as an expression of the emergence of a social group (Burghart 1987) which, in turn, facilitates an intensification of interaction.

Often a protective concern is shown for the survival of the religion into the future. The language sometimes resembles that used in ecological studies of endangered species. Recurring words are preservation, persistence, re-establishment, survival. I quote some examples. "Sikhs *suffer from* internal differences but are not divided by ethnic allegiance like Hindus. The Hindus do not have the same natural *advantages*" (Knott 1987, 159). "Without the temple the *maintenance* of the tradition would depend on the efforts of individuals to consolidate and transmit the *important* features of Hindu religion and culture. While this might result in the private retention of *valuable* vernacular traditions ignored in the temple's current religious provision, it is difficult to see how Hinduism as a religious and social *system* could be perpetuated ... without undergoing some kind of institutionalisation." "The process of giving new meaning ... is *the price of its survival* as a socially meaningful tradition" (1987, 177–79). Such sentiments are expressed in many of the Burghart contributions and also by Nesbitt. "Many British born Valmikis find aspects of their parental tradition boring and meaningless ... how might this gulf be *bridged*?" (Nesbitt 1994, 135). The findings of earlier research (that Hinduism is dying out) are "*gloomy*" and can be rejected (Jackson and Nesbitt 1993, 10, 12). Dwyer speaking of the Pushtimarg sect, says "its survival is *endangered unless long-term action is taken soon*" (1994, 188). These are deeply conservative sentiments of the kind one might associate with a heritage document. Outside folklore studies, which have often been associated with nationalist movements, or the writings of nationalist historians, it would be unusual to encounter such an academic approach in relation to the cultural practices of whites. What is curious here is that the concern and protectiveness relates not to the cultural traditions of the researcher her/himself, nor does it relate to individuals and their civic rights. Would researchers adopt such an attitude to Christian denominations not their own? Though it is understandable that many Indians are concerned with issues of cultural continuity, it is surprising that a survivalist problematic forms the focus for an academic text, as it does in Burghart's book, subtitled *The Perpetuation of Religion in an Alien Milieu.* This approach is often based on the view that religion, in any form, is primarily benign and positive, with socially integrative functions. It derives from a combination of the influences of both Durkheim and the discipline of Religious Studies.

Rarely is there more than a perfunctory consideration of the way in which religion may serve as a vehicle for the expression of conflicts, or of the ideological functions of "religious" behavior. We are told of miracles, homes being visited by deities and becoming semi-public places of worship, without any attempt to consider possible economic or social dimensions of this (Michaelson 1987, 39–40), though there is abundant evidence that in India, at least, a common way of expressing a rise in social status is by accentuating religious practice, by sponsoring the performance of elaborate rituals, or building of places of worship. Another contributor to the Burghart collection tells us that there are "many possible stories about the founding of the Community of Many Names of God." This variety is not narrated, let alone related to any social base (Taylor 1987, 104). We are presented with the Guru's version as a way of understanding "the community's relation to god" (1987, 101), as if this is the only version needed. Reference is made to very large sums of money which appear mysteriously as a result of prayer, sufficient to enable purchase of a London flat, the flying over of an elephant from Sri Lanka, and purchase of a center, but no attempt is made to consider where these funds might have come from (Taylor 1987, 106).

9. Religion and Politics

The phenomenological approach common in Religious Studies (see Smart 1973; Knott 1986) places complete reliance on the accounts of key "insiders" and ignores the fact that "insiders" always diverge in their interpretations. This is seen where Bowen refers (1987, 16–17) to the Hindu Swayamsevak Sangh (HSS), conceding that its counterpart in India, the Rashtriya Swayamsevak Sangh (RSS), had strong political overtones but assuring us that in the UK these have been neutralized. Such a claim is, indeed, put across by HSS members but on what grounds does an academic researcher report it uncritically? The HSS and the Vishwa Hindu Parishad (VHP) in Britain have never *publicly* disassociated themselves from the activities in India of their counterparts. Bowen comments "differences are subsumed within the idea of Hindu society, transcended by the notion of sanskritic civilisation of which all Hindus irrespective of regional culture are a part" (1987, 28–30). This is a very particular "high" caste viewpoint, specifically associated with north

Indian urban Brahmans and secondarily with merchant castes (Dirks 1996). He romanticizes a particular "insider" view which he takes to be a universal. "In this movement between unity and diversity one finds among the Gujaratis of Bradford evidence of a characteristically Hindu paradigm for the structure of a plural society in Britain." His work contrasts with that of Carey in the same volume who dearly detaches himself from his informants despite showing imaginative empathy (1987, 99).

One might concede that this was 1987 and political innocence was therefore understandable. Bowen's comments on the HSS and VHP are, however, quoted again by Knott in 1994 who states authoritatively that the VHP and HSS have been politically neutralized in Britain. What is the evidence for this? Once again it reads as the words of key informants. By the late 1980s there were clear signs of political dimensions to moves for Hindu unity. In 1989 the VHP held a vast assembly at Milton Keynes (the Virat Hindu Sammelan), at which leaders of the rightwing political party, the BJP, had a prominent role, and at which the program was dedicated to Hedgewar, the founder of the paramilitary RSS. The program advocated the building of a Ram temple on the site of the Babri Mosque (Dwyer 1994, 185–86, 189), in other words, demolishing the mosque. Vertovec, too, as late as 1995, refers to the Council's moves towards unification but ignores its involvement in rightwing political movements:

> [T]hus far little actually exists to safeguard common interests across the board of regional, sect and caste groups … . The National Council of Hindu Temples comes closest to this … though some complain it is Gujarati dominated. Large-scale mobilisation has not been given cause or opportunity to take place in society-wide public space (1995, 144–47).

Dwyer and Banks are exceptional in showing awareness of economic and political uses of religion in the case of Swaminarayans and Jains (1994).

Neglect of political dimensions of religious action may partly be a consequence of researchers in Britain not taking note of subcontinental politics. Communist parties exist in every Indian state: Kerala and Bengal often have communist governments. The use of religious symbolism as a basis for political mobilization is one of the more powerful tools at the disposal of anti-left movements. Middle-class Brahmans and merchant castes provide the backbone for Hindu nationalist organizations. It is no coincidence that they are particularly active in the Bombay region with its long history of "low" caste anti-Brahmanical movements (Basu, *et al.* 1993, 4–12, 16). It is revealing that the advertisements in the nationalist Savarkar memorial volume were addressed to extremely wealthy entrepreneurs (Savarkar 1989).

Political innocence is now no longer acceptable for it appears to legitimize forms of religious nationalism. It is possible that the "Islamophobia" entrenched in European culture, and reinforced by various recent conflicts and movements, may blind academics in the west to the significance of religious nationalisms of other kinds.

One of the claims of the Hindu nationalists which alarms other religious groups in India (as well as many non-nationalist Hindus) is that Hinduism is the "way of life" of the people of India, that Hinduness or "Hindutva" is a matter of culture rather than of religious commitment, an ethnic marker of peoplehood, rather than a rich reservoir of symbols, values, and practices from which individuals may draw. Bowen referred favorably to this HSS claim that they are not concerned with Hindu religion but simply with the values of Hindu civilization (1987). He appeared to be unaware of its history and significance. Its implication is that all true Indians, regardless of religion, ought to be able to accept that they are Hindu. If they cannot do this their right to citizenship is questionable. Academic discussion of whether Hinduism is, or is becoming, an "ethnic religion" in Britain may have implications for this claim. In the older "Comparative Religions" literature it was common to refer to Hinduism, like Judaism, as an ethnic religion in that it was associated with people of a specific geographical origin. Ninian Smart's description of Hinduism as a "world religion" rather than a "group-tied" one (1973) counteracted that approach. Burghart took up this issue for discussion, recognizing that some prominent groups of Hindus in Britain, particularly the National Council of Hindu Temples (NCHT), were now claiming that Hinduism is the "timeless spiritual culture of India," a marker of Indianness (Burghart 1987, 231, 246f., 251). He had a slightly unclear position on this, noting that these lay spokespersons were ceasing to make universalist claims to truth unlike the ascetic spokespersons of redemptive Hinduism who have never claimed that it was an ethnic religion, that is to say restricted to a particular people (1987, 233–34, 237). What is surprising is that he did not consider the political implications of the NCHT claim, that is, that only Hindus have rights to full Indian citizenship. Such a hegemonic claim has existed since the 1920s and derives from Savarkar (1942 [1923]), though it has been heard much more since 1985. For British whites, Hinduism *is* an ethnic religion, that is to say of a particular bounded group of people. That is why Indians are considered to be its most appropriate spokespersons (Burghart 1987, 233). In the end, Burghart argued that though British Hindus identify with ethnic groups based on region or caste, they do not in general see themselves as constituting a single people or ethnic group.

The National Council of Hindu Temples imagines and attempts to create a community of Hindus on the basis of what was, and is, generally only a category used contextually and intermittently. For the Council, as for the VHP and RSS/HSS, this is to be the prime identity of all Indians. The work of academics should not be blind to the importance of this idea in representing a political interest likely to be more prominent in the future. Unification is a political project, enabling mobilization against low caste, or leftwing movements (in India) and differentiation from stigmatized or low-status Muslims (in Britain). The western reader may not be aware of the complex relationships between class and religion in South Asia (see Fuller 1992, 260–61; Lieten 1994; Searle-Chatterjee 1994a). Although in India there was always a landed Muslim feudal class, as well as Muslim merchants and professionals, Muslims were, and are, more likely to be of the "lower" classes than are Hindus (Imam 1975; Banerjee 1992, 58). This pattern continues, not surprisingly, in Britain too (Modood 1992), though here this is partly related to the region of origin of the migrants, and timing of arrival.

Conclusion

Although there is much detailed description and analysis of interest in academic writing on the lives of Hindus in Britain, I have focused on the wider implications of much of that literature and on some of the problems implicit in it. I have argued that it needs to free itself from the influence of the "world religions" paradigm common in Religious Studies and from the Durkheimian model, with its assumption that religion primarily has integrative functions. It is common to refer to the influence of Social Anthropology on Religious Studies. What is often not recognized is the influence of Religious Studies on Anthropology. Much of what I refer to is the product of disciplinary drift and market demand, coupled with political innocence. By reifying religious action and prioritizing it, rather than seeing it as a contextualized dimension of social action, we are leaving out *individual* actors' frames of reference and inadvertently providing legitimacy to the hegemonic endeavors of rightwing Hindu nationalists. Nowikowski and Ward (1979), Werbner (1991) and Baumann (1996) provide examples of some alternative paths that can be followed. Though it is essential to retain awareness of the racist context in Britain, should this make us treat the religious activity of racialized minorities with special intellectual tools? Is the western academic being patronizing by refusing to recognize that Hindu individuals, too, may have a will to power? If Religious Studies specialists wish to study religious practice in contemporary society, they will have to take on board the wider social and political awareness which is part both of sociology, and of the best traditions of social anthropology.

Note

1. This article owes much to discussions with Chetan Bhatt, Parita Mukta, Ursula Sharma, and Jacqueline Suthren Hirst. Thanks also for the comments of Malory Nye. The views expressed are my own.

8

INTRODUCTION TO *DALIT VISIONS*

Gail Omvedt

For most people, even scholars, "Hinduism" has been a taken-for-granted concept. Hindus are the people of India. Hinduism is their religion. Beginning with the Rig Veda to the philosophers and even contemporary political leaders, it has been seen as a unique phenomenon of spirituality linked to a practical life; and with a solid geographical base in a diversified subcontinent. Although its stability has been broken from time to time by invasions, conquests, and disturbances, it has nevertheless maintained a fair continuity. It has given birth to rampant and unjustifiable social inequalities but has also spawned the protests against these. Its greatest virtue has been its elasticity, its pluralism, its lack of dogma. Hinduism, it is said, has no "orthodoxy" (though it may have an "orthopraxy"). With a core in the religious tradition going back to the Vedas and Upanishads, it has brought forth other sister/child religions—Jainism, Buddhism, Sikhism—all born out of the same fertile continuate of tradition, all part of India and Hinduism's contributions to the world.

This image, encompassing the cultural diversities of the subcontinent and subordinating them to a Vedantic core, has pervaded both popular and scholarly writings on India. To take but one example, two scholars (Zelliot and Berntsen) of "religion in Maharashtra"draw together dalit, Marxist, and *bhakti* traditions in a book entitled *The Experience of Hinduism*, only to give Vedanta the last word:

> Buddhists, Jains, Muslims, Christians, nay even the Marxists, of today's India cannot help partaking of it—they are all Hindu-Bharatiya at heart. … What is it to be a Hindu-Bharatiya? What does it involve? Chiefly, the accepting of the other world as well as this world, the attempt to

reconcile the two. But between the two the other world comes first. *Brahman* and *maya* are both real, but brahman is the ultimate reality. ... This ultimate/provisional duality has been resolved into a unity in the Vedanta of nonduality (Bhave 1988, 318–19).

There are many who would contest this violently. What is more striking, though, is that behind the image of flexibility and diversity is a hard core of an assertion of dominance. "Between the two the other world comes first." This assertion leads to the political line of the Vishwa Hindu Parishad that there may be various versions of what is defined as the "Hindu tradition" (Sikhism, Buddhism, Jainism, Arya Samaj, and Sanatan Dharma are the ones usually mentioned), but there is no question that the core is "traditional" Hinduism—*sanatan dharma*.

Out of the pleasantries of the official ideology of Hindu pluralism and tolerance, and under the pressures of contemporary material deprivation and economic turbulence, has grown the modern politics of *Hindutva*—militant Hinduism, Hinduism as nationalism. It makes a simple addition to the claim that Hinduism is the main religion of the people of India: Hinduism is the national religion, the people's tradition in the subcontinent, but it has been attacked, smothered, insulted, dishonored, first by Muslim aggressors, then by British colonialism, and now by the contemporary State which in its self-definition as "secular" is dishonoring it in its own land and pampering Muslim and Christian minorities. Hinduism's great virtue was its generous tolerance of other faiths, but its enemies have taken advantage of this; Hindus must now be strong, fierce, and proud, and not hesitate to assert themselves.

Today, large sections of left and democratic forces and all new social movements are trying to argue and organize against the growing influence of *Hindutva* or Hindu nationalism. The majority of these have taken a position against "communalism" but not against "Hinduism" as such. The "secular" version of this opposition argues that Indians must come together beyond their religious identities, as citizens of a nation and as human beings. It is exemplified in the popular anti-communal song *Mandir-Masjid*:

In temples, mosques, gurudwaras
God is divided.
Divide the earth, divide the sea,
But don't divide humanity.
The Hindu says, "The temple is mine,
The temple is my home."
The Muslim says, "Mecca is mine,
Mecca is my loyalty."
The two fight, fight and die,
Get finished off in fighting.

The song goes on to describe the machinations of political leaders and the perpetuation of exploitation through communalism, but, interestingly enough, even its appeal to a common identity draws on (and reproduces?) the notion that India is the home of the Hindus while the Muslims find their loyalties elsewhere.

Another mode of opposing communalism is to re-appeal to Hindu traditions themselves, a position that has been developing among several anti-communal Delhi intellectuals over the last few years. This has been eloquently voiced by Madhu Kishwar in a number of *Manushi* articles which argue "in defence of our dharma." Agreeing with the condemnation that Nehruvian and modern left secularism are insufficient to deal with the need for identity, she appeals to *bhakti* traditions as the "true Hinduism," and argues that the militaristic image of Rama is a distortion, and that much of casteism is in fact a colonial heritage. This position has antagonized many secular feminists, but there is no denying that it is persuasive to many, particularly to middle-class, upper-caste Indians. Even the upper-caste left is being increasingly drawn to it. This is illustrated by the poster of the Sampradayikta Virodhi Abhyan: the mask of Rama, the form of Ravana. The SVM thus appeals to the "gentle" image of Rama and takes for granted the demonical quality of Ravana.

These two forms of opposition to Hindutva, the "secular" and "Hindu reformist" versions, draw respectively upon Nehruvian and Gandhian traditions. While there is no reason to doubt the genuineness of their attempts to oppose the aggressive politics of the Hindutva forces, one can question the validity of their picture of Hinduism: the validity of the general identification of "Hindu" with "Bharatiya," of Hinduism with the tradition of India.

Beyond this debate between the secularists and the Hindu reformists there are many voices in India today which not only query the BJP/VHP interpretation of Hinduism, but also contest the very existence of Hinduism as a primordial force in India. A Tamil dalit scholar-activist, Guna, writes:

> The very concept of Hinduism, which took shape in the north only when the Muslim rule was being consolidated ... was never known to the Tamils until the period of British colonization. ... The Brahmans, who had English education and had the opportunity of studying abroad, took some threads from the Europeans who conceived of a political entity called "Hindustan." With the borrowed idea, they could clumsily merge the divergent cults and Brahmanic caste apartheid to term it as Hinduism. This concept ... resulted in formulating a pseudo-religious-political concept called "Hinduism," based on which they sought to define their myth of a "Hindu" nationhood. ... The "Hindu" was thus born just two centuries back; and he is still a colourless, odourless and formless illusory artificial construction (Guna 1984, 124–25).

Guna is part of a broader tradition or set of traditions which have put forth alternative interpretations of Indian identity (or identities). These have been socially based among the lower castes, dalits, and non-Brahmans, drawing on peasant (and women's) traditions, mainly in the southern, western, and outlying regions of the subcontinent. In contemporary times they draw on such leaders as Phule, Ambedkar, Periyar; they appeal to heroes of revolt such as Birsa Munda and Veer Narayan Singh; they claim the traditions of Buddha and Carvak, Mahavir, Kabir and Guru Nanak, and Basavappa; they claim heroes like Shivaji but contest the Hinduist interpretation of him; they claim the glories of Mohenjo-daro and the heritage of the pre-state tribals as opposed to that of plundering Aryan tribes. In contrast to the secularist opposition to Hindutva they proclaim a politics of identity, and in contrast to reformist Hindu identities *they define "Hinduism" itself as an oppressive class/caste/patriarchal force.*

The dalit movement, based on ex-untouchables and widening to include non-Brahman castes of many southern and peripheral areas, has in recent times brought forward most strongly this ideological challenge, this contesting of Hinduism. Indeed the impetus to challenge the hegemony and validity of Hinduism is part of the very logic of dalit politics.

It is insufficient to see dalit politics as simply the challenge posed by militant organizations such as the Dalit Panthers, the factionalized Republican Party, the rallies of the Bahujan Samaj Party, or even the insurgencies carried out by low-caste based Naxalite organizations. Dalit politics as the challenge to Brahman hegemony took on wider forms throughout the 1970s and 1980s, its themes sweeping into movements of "backward castes" (the former Shudras of the traditional varna system), peasants, women, and tribals. Dalit politics in the sense of a challenge to Brahmanic tradition has been an aspect of "several new social movements." Strikingly, if we take 1972, the year of the founding of the Dalit Panthers, as a beginning year for the new phase of the dalit movement, it was also a crucial year for many other new social movements—from the founding of SEWA in Ahmedabad to the upsurge of a new environmental movement in the Tehri-Garhwal Himalayan foothills, from the agitations and organizations of farmers in Punjab and Tamil Nadu to the rise of tribal-based movements for autonomy in the central Indian region of Jharkhand. These movements, though not as directly as the dalit movement, came to contest the way in which the Hindu nationalist forces sought to depict and hegemonize Indian culture. They often linked a cultural critique to a broader critique of socio-economic development and an opposition to the overcentralized political system. By the late 1980s, an intermixing and dialogue of all these themes could be seen. The events of 1989–1991 ended with a setback resulting in the renewed aggressiveness of the forces of Hindu nationalism, but we continue to hope that the setback has been temporary.

9

Problems with "Religion" as a Category for Understanding Hinduism

Timothy Fitzgerald

Introduction

In this article I argue that the term "religion" is an ineffective category for the analysis of Hinduism. Much of the problem concerns how religion is distinguished from nonreligion—whether social or secular. This issue bears relevance for both religious studies and anthropology/sociology. Hinduism is consistently classified in books of the religion genre as one of the major five world religions. Despite the literature's format, its conclusions remain the same. The selection of the data, the format, and the generalizations reflect an unacknowledged ideological commitment on the part of the comparative religionists. The collision between comparative religion and anthropology has produced a notion of religion which does nothing to clarify the complexities of the data.[1]

I begin by establishing some alternative categories which, I propose, can replace the concept of religion. Then I look at four typical productions of the religious studies genre by John Hinnells and Eric Sharpe (1971), R. C. Zaehner (1971), Glyn Richards (1988), and Klaus Klostermaier (1994, 1998). Next, I discuss anthropological attempts to distinguish between the religion of Hinduism and the Indian social institutions, in particular those of Lawrence Babb (1975), C. J. Fuller (1992), and Brian K. Smith (1987). This will necessarily involve some discussion of Louis Dumont (1980). Finally, I argue—in part using my analysis of Ambedkar Buddhism as an example of a caste movement seeking minority status (Fitzgerald 1996, 1997b)—that the category religion does not effectively demarcate any *nonreligious* institutions; nor does it clarify the sense in which Buddhists, Christians, Jains, Muslims, or Sikhs constitute separate minorities in India.

Ritual, Politics, Soteriology, and Economics

I argue that the distinctions between ritual, politics, soteriology, and economics bring greater clarity than religion—which is used in many texts to cover (and thus to obscure) all four. These categories seem to resolve many of the conceptual problems I have encountered in my research on Ambedkar Buddhism, and I believe they may find wider relevance. The underlying assumption posits that religion can be abandoned and replaced by such categories without significant loss.[2]

I have not found the concept of religion useful as an analytical category for understanding the situation of the Ambedkar Buddhists. If I was a comparative religionist, the first thing I would notice if I visited their communities would be their temples and their *pujas* performed to pictures of Gautama Buddha and Ambedkar side by side on the shrines. And there is no doubt that many Buddhists conceive of Buddha and Bhimrao Ambedkar as supernatural beings who can bring benefits. In this sense they fulfill the same function as some Hindu deities. On the other hand, many completely reject this interpretation.

The thought of Ambedkar as a supernatural being who brings liberation to all backward classes is widespread among Buddhists. However, Ambedkar himself was entirely against supernaturalism, seeing it as a form of dependency induced by the traditional oppression of Indian caste culture. And the dominant understanding of present-day Buddhists, especially educated Buddhists, is explicitly against the idea that Ambedkar is a supernatural being. Some Buddhists believe Ambedkar was enlightened in a way which stresses his humanity and refrains from declaring him a god. When such Buddhists perform *puja*, they are recalling Buddha's and Ambedkar's outstanding life examples. Many educated Buddhists interpret Ambedkar's enlightenment as the product of education and the full realization of his potential as a human being. It is significant that the dominant mode of artistic representation of Ambedkar is not as a renouncer with a begging bowl or a meditator beneath the Bodhi tree but as a middle-class intellectual wearing a blue suit and glasses and carrying a book that symbolizes the Republican Constitution and the power of education and literacy.

The concept of religion either as a traditional soteriology or as an interaction with superhuman beings is patently inadequate for the realities of Ambedkar Buddhists. This is true even though transcendentalist or supernaturalist aspects of the movement exist. And when one realizes that the vast majority

of Buddhists are members of the same untouchable caste, it be
ous that caste hierarchy must be a fundamental part of the
reflects Ambedkar's focus on liberation as an institutional problem.

I have developed a typology of ritual, politics, soteriology, and econom.
to make sense of these issues in my own research. I propose that, whereas the
hazy distinction between "religion" and "nonreligion" obscures the analysis
of institutions, social movements, and minorities, these alternative categories
bring greater analytical clarity.

Ritual

It seems to me that Ambedkar's analysis of traditional Indian society found
that it is fundamentally a ritualistic—rather than moral—system and that
caste, untouchability, and supernaturalism were its main institutional expressions. Though he did advocate some simple Buddhist rituals such as *puja* and
simple weddings and funerals, he believed that these should be cheap (to
avoid dowry problems, for instance), transparent, and nonmystifying. The
rituals referred to in this category include the whole spectrum of practices
that Ambedkar condemned—worship of the supernatural, exorcism, possession states, caste ritualism; the location of the untouchable quarter on the
boundaries of the villages; the duties of scavenging and night soil removal.
Thus, for Ambedkar, ritual is as much about power as "irrationality."

Ideologically, when we identify the form of life indicated by ritual, we are
not talking about Buddhism as understood by Ambedkar but about a de facto
form of life that many Buddhists practice. For example, caste and even subcaste endogamy is widespread among all Buddhists. It is part and parcel of
contemporary Buddhist identity, though Buddhists themselves deplore it.
Another example is that Buddhists who have exposed themselves to the dan-
gers of high-caste anger by refusing to perform some ritual services (scavenging, for instance) may still be practicing untouchability against other untouchable castes or be worshiping Buddha and Ambedkar as Hindu gods.
The importance of this element of ritual, though it is incompatible with
Ambedkar's teaching, lies in the fact that it is part of the actual situation and
identity of Buddhists and, consequently, must be investigated as such.

Politics

It seems to me that humanistic rationalism and social democracy are central
to Ambedkar's understanding of Buddhism. I call this a modern concept of
politics in order to contrast it with the traditional legitimation of power
mediated by ritual status. Modern politics in India is also about power, but
power mediated by egalitarian values. Conversely, power is also still mediated
through ritual status as a result, for example, of the dominance of certain

caste groups in a particular area. Thus, at the level of ideas, politics and ritual are based on conflicting principles. This central political component of Ambedkar's understanding of Buddhism is, to some extent, recognizable in most Buddhist groups in Maharashtra. I believe that "politics"—that is, social activism directed toward the democratic exercise of political power for peaceful social revolution—may be the single best term to encapsulate this element of Ambedkar Buddhism. This notion of politics is not arbitrary, for it is closely linked with the fundamental principles of a democratic constitution, an independent judiciary founded on equality before the law, democratic representative legislatures and universal suffrage, the principles of human and civil rights, the sovereignty of the nation state, and the right to self-rule by groups claiming historical, linguistic, ethnic, and cultural independence.

Soteriology

Though politics is the pursuit of power, it is power which liberates. It liberates individuals and collectivities from ignorance, exploitation, and degradation. Soteriology is traditionally a doctrine of spiritual salvation or liberation from the world of suffering and evil. It is a doctrine concerned with the individual, for it is the individual consciousness that is constituted by the karmic factors of suffering. It is the individual who practices moral restraint, social concern, and meditation along the path to enlightenment. However, in Ambedkar's writing social concern is given a distinctively political emphasis. The institution of caste hierarchy and its ritualistic mechanisms are particularly identified as major causes of suffering. The concept of individual liberation is closely linked with sociopolitical liberation, and the factors of suffering are identified more broadly with institutionalized exploitation—particularly caste, bonded labor, and untouchability. Therefore, in Ambedkar's writing soteriology and politics are closely identified—politics understood as the pursuit of power within the jurisdiction of a democratic constitution, soteriology as liberation from inequality and exploitation.

Nevertheless, many Buddhists hold strongly that soteriology is not only political and social activism in Ambedkar's thinking but has an important spiritual or transcendental element as well. This spiritual element is pursued through reading Buddhist texts, practicing meditation, and going on retreats. Sociopolitical activism and a more "spiritual" understanding of liberation are often seen as complementary, even dialectically implicated. One highly organized expression of this idea of soteriology is the Trilokya Bauddha Mahasangha, which has developed a sophisticated interpretation of Buddhist soteriological doctrine based on both Ambedkar's teaching and the scholarly writing of Sangharaksita (1957, 1986, 1988). This teaching sees the social revolutionary and the transcendental goals as complementary.

Economics

This substitution of ritual, politics, and soteriology for religion does not mean that other categories such as "economics" are not important in the analysis of any specific Indian institution or movement. However, the economic sphere must be specified in relation to ritual, politics, and soteriology. For example, the economics of a village may be characterized by wage labor and a market economy, but many aspects of a local economy are still embedded in local caste hierarchy. Contemporary bonded labor is not economics in the sense of wage labor or market economy but a form of slavery that stems from a ritual system of dowry, partially controlled by high-status castes. And some forms of exchange are descended from the old *balutedari* system, which was deeply embedded in ritual status and the power of the local dominant caste. Thus I believe that the meaning of "economics" as a category can be clarified only in relation to these other categories.

Hinduism as the Creation of Ecumenicists in the Religion Genre

It is obvious that analyzing Ambedkar Buddhism in terms of the above categories cuts across the simplistic distinction of religion and nonreligion (religion and the secular or religion and society). It is clear that many books on Hinduism in the religion genre either have no interest in anthropology (or ethnographic studies) or relegate it to a subdiscipline. This relegation implies that "society" was something essentially extraneous though with which "religion" connects at various points, one of a number of dimensions of the separately existing object religion. I have argued elsewhere (Fitzgerald 1990, 1997a, 2000) that the study of religion is fundamentally a theological enterprise which has attempted to disguise itself as something akin to—though distinct from—a social science. Most of the leading theorists from the time of Friedrich Max Müller have been explicitly involved in theological ecumenical activities. In this way, religion has been mystified as a sui generis reality (see McCutcheon 1997) which, though connected to society and politics, is conceived as essentially independent of them.

Thus there is a thinly veiled ideological agenda that has succeeded in mystifying the word "religion," investing it with an appearance of self-evident reality it does not possess. This process of mystification carries over even into the social sciences, where a concept which has originated in a modern form of theology and wrapped itself in the mantle of common sense is used as though it were just another of those useful categories, a virtually unavoidable feature of the sociocultural landscape. As such, the use of the word appears without question in many of the general surveys of

Hinduism. Though such books are sometimes erudite and, indeed, profound in the scope of their learning, they usually lack a convincing theoretical focus to differentiate between Hinduism and the entire history and culture of India.

I now look at a sample of texts from the religious studies genre.

Hinnells and Sharpe

John Hinnells and Eric Sharpe's *Hinduism* (1971) is an old book, edited by authors who were involved in the formation of the Shap Working party on religious education in Britain. It is still on various school and college syllabi, in conjunction with books typically entitled *The World's Religions*. The lack of theoretical focus of these books makes it problematic whether there are any nontheological principles guiding inclusion or exclusion of material. Is the study of religion something different from the study of culture? Or, is it, in fact, part of an ecumenical theology created by a long line of comparative religionists since Max Müller? The problem I wish to explore impacts the way religion is taught in schools, colleges, and universities.

Time and again books on Hinduism—written for the religious studies market—acknowledge that, in crucial respects, Hinduism defies their categories. Hinnells and Sharpe's textbook is a case in point. It attempted, with considerable skill, to isolate and describe a coherent and manageable entity from the mass of data provided by Sanskritists, historians, and others. But because the editors were a priori guided by an essentially theological concept—which I gloss as "belief in a god who saves and who gives meaning to human history"—they cut across the available data in the wrong places.

Actually, they themselves acknowledge this problem. And the same problem is repeatedly reproduced in world religions publications. At its simplest, the problem arises most evidently around caste. The editors acknowledge the problem of caste in this way: "A Hindu is a Hindu not because he accepts certain doctrines or philosophies but because he is a member of a caste" (1971, 6). Given the actual contents of the book, this is a surprising admission. There are less than three pages on caste. The section on caste is no longer than the average length of the other fifty-two sections. Generally speaking, ideology and ritual are described for their theological and soteriological significance, as though the salvation of the individual soul is central and fundamental and Hinduism exists as a theosophy with universal relevance. The centrality of Hinduism as an ideology belonging to the social relations of a particular group or set of groups is acknowledged but not addressed. Virtually everything that anthropology has revealed about Hinduism is ignored in the quest for a soteriological belief system, a world religion, that transcends any particular social group.

Zaehner

The same criticism can be made of R. C. Zaehner. Zaehner's translation of, and commentary on, the *Bhagavad Gita* (1969) is a brilliant work, providing the reader with a fascinating exploration of the profound theological and metaphysical thought-world of India. In this case it would be unreasonable to expect such a work to also be concerned with the analysis of institutions. However, his *Hinduism* (1971) offers itself as an introduction to a religion. Right at the beginning of the book he says, "It is perfectly possible to be a good Hindu whether one's personal views incline towards monotheism, monism, polytheism or even atheism" (1971, 1). He may mean that to be a "good Hindu" one must be ritually pure, and ritual purity is related to caste status. Hinduism is an orthopraxy, not an orthodoxy. Yet the book contains virtually nothing on caste, focusing upon myths and doctrines and philosophies presented as though they did not exist in a social reality. In this case further explanation is needed.

I argue that the ideas of a religion and a world religion are highly dubious—to say the least—when applied to Hinduism. There are some sectarian neo-Vedanta soteriologies which propagate universalistic missionary messages. These theologies correspond, as suggested by Richard Burghart (1987, 6), to the idea of a religion held by many Christian theologians and religious studies academics. One can see the influence of the neo-Vedanta view of Hinduism as a world religion in Hinnells and Sharpe's *Hinduism*. Such sectarian viewpoints, with their "universal" soteriologies, are one important component of the study of Hinduism, but they are distorted when made synonymous with the subject.

We should consider that millions of Hindus have probably never even heard of the trio of Shankara, Ramanuja, and Madhva—medieval philosophers whose names are ritually chanted by religion scholars on Hinduism. I do not mean that they should not be studied as theologians; they were indeed profound thinkers. But their influence survives because of their sectarian theologies. We are, therefore, dealing with an aspect of Hinduism that can, to some extent, be analytically separated from caste, politics, ritual, and communalism but still requires sociological, contextual analysis before it can be abstracted for the purposes of theological comparison or ecumenism. In religion books they are prematurely plucked from their nests and transferred to the ecumenical basket for various purposes ranging from race relations to the construction of a world theology.

Richards

In an article entitled "Modern Hinduism," Glyn Richards (1988) takes an approach that is—in several ways—typical of the religious studies genre. He merely lists the names and theological principles of the standard set of theologians who seem to have acquired the status of saints in the ecumenical vocabulary: Vinoba Bhave, Dayanand Sarasvati, Mohandas Gandhi, Aurobindo Ghose, Sarvepalli Radhakrishnan, Ramakrishna, Rammohan Roy, Keshab Sen, Devendranath Tagore, Rabindranath Tagore, and Vivekananda. I mention this article because it illustrates how an ecumenic theological concept impoverishes our understanding of India, separating big names and their theologies from the everyday realities of power and hierarchy in Indian life. This idealization continues the ecumenic ritual tradition of repeating name litanies and studiously avoiding any suggestion that the saint theologians of modern times were interested in power or that they had vested interests of any kind. To suggest this would doubtless be considered cynical and unworthy.

But one does not have to go this far. One can investigate the relationship between, say, a theological position of the high-caste metaphysician Radhakrishnan and his view of caste. "Caste," says Radhakrishnan, "stands for ordered complexity, the harmonized multiplicity, the many in one which is the clue to the structure of the universe" (cited in Gore 1993, 275). It is interesting to compare this idealization, as M. Gore does, with the perspective of Ambedkar, who saw in caste a mechanism of repression and in the sacred Smritis a sanctification of that repression. Gore comments:

> Thus for Radhakrishnan, the caste system represented a process of fostering unity in the midst of diversity. To Ambedkar, it was a process of dividing what was homogeneous. Radhakrishnan saw the learned Brahmanas as the great synthesizers. Ambedkar first saw them as the providers of a "glib philosophy" for division and later as in fact the class responsible for strife and division (1993, 275).

Richards, in his tendency to idealize Gandhi, says that Gandhi's:

> metaphysical presuppositions point clearly to the interrelation of morality and religion and imply that we have an inescapable moral obligation towards our fellow men. This is illustrated in Gandhi's emphasis on *sarvodaya*, the welfare of all, which is revealed in his concern for the status of Harijans (Untouchables) and women in Indian society. He proclaims the need for the abolition of the caste system, child marriages, enforced widowhood and *parda* which were harmful to the moral and spiritual growth of the nation. Radical social changes were required to improve the lot of the outcastes and the status of women and only the restoration of the purity of the Hindu way of life would suffice to effect the changes needed. The social, economic and political implications of Gandhi's emphasis on *sarvodaya* are far reaching. His economic policy is people-oriented and rejects developments that dehumanize

and degrade people's lives, including unbridled industrialization; his alternative educational system fosters rather than undermines the cultural heritage of the nation; and his political goal of Svaraj, self-rule, promotes Indian self-respect and the determination of his people to accept responsibility for managing their own affairs (1988, 711).

We can see how ecumenic theological principles determine the presentation of the data. I do not mean only that Hinduism is presented as a series of theological positions—though there is some truth in that. I mean also that the writer himself is acting as a tacit theologian by selecting certain kinds of data to present in a certain way, without explanation. It is, in short, an ideological position—but unacknowledged.

There is no doubt that Gandhi was a remarkable man. But Richards seeks to put Gandhi beyond criticism by excluding any view but the ecumenically acceptable one. For example, George Orwell—in his essay on Gandhi (1991)—was well aware of Gandhi's stature as a human being, though—as a humanist—he found some of Gandhi's moral principles *inhuman* and some of his political assumptions naïve and even disingenuous. Jiddah Krishnamurti, who knew Gandhi personally, once described him, in an interview, as "a very violent man" (cited in Lutyens 1988, 70) and elsewhere said, "The whole philosophy of non-violence is warped, both politically and religiously" (Krishnamurti 1978, 205).

Richards asserts that Gandhi's views foster the cultural heritage of the nation; but what is the cultural heritage? Ambedkar Buddhists and Dalits would say it includes discrimination and oppression aided and abetted by high-caste reformers. This process of idealization is sometimes promoted by factually dubious information. For example, Richards says that Gandhi wanted to abolish the caste system, but how does one square this with his article "A Vindication of Caste" (1936)? Some of his views changed over the years. For instance, in 1920 he was advocating the traditional bar on intermarriage and interdining between castes, but by 1946 he was encouraging intercaste marriages (Zelliot 1992, 153). What did not change was his commitment to *caturvarnya (varnashramadharma)*, the ideal *varna* system. He believed this division of different functions is inherent in human nature, is essential in all societies, is taught in the sacred texts, and was the original order of Hindu society. He was also consistent, as Richards says, in his condemnation of untouchability, which he saw as a degeneration from the original ideal division of social functions. He claimed that this ideal did not imply hierarchy, which was a subsequent development. He deplored that different functions had come to confer superiority and inferiority. All occupations are equally honorable: "The calling of a Brahmana ... and a scavenger are equal" (Gandhi 1936, 136). Yet he also upheld the birthright of *varna* and indeed the birth duty. People must follow their hereditary occupations: "One born a scavenger must earn his livelihood by being a scavenger, and then he do whatever else he likes" (cited in Zelliot 1992, 154).

Nobody could doubt that Gandhi genuinely wanted to abolish untouchability. But it is difficult to see how Gandhi imagined that superiority and inferiority could be eliminated from such a picture. And Richards, like most writers in the ecumenical religion mode, presents Gandhi as the emancipator of the untouchables while ignoring Ambedkar. The latter replied (see Ambedkar 1936, 143–60; see also 1945).

In Ambedkar's view the oppressors of untouchables were mainly the high-caste Brahmans who controlled the Indian National Congress and who put independence of India above genuine reform. Another group whom Ambedkar saw as the enemy of the untouchables were the non-Brahman, high-caste reformers with whom he worked in the earlier years but from whom he became increasingly alienated. However, the figure who Ambedkar came to see as the most dangerous to untouchable liberation was the one who claimed to be their leader and emancipator—Gandhi.

Though Gandhi was not himself a Brahman, his influence over both the Congress and the non-Brahman reformers was considerable. Essentially the problem was reformers who believed that untouchability could be eradicated on the basis of high-caste goodwill alone, without giving real power or constitutional rights to untouchables, and without abolishing the caste system or the hierarchical values on which it is founded. As an untouchable himself, Ambedkar had experienced the effects of this system on those at the bottom of its hierarchy, and he was confident that enforced untouchability was a fundamental aspect of the very structure of Indian caste relations. In his view it was impossible to remove untouchability by merely reforming the system. He believed that only through a program of radical political democratization—involving a revolution in the sphere of values, and the subsequent abolition of caste—could untouchability be removed. All his life he tried to achieve this not merely by moral persuasion but also through constitutional change and political activism. It was this revolution in the sphere of values which he gradually came to identify with Buddhism.

It is not necessary for us to agree with Ambedkar, Krishnamurti, or Orwell, but it is necessary to be aware of the fuller context and the criticisms.

Klostermaier

Klaus Klostermaier's *A Survey of Hinduism* (1994) was followed by a condensed *A Short Introduction to Hinduism* (1998). Both books contain discussions of theoretical issues. It is upon these issues that my own discussion is directed. The *Survey*, in particular, is a work of compendious knowledge, an invaluable source-book on Indian history and culture. However, its comprehensiveness should not blind us to the theoretical confusions which

Klostermaier displays in the introduction to the 1994 volume and which resurface in the 1998 one. Indeed, so comprehensive is the *Survey* that it is difficult to distinguish the "religion of Hinduism" from the entire history and culture of India. At one point he says that he "did not choose the framework of any one particular contemporary Western academic discipline" (1994, 4). But perhaps this is part of his problem; he wants to be all things to all people and ends up with a nebulous object.

I am concerned about the following issues: the sense in which Hinduism is a religion; how it can be demarcated from culture (if at all) and from the sociopolitical system(s) in general; what validity should be attributed to which nonindigenous, analytical categories; what editorial principles guided the inclusion and exclusion of material.

An important question to pose is: Why do scholars persist with a concept of religion that obscures their data and leads them into absurd conceptual entanglements? I suggest that this can only be explained by the mystifying role of religion as a category in western ideology, all the more powerful because it rarely gets subjected to serious critique by those who regard it as a self-evident aspect of human experience.

Klostermaier is aware that some kind of theoretical statement ought to be made on these issues. But his statements seem slippery and inconclusive. His ambition is "to offer correct information on Hinduism as a whole and also to make a modern westerner understand some of its meaning" (1994, 3). And later he says, "If one entertains the ambition to deal with Hinduism as a whole, comprehensively and topically, philosophically and sociologically, one has to find one's own disposition and must justify it before one's readers" (9).

He describes himself as an "insider-outsider," and from this position he "has attempted to pay attention to ... [the concerns of the western investigator and the Indian scholar], fully aware of the fact that it is not always possible to avoid taking sides" (1994, 4). There are important issues here, regarding who has the right to make interpretations of people's behavior and statements. But then what is his position on these issues? His statements do not make it clear.

For example, the author deplores "scholars playing around with structuralist, functionalist, or other theoretical models that are clever and appear plausible to western intellectuals, but explain little and often distort a great deal of Hindu reality," and contrasts this attitude with his own approach: "Here the attempt is made to describe Hinduism as the living tradition of the Hindus; a tradition with its own logic and purpose of its own" (1994, 3). A little later he says: "Hinduism is not a 'case' to be studied and brought within preformed and preset categories (taken from Western culture) but an expression of human nature and culture to be accepted on its own terms" (11). Yet on page 4 he acknowledges that, in order to understand something, we have to translate it into "known categories" and "identify certain struc-tures." Then he sympathetically quotes Dumont (and again on page 5) without making his views on Dumont's structuralist interpretation clear. Therefore his position on the use of nonindigenous categories to interpret Hinduism remains unclear, and he seems to constantly shift his ground about the legitimacy of nonindigenous categories for interpreting Hinduism.

This brings me to the more specific issue of the category "religion" and the concept of Hinduism as a religion or as several religions. As far as I am aware, he does not subject the legitimacy of religion as an outsider category to analysis. Instead he gives ambiguous and contradictory indications of his meaning. He says: "Hinduism has always been more than mere religion in the modern western sense and it aims at being a comprehensive way of life as well today" (1994, 2). What he means by "mere religion in the modern western sense" is not explained, but here he seems to want to convey the idea that Hinduism is "a comprehensive way of life" rather than an area separated off from the secular or nonreligious. Again on the same page, Hinduism:

> was meant to interpret reality to Hindus, to make life more meaningful to them, to provide them with a theoretical and practical framework for their individual and corporate existence, to educate them intellectually and morally, and, finally, to fulfill their longing for ultimate freedom and salvation.

Ignoring the attribution of agency or anthropomorphic purpose to Hindu-ism ("Hinduism was meant to … ," for instance), it can be suggested that this notion of Hinduism is so comprehensive that it would fit communism without much trouble and arguably free market capitalism as well. This comprehensive concept of Hinduism is reinforced by "Hinduism as a way of life embraces virtually all aspects of culture" (1994, 5). And again he refers to "the pervasive presence of religion in all aspects of daily life" (7).

However, he also wishes to introduce the idea that, though Hinduism is a comprehensive way of life, there are more-and-less religious components to its pervasive presence. The more religious components are the metaphysical heart or core of the religion, and the less religious are—generally speak-ing—the historical, the structural, and the sociopolitical aspects. He says:

> This survey focuses on those aspects of Hinduism that are "religious" in a more specific sense, without either leaving out or completely sepa-rating it from other aspects of life that in the West are no longer con-nected with religion. Hindu religion has, in spite of its all-inclusive character, a metaphysical core, and there is no denying the fact that it provided a religious interpretation to the whole of life. Hinduism always left much freedom to its adherents to choose among many

options and exerted, except in matters that had to do with sectarian disciplines and caste rules, little pressure on its followers (1994, 5).

What does all this mean? Klostermaier wants to have everything without making clear choices. On the one hand, Hinduism is virtually the same as culture; it is all-inclusive. It is an interpretation of the whole of life. On the other, it is religious in a more "specific sense." This more specific sense appears to be its "metaphysical core." What is this core? How does Hinduism the religion differ from India as a "great old civilization" (1994, 7) and from that which is "the pervasive presence of religion in all aspects of daily life"? Later he identifies this core—"Hindu religion in the more specific sense"—as "the time-honored *trimarga* scheme. ... The path of work, knowledge, and loving devotion" (9). Does he mean that the metaphysical core can be identified with the three paths to salvation? For the metaphysical core of Hinduism might be taken to include a whole cluster of important Hindu concepts centered on *dharma*. Concepts which inevitably involve the world order and the social or ritual order (*varnashramadharma*)—which, in turn, include the legitimation of the power of kings and the ritual status of Brahmans and untouchables. And would "Hindutva" be included or excluded from this metaphysical core?

These are not idle questions. In his *Short Introduction* (1998) in a section called "Is There a Religion Called Hinduism?" (12–13), Klostermaier seems to say that the Hindu religion can be identified with those aspects of Hindu culture which distinguish Hindus from minorities. He mentions, in particular, Hindutva and Vishwa Hindu Parishad. However, elsewhere (47–56) Klostermaier identifies the heart of the religion with the Epics and Puranas.

The discussion in the introduction concerning what constitutes Hinduism the religion continues to be unclear. For Hindus, Hinduism is:

> a way of life, a large and rich culture, an environment that envelops a Hindu from before birth to after death. What we call Hinduism, Hindus themselves designate as *sanatana dharma*, "eternal law." It is identical with universally valid and generally binding insights and precepts, specified so as to accord with individuals' standing within society (1998, 2).

One could hardly have a broader definition than that, and it is difficult to see how, on this understanding, Hinduism can be analytically distinguished from Indian culture, society, or history in general. And this need for clarification is not provided by the statement: "The real Hinduism of the Indian people is the accumulation of many different layers of religion. To consider one aspect only would be to miss out on Hinduism as such" (6).

If "the real Hinduism," that is Hinduism "as such," includes all the historical layers of religion (which is itself one of the terms requiring clarification), then we are kept in a perpetual circular argument where what requires definition (the religion of Hinduism) is being defined by one of the words requiring definition, that is, "religion"; which is simultaneously both an essence ("the real Hinduism," "Hinduism as such") and an all-inclusive phenomenon requiring all historical levels to be included for proper understanding.

At other times, instead of talking about Hinduism the religion, Klostermaier talks about "the great diversity of religions, such as Vaishnavism, Shaivism, Shaktism and their subdivisions, which separates Hindus into many different competing communities" (1998, 3).

So we find that the word "religion" is operating at multiple levels of analysis and even identified with the plural "communities" (a vague word which might mean castes, sects, regions, villages, ethnic identities). Yet even so, the reader is supposed to understand what it means to say that "As a community ... Hindus are arguably the most intensely religious people on earth" (1998, 3). Here the word "community" has become singular, but it is impossible to know what is meant by "intensely religious." What is being compared with what? How is this judgment being made? This is not primarily a psychological question but a conceptual one. There is so little clarity attached to the words "religion" and "religious" that we cannot understand what kind of intensity is being discussed. And how would we distinguish between, say, religious intensity and political intensity? Here are some random examples which we do not, on the grounds offered here, know whether to include or exclude as exemplifying "religious" intensity: the practice of yogic meditation while buried alive underground; the practice of *sati*; the routine chanting of holy texts by Brahman funeral priests; the Dalit veneration of Ambedkar; necrophagous asceticism of the Aghori sect of Benares; the destruction of the Babri Masjid; the suicides of high-caste Hindus protesting at the Mandal Commission findings.

In his *Survey* and *Short Introduction*, Klostermaier has many interesting things to say. I respect his knowledge and the depth of his research. The point concerns theoretical clarification. The actual use of the word "religion" in the *Short Introduction* renders the statement "Hindus are arguably the most intensely religious people on earth" entirely vacuous. It may have a superficial appearance of meaning, but that derives not from scholarly and analytical usage but from some prior, unexamined commitments which lie undisclosed in the writer's (and, perhaps, the reader's) mind.

The author generalizes: "Religions mean to provide their followers with notions of human perfection and ideals of life" (1998, 3). Apart from the ideological implication of "mean to provide"—which seems to attribute religion not only with an essence but also with purposeful activity—the reader might be justified in thinking that any ideological systems might be contained in the same characterization. It could, I think, be argued that the ideal of human perfectibility lies behind the notion of progress in many different western systems of thought, stemming from the Enlightenment and the French Revolution. There is no clear way for the reader to be sure that Klostermaier would want to exclude these from religion or religions. So not only can we not distinguish religion from religions, or religion from cultures and civilizations, or religions from social and ritual order, but also it is doubtful whether any clear distinction is being made between religion and ideological value systems in general.

Nor can the reader distinguish analytically between what the author means by religion and what might otherwise be called communalism, nationalism, or politics. The author asks: "Is there a religion called Hinduism?" (1998, 12). The question is focused primarily on the meanings of Hindu and Hinduism, but of course it implies a concept of religion. Klostermaier tries to define Hinduism in communal terms, whereby Hindus distinguish themselves from Buddhists, Christians, Jains, Muslims, and Parsees. He suggests that this communal distinction is significantly related to the concept of Hindutva and the attempts of such an organization as Vishwa Hindu Parishad to create a Hindu sense of nationalism. In this case, Hinduism is apparently being tied to nationalism and communalism, and the implication then is that these count as religion (for example, the Hindu religion). This bewildering jumble of usages is then capped by the reassuring statement: "To call oneself a Hindu definitely means something, and to talk about Hinduism is fully acceptable to Hindus" (13). The only problem is that we do not know what it means.

The "Heart of Hinduism" (1998, ch. 5) is identified as the Puranas, together with the Epics. The *Bhagavad Gita* has "an extraordinarily important position" (47) in the heart of this heart. The problem with making these voluminous texts the heart of Hinduism is that they include so much. If we were to take the *Bhagavad Gita* alone, we find there not only a detailed philosophical discussion of the various paths to liberation but also a discussion (stemming from *karmamarga*) on caste duty and the social and ritual order of *varnashramadharma*. This, in turn, has political implications, in the sense of the legitimation of power because it can be, and indeed is, used to justify a particular ideology of social order. Thus, for example, both Gandhi and Ambedkar wished to eradicate untouchability, but they had different political programs. When Ambedkar wrote *Annihilation of Caste* Gandhi countered with "A Vindication of Caste." Gandhi's claim was that *varnashramadharma* had degenerated from an originally pure ideal as revealed in the sacred texts. How could anybody doubt that such texts legitimize a specific concept of social order—that is, power relations and the dominance of the Brahmans and higher castes? It is not clear that Klostermaier wishes to include questions of power, dominance, or untouchability as the heart of Hinduism. Is the dragging of dead cattle and the removal of night soil at the heart of Hinduism? Ambedkar would say yes, and indeed he did. But supposing one wanted to exclude these from Hinduism's heart, on what grounds can one do that? Klostermaier has failed to explain these important issues because his theoretical position slips and slides and is riddled with ambiguity.

Hinduism, Religion, and Indian Society

I now look at a sample of texts from the anthropological genre.

Babb

Lawrence Babb's *The Divine Hierarchy* (1975) is an ethnography of a specific region of Madhya Pradesh called Chhattisgarhi. Though it is now over twenty-five years old and reflects many of the theoretical assumptions of the time, it is well known within the religious studies and anthropological communities and provides an excellent example of the kind of usage I wish to examine. It is clearly written and relatively lucid theoretically, the analysis of the ethnography explicitly related to theoretical issues current at the time and still relevant for our discussion. Furthermore, it is obvious that, as an anthropologist committed to a sociological theoretical position and methodology, Babb has no theological intention.

The title might suggest that he is primarily concerned with religion in the conceptions of relations with the gods. Up to a point this is true. The title refers, in part, to the hierarchical pantheon and the relationships that exist between various beings of both genders, relationships that can loosely be called "supernatural" or "superhuman." These vary from the remotest and most transcendental gods of the texts to the local goddesses, demons, witches, and ghosts. Furthermore, there are uses of the words "religion" and "religious" that occur throughout the book, implicitly or explicitly tying "religious" to the superhuman beings or to ritual relations with the super-human beings. For example: to be pious and "religious" is to rise early every day and perform *puja* to the gods (1975, 104); the Brahman and the Baiga are described as "religious specialists" because they have a special relationship with gods, ghosts, or witches (187); "religious" is linked to the gods as distinct from "the social order" (189); and renunciation and fasting are described as "religious" observances (208–209). Again, an explicit distinction is made between "ritual behavior" and "religious ideas," the latter referring to the divine hierarchy (215).

Yet these casual connections between the supernatural and the use of the words "religion" or "religious" is not consistent. First, Babb explicitly relates, at the theoretical level, religion to ritual and symbolic systems, and he finds, at a deeper level of analysis, a single paradigm based on concepts of hierarchy and the opposition between purity and pollution. This paradigm undercuts supposed distinctions between religion and society and provides a unified theoretical perspective. Second, his whole method of analyzing the pantheon is designed to bring out the structural homologies between the divine hierarchy and the human hierarchy and to show how the relationships between divinities symbolizes the domestication of the wild—the creation and recreation of social order from the dangerous and chaotic contingencies of nature. In short, he is trying to analyze a total ritual system whereby human institutions are reproduced and, in the context of which, relations within and between deities can be understood and interpreted.

To prove my point, first let me quote from Babb's introduction. Here he is talking about the problem of grasping the unity and diversity of Hinduism and the advantages of a specific area where certain general principles and structures emerge into view:

> Many of the analytical problems relating to the diversity of Hinduism are fully exemplified in the Chhattisgarhi setting, though on a far smaller and considerably more tractable scale. My emphasis will be on systemic aspects of religion in Chhattisgarh. ... In the course of my analysis it will become clear that Hinduism in Chhattisgarh is related in the most intimate way to the social structure that forms its context. Nevertheless, my analysis is not primarily concerned with religion in relation to social structure, but rather is an effort to understand popular Hinduism as a system of concepts and practices in its own right, as an autonomous cultural domain which displays a pattern and consistency of its own. This is in no way intended to minimize the importance of connections between religion and society in Chhattisgarh, nor is it to be construed as a denial ... that an understanding of social structure is a vital opening wedge to the understanding of religion. Indeed we shall see that nowhere is this assumption more applicable than in Chhattisgarh, where a single symbolic and conceptual paradigm underlies understanding of human and divine hierarchy and supplies the structural core of most if not all Chhattisgarhi ritual. Thus, in Chhattisgarh, as elsewhere, religion and society converge. But the full implications of connections of this sort can be seen only when the religious system itself is understood on its own terms. Such is the goal of this book (1975, xvii–xviii).

It seems to me that there are three different ideas or levels of analysis here. At Level 1 religion is a cultural system, an autonomous domain that has its own separate logic and consistency and can be "understood in its own terms." An extension of this idea is Level 2 where this distinct system is "intimately" related to society. Depending on what is meant by "intimate," this would suggest that it would be difficult to understand religion only on its own terms. In this connection one needs to know what "autonomous" means. A third idea (Level 3) is that religion and society are not only connected but also "converge" in a structural core of symbolism and ritual.

I believe Level 3 is central to Babb's theory and methodology, and I will give my reasons. However, it seems to me that he is keeping his options open by juggling with the concepts of religion, society, culture, and ritual in a way that obscures his real theoretical goal. We sense that he is trying to please different parties, such as the "social structuralists," descended from A. R. Radcliffe-Brown; the religionists, who insist on the autonomy and irreducibility of religion to sociological categories; and Dumont, whose concept of hierarchy became important in India studies in the 1970s (and indeed still is). However, if we move on, I think we can easily find where his real allegiances lie.

Hinduism as a religion, Babb tells us, is fundamentally a ritual system or rather many ritual systems that share a common core structure (29). Religion is "a thing done, not 'believed'" (31). Ritual is "symbolic activity that conveys information" (32). The basic core of all the rituals, however diverse, is found in the value of purity and its opposite, pollution. This value of purity and the eradication of pollution is the point at which society and religion "fuse" (47). The value of purity is equally fundamental in relations with a deity and in hierarchical caste relations (47–48). This concern with purity is found in the whole range of rituals that he analyses, including *puja*, life-cycle rituals, and rituals connected to special time frameworks.

That the whole thrust and direction of Babb's analysis is towards a holistic, sociological, and contextual analysis of ritual institutions can be seen from his discussion of the divine hierarchy itself. He makes a distinction between textual and local complexes of divinities. These he distinguishes according to various criteria. One is the degree of abstraction and distance from everyday concerns. The textual deities are more distant and are more concerned with the general welfare of the world, the encompassing order, and "the ultimate validity of social values in general" (238). These deities are regarded as pure and vegetarian. Ritually, they are served by the Brahman priest who, being ritually pure himself, is less likely to endanger the god with pollution (189). At the other, more local end of the supernatural spectrum are the smallpox goddesses and the dangerous ghosts and witches. These are related to immediate danger, uncertainty, disease, death, and chaos. These are themselves polluting, dangerous, meat-eating, demanding propitiation by blood sacrifice.

Babb points to the homologies between the hierarchy of deities, temple organization, and social and geographical segmentations (family, neighborhood, village, caste). Thus he says that, despite Maratha and British disruption in that area in modern history, "even today it is possible to speak of deities as objects of worship of ascending and descending degrees of social and territorial 'spread'" (187). Each god has a "constituency" (194).

Thus the stratification of the deities is related to human hierarchy and levels of social organization, the key terms in these sets of relationships being relative degrees of purity and pollution. Furthermore, relative purity and pollution is itself symbolically related to levels of order and disorder. The highest gods ensure the continuity of the entire overarching order, while the lower gods explain and symbolically represent the dangerous contingencies of everyday life. But the lower beings are encompassed by the higher beings, for ultimately the higher gods can be called on to bring protection and to restore the disruption caused by the dangerous elemental spirits.

In Babb's description, the goddess supplies a key to understanding the structure of the pantheon and the symbolic relation of the pantheon to the social order. This is because she both differentiates and unites the textual and local levels. In the ancient myths the gods (who are "essentially magnifications of human beings" [220]) brought the goddess into existence in order to defeat the demons who were threatening to overpower them. She emerges as a wild, dangerous, uncontrollable power filled with black anger. As such, she is more powerful than the gods themselves, and when they accompany her in the temple iconography they are subservient to her. For example, the great god Shiva will appear as Bhairava (223)—a terrible form of the god but subservient to the goddess. This single, destructive image of female deity is reproduced at the local level in many cholera and smallpox goddesses, witches, ghosts, and demons that attack people and cause calamities. Babb points out that even where the ghost is believed to be that of a dead man, it will frequently take the form of a girl or woman (200).

But in other iconography the goddess appears beside her husband, whether it be Shiva or Vishnu or Rama, as the dutiful and subordinate wife. Here she has been transformed from the sinister and uncontrollably dangerous polluting power of nature, conceived as feminine, to the domesticated wife representing the central values of Hindu civilization. She becomes vegetarian, pure, benevolent, "an exemplar of passive devotion to her husband" (223). "An appetite for conflict and destruction is thus transformed into the most fundamental of social virtues, that of wifely submission which, on the premises given in Hindu culture, makes the continuation of society possible" (225–26).

We see from this analysis of Babb that there is an ambiguity in his use of the concept of religion which is instructive, since we can expect to find similar ambiguity in the texts of other anthropologists too. He explicitly uses religion to mean a core ritual symbolic structure that expresses hierarchy in terms of purity and pollution. This structure is common to relations with gods and relations in the context of caste. In this case he says that both religion and society merge in the common ritual structure. This ritual structure

189

creates and recreates enduring human institutions (centrally marriage and all that is implied by marriage in the Hindu context) in the face of the contingent and dangerous realities of daily life.

Yet throughout the text he continuously (and I suspect almost automatically) uses the words "religion" or "religious" in such a way as to indicate a distinction between religion and society, based on the distinction between supernatural and human. It seems to me that here we have a good example of an anthropologist who, feeling "naturally" obliged to accept the legitimacy of "religion" as a common-sense referent, creates unnecessary confusions in his otherwise lucid text. This results from the common-sense notion being at odds with his more interesting theoretical analysis.

In the context of his more fundamental analytical core structure, the concepts of both religion and society become effectively redundant, replaced by other more precise categories such as ritual, hierarchy, gender, caste, ritual specialist, purity, and pollution. These confusions are not so serious in a book of this kind, perhaps, because the book obviously does not have a theological agenda and remains full of interesting data and careful analysis. Nevertheless, for my purposes, the confusions indicate the way in which the illusion of "religion's" analytical validity is perpetuated. The word is juggled backward and forward between a reference to the gods (thus appealing to common-sense notions deriving from Christian theological origins and the established theological meaning of religion as something like faith in God) and a reference to a fundamental symbolic system underlying the whole range of ritual institutions.

The latter is arguably closer to indigenous Hindu ways of thinking, too. I would suggest that the fundamental ritual structure that Babb is indicating is *dharma*. *Dharma* is often translated as "religion" in the modern sense, as a sui generis and distinct faculty and set of institutions defined by belief in the supernatural and in principle separable from nonreligion, from society. But *dharma* corresponds more closely to a notion of cosmic, social, and ritual order. If we were looking for the fundamental principle or value to provide an entry into the vast complexity of Hindu civilization, the concept of *dharma* might be a good place to start. It is mentioned in most religion books on Hinduism, but its rootedness in the ritualization of everyday life is not explained. The creation and recreation of *dharma* is described in different ways in the Vedic, Epic, and Puranic myths. *Dharma* is an eternal ritual order that defines the correct condition of all beings, their status. *Dharma* is fundamentally an ideological expression of hierarchy, or ritual order that embraces the whole mythical cosmos but is manifested to the observer most evidently in caste, including the traditional power exercised by the king or by the dominant castes. If Hinduism can be said to have a fundamental unifying principle, then this must be high on the list of candidates.

Dumont

Babb's work is heavily influenced by Louis Dumont, as is that of many sociologists of India. This is true even where criticisms or modifications of Dumont's theory have been made. Yet Dumont himself is, in my view, unclear about how the term "religion" should be used in the context of India. In his influential article "World Renunciation in Indian Religions" (included in 1980, 267–86), Dumont asserts that "the fundamental institution is caste: the caste system is based upon a hierarchical opposition of the pure and the impure, it is essentially religious" (270). It is "the religion of the group" (275, 278, 286). On the other hand, the renouncer also represents a religion, but a different kind of religion, "an individual religion" (275, 286), which (following L. de La Vallee Poussin) Dumont also calls "the disciplines of salvation" (274, 278).

It is easy to find subsequent reference in Dumont's work to religion in these two different senses. Furthermore, though the renouncer is represented in Indian thought as being outside the world, from the sociological point of view he is a kind of social institution. When one considers the full theoretical implications of these distinctions within the "Indian configuration of values"—both of which are called religion—one might ask what lies outside religion? Even power, which is distinct from ritual status, is subordinated to it at the primary level of values and ideology (75–79). The king—or his structural equivalent, the dominant caste—cannot be understood without the notion of the encompassment of power by ritual status. Thus, though power is in one sense separated from ritual status, it is conceptualized within the context of the overall dominant configuration of values: "In the traditional perspective, the essential perspective here ... the politico-economic domain is encompassed in an overall religious setting" (228). Surely religion becomes a redundant expression in such a context since it is equivalent to the configuration of values.

The theoretical distinction Dumont is making between hierarchy and renunciation is enormously powerful and necessary. But to call them both religion has unnecessarily confusing ramifications because hierarchy—as "purely a matter of religious values" (66), that is, the "religious" principle itself, expressed in terms of the opposition between purity and impurity—underlies the ranking order of caste and *varna* and provides the fundamental value of the entire social order. It can easily be called ritual status. Indeed it represents the cosmic order (*dharma*), of which the social order is a microcosm. This concept also represents the order of the gods, that is, their relations with each other and with humans (270). On the other hand, the *sannyasin* represents the religious principle of the individual, where religion is understood as a path to salvation undertaken by the individual rather than a sacred ritual order governing the whole cosmos. This distinction, which is seen as a distinction within a conceptual totality, can easily be marked by the terms such as *"moksha"* and *"marga,"* which express the goal of renunciation (or the differently formulated [sectarian] paths to salvation). Another western term would be "soteriology," conceived as a doctrine concerning what one must do to be saved. Soteriology corresponds to the "disciplines of salvation" or renunciation. This opposition between renunciation and ritual order or hierarchy also determines the distinction, and the relations, between caste and sect (284–86).

So far I have argued that in Dumont's writing "religion" exists at every analytical level, and consequently it appears to be a redundant category. On the other hand, the structure of his analytical model is clearly articulated in other terms, rendering the potentially confusing term "religion" (with its historical and semantic connections to privatized Protestant piety) relatively harmless.

The question, then, is: How is it that any group that defines itself in relation to a set of values different from the dominant hierarchical ones can exist in such a society? This brings us to the issue of minorities, such as Buddhists, Christians, Jains, Muslims, and Sikhs, whose values may seem different or antithetical. Let us consider Dumont's view of the matter. Here the term "religion" seems to get shifted to a different plane (for example, when he talks about "groups adhering to other religions" [210]). If, like Christianity and Islam, these "religions" originated outside India, he refers to them as "the foreign religions" (211). However, this extends our problem, for religion is already being overused. What is meant by calling these minorities different religions or groups having different religions?

There is a suggestion that we should think of "foreign" religions as bearing a sectarian-like relation to the caste system. "Sects" have tended to start off as egalitarian yet have over time inevitably developed caste-like characteristics: "Everything happens, or happened, as if the foreign religions had brought a message similar to that which the Hindu could find by adhering to a sect, a message which only made the social order relative, without abolishing or replacing it" (211). My understanding is that Christians and Muslims (foreign religions) and (ancient) Buddhist, Jains, and Lingayats (Indian sects) inevitably modify the dominant Indian or Hindu system but can never escape it or completely destroy it. Dumont makes the point that Buddhists in particular were never traditionally concerned about reforming caste but located equality within the *sangha*—defined as the quest for otherworldly liberation. And, talking about Lingayats and Muslims, he says:

> On the one hand the Hindu ideological justification is lacking, or at least much weakened and contradicted in theory (denial of impurity among the Lingayat, equality of believers among the Muslims), and on

192

the other hand the system of groups is subjected to alterations (no strict endogamy in the Ashraf categories of UP, no disjunction between status and power among the Lingayat, everywhere a relaxation of commensality). Therefore we must recognize that these communities have at the very least something of caste despite the modification in their ideas and values. Caste is weakened or incomplete, but not lacking altogether. … One is therefore led to see the caste system as an Indian institution having its full coherence and vitality in the Hindu environment, but continuing its existence, in more or less attenuated forms, in groups adhering to other religions (210).

I think it is clear that, despite Dumont's continuing and confusing use of religion as a category on several different levels, the basic structure of his theory is sound: He is asking us to consider caste and the hierarchical values underlying it as a total structure into which all groups located in India are inevitably, in one way or another, connected. These groups are also differentiated from one another, in a way analogous to sects, by their different ultimate values. Since these ultimate values have to become compromised and Hinduized, it is the soteriological aspects (the sectarian disciplines of salvation) that survive to provide a major component of their different identities within the total Indian environment.

However, describing the differences between Christians, Hindus, Muslims, and Sikhs solely in terms of different sectarian-like soteriologies clearly would not be enough for definitional purposes. True, isolated groups of Muslims living in Hindu-dominated areas of rural India, practicing subcaste endogamy and commensality and sharing many festivals, saints, and deities common to that region, may look like Hindu. They may be distinguished more by soteriological conceptions (Allah's salvation and the *masjid* instead of Brahman/Shiva and the *mandir*) than ritual ones (caste). Such a scenario would allow for ritual modifications but not complete eradication of the dominant ritual order. But in the densely populated Muslim areas such as Kashmir clear political factors—like nationalism—must also come into the equation. In this case the ultimate values have become highly politicized and the identity of different communities runs along a soteriology-political axis where salvation has developed different degrees of individual and collective nuance. The separate Islamic nation state has become virtually a soteriological goal itself (see Dumont 1980, 314–34).

Ambedkar Buddhists and Dalits, unlike Muslims, do not usually seek a separate nation. They do, though, seek separate electorates and a revolution in the sphere of values. Some wings of the Dalit movement proclaim a different ethnicity from high castes and even a separate nation, Dalitastan (Rajshekar 1987, 8). They follow an egalitarian ideology that is in direct conflict with the dominant hierarchical ones. Ambedkar Buddhists are soteriologically and politically egalitarian but ritually untouchable. For them, soteriological goals (*moksha*, for instance) are expressed in terms ranging from traditional (studying the Buddhists texts, practicing the Buddhist virtues, and seeking individual enlightenment through meditation and awareness) and modern political (collective liberation from untouchability through enactment of the Constitution, adjudication by the courts, and government anti-discrimination policies). On the other hand, virtually all Ambedkar Buddhists belong to one ritual status (caste), are still known by their old Hindu name Mahar in most local contexts, and are subordinated to the Brahmans and dominant castes. In other words, their relationship with the Hindu ritual hierarchy is highly problematic. If the Ambedkar Buddhists can be used as an analogy for minorities in general, then I argue that we can abandon the word "religion" altogether in seeking to determine the distinct identities of such groups and instead use such analytical concepts as soteriology, politics, and ritual. (More on this later.)

Fuller and Smith

I have been suggesting that Dumont's use of the word "religion" was unnecessary and confusing and that at the same time he provides us with alternative analytical concepts that are also in wide current usage. I want to pursue this discussion in connection with an article on defining Hinduism and religion by Brian K. Smith (1987) and a book on popular Hinduism by C. J. Fuller (1992). Both the article and the book are well informed, well written, and transparently concerned to give a nontheological, humanistic account of their subject. Both, however, fail to resolve the confusion created by "religion." Both wish to distinguish between Hinduism and the Indian social system. By this, I think they do not mean that Hindu institutions are not social institutions; they mean that there are some institutions in India that are not Hindu. For example, they might be Buddhist, Christian, Jain, Muslim, or Sikh. The issue here, as with my discussion of Dumont, is whether religion is the concept that will allow us to make valid analytical distinctions in this complex arena. By asserting that these are different religions, they can then argue that religions are a distinct kind of sociocultural institution. Fuller slides from this into the claim that Hinduism, as a religion, has an "interdependent relationship with society" (1992, 7). It seems that as long as the concept "religion" is on the scene, this tendency to reification almost inevitably arises. But it is difficult to understand how a social institution can have an interdependent relationship with society, except in the sense that all social institutions are to some degree interrelated with one other. The issue becomes whether "religion" genuinely picks out a distinctive set of institutions that demarcate it from other institutions or whether we need concepts that can pick out the finer distinctions that pervade many institutions.

For one thing, these writers have a different and contradictory criterion for defining "religion." Fuller, who is only concerned with Hinduism in India, falls back on the notion that Hinduism as a religion is a theistic construction and is distinguished from other cultural constructions by "beliefs and practices focused on the multiplicity of deities with whom Hindus interact and communicate in ritual" (1992, 5). Presumably, then, he would distinguish between the religion Hinduism and the various other "religions" on the basis that they worship and perform rituals to different deities. But, as Dumont suggested, this is not entirely true. Much ritual is shared by all groups in India, not least because all groups have an identity that is at least partly determined by caste. Further, much of the ethnographic data presented in his book presents a world in which deities, humans, and all living creatures are inextricably interrelated in a cosmic hierarchy, such that it would be difficult to find any institution which is not religion in that sense. In that case, what would fall outside religion? Conversely, there are movements in India (and here I have Ambedkar Buddhism primarily in mind) that are defined as religions both by those inside and those outside but that consciously reject all ritualism and belief in gods. Thus so much can be called religion in India that nothing distinctive emerges. Indeed Ambedkar (1936)—like Dumont (1980, 316)—called the values of individual equality religious.

Smith, on the other hand, is concerned more widely with the definition of religion. Perhaps because he is more conscious of the problems surrounding the many uses of this term, he explicitly rejects the idea that Hinduism—or religion more generally—can be usefully defined in terms of beliefs in superhuman agents (1987, 52). Smith believes—like Fuller—that religion can be used as an analytical concept, but—unlike Fuller—he requires it to be freed from any necessary association with the supernatural. After critically reviewing various previous attempts at definition, Smith comes up with a definition based on the notion of the canonical authority of the Veda: "Hinduism is the religion of those humans who create, perpetuate and transform traditions with legitimizing reference to the authority of the Veda" (40). He then goes on to argue, on the basis of this definition, that Marxism and Freudianism can equally be considered to be religions.

Thus the issue is not only whether western researchers can use western concepts for crosscultural analysis but also *which* western concepts can be illuminating and *which* tend to obscure. Thus, when Fuller says that "a large proportion of Hindus—even though most of their religious activity involves them alone—do have significant social relationships with Muslims, Christians, Sikhs, and other minority groups" (1992, 7), it is not entirely clear what "religious activity" and "social relations" demarcate. Undoubtedly there are important things that differentiate Hindus and the minorities, but are these distinctions best served by describing them as different religions? As we have seen, many scholars, including Dumont, refer to hierarchy as itself a religious principle; some saints and deities are shared; and, at the same time Hindus and Muslims are not only divided by deities but also by politics and ethnicity.

Fuller gives the example of *namaskara* as his starting place:

> Thus the principle of hierarchical inequality, as well as the partial continuity between divinity and humanity, is always symbolically present in the gesture of greeting and respect, and although these are not the only important themes to be explored ... they are certainly central (1992, 4).

Given the centrality of this principle of hierarchy and the degree of continuity between deities and humans, the distinction between religion and society seems highly problematic. The fundamental value seems to be hierarchy, and I am not clear that Fuller would deny that this is, in some Dumontian sense, a "religious" or sacred principle. What, in the ritual relations between humans and deities, is additional, extra, over, and above ritual relations between superior and inferior people? The answer appears to be "devotion or adoration" (4), which is presumably strongly associated with some concept of salvation, bringing us back to *soteriology*. Furthermore, even the worship of deities and saints is frequently shared. John Stanley (1988, 41–52) describes how in Pune different castes, such as Brahman, Chitpavan, Dhobi, Koli, Maratha, Sarasvat, Vanjari, and Muslim, participated in *angat yene* (ecstatic possession by a god, *pir*, or saint). K. Kadam (1988, 280–83), an untouchable Mahar who converted to Buddhism, describes the many Hindu-Muslim practices, including the worship of Muslim "gods" and possession states.

Fuller stresses "all symbolic interaction with the gods and goddesses of popular theistic Hinduism is about relationships among members of Indian society, as well as between them and their deities" (1992, 8). He goes on: "In the anthropological investigation of worship and popular Hinduism in general, we can focus on the deities, ... but we cannot understand them properly unless we also look at their priests and other members of society" (9).

It is difficult from this to understand how the content of relationships with deities is substantively different from the content of relationships with other humans. If the principle of hierarchical reciprocity—mainly formulated in terms of purity and pollution—operates at every level, then in what sense are relations with deities something more than symbolic statements about the social order? Does the difference lie in the fact that they are invisible? Or that they are superior in power? In what sense is it useful to maintain that there is an analytical distinction between religion and society, if any significant content of the relations with deities is also "about relationships among members of Indian society"? What is, in fact, left out of the social relationships and the symbolic statements of purity, hierarchy, and the legitimation of power?

As far as I can tell, there are two things which Fuller has in mind. One concerns what might be more satisfactorily called soteriology either in the pragmatic sense of removal of suffering or in the more metaphysical sense of liberation from conditioned existence. In this latter context, *marga* would be the relevant indigenous concept. In addition to the traditional concepts of the *marga*, there is also a modern notion of public service as a form of *karma marga* and therefore a way to salvation. This notion of public service can also have a *political* dimension. These senses of soteriology would help to analytically distinguish between a caste and a sect, between sects of many different colors, or—in the more pragmatic sense—between the different elements of a festival. Again, some festivals might have a political element as well. Thus, in the modern context, soteriological messages take on a political nuance, in the form of collective salvation. To what extent the Indian ritual identity is actually modified is a matter of ethnographic investigation.

Therefore, these senses of soteriology, and the relationship between soteriology and politics in the modern sense, may help to distinguish between different ethnic minorities. Smith is also concerned about this problem but tries to distinguish between them on the basis that they adhere to different canons. What is it that Indian Christians, Muslims, and Sikhs share, and what distinguishes them? Fuller and Smith seem to want to say that they share the Indian social institutions but are distinguished by religion. I would suggest, instead, that they share many of the *ritual* institutions (what traditionally has been covered by the term "*dharma*"), including what at the more formal textual level are called *caturvarnya* or *varnashramadharma*, and which might sometimes include the traditional systems of village service (*balutedari* or *jajmani*) in which castes are implicated—but are distinguished by different sectarian *soteriologies*, which, in turn, are connected to what have become translated into different *political* goals, such as an independent nation state or separate electorates with reservations. Different soteriologies may modify the ritual institutions to some extent, but they all belong to castes, generally recognize hierarchy, live in separate quarters, have different water wells, practice endogamy and commensality, participate in some of the same festivals, worship many of the same gods and *sants*.

Hew McLeod says this about Sikhism and caste:

> In terms of status or privilege caste is explicitly rejected by Sikhs. Nanak denounced it, subsequent Gurus reinforced his message and ritual observance confirms it. ... At baptism all must drink the same water; and in Gurduaras all sit together, receive the same Karah prasad, and eat in the same Langar. Caste is, however, retained within the Panth as a social order. The Gurus were married according to caste prescription and gave

their children in marriage similarly. This convention has survived virtually intact, with the result that practically every Indian Sikh belongs to a particular caste. An absolute majority are Jats, members of rural Punjab's dominant caste (1995, 93).

One thing to note about this description is the weight which falls on the word "convention." What does it mean to say that caste is a convention? Does it imply "merely"? Are all castes merely conventions? And in this context what does "dominant"—as in "dominant caste"—mean? One possibility is to say that in the Gurduara Sikh rituals are egalitarian but in the wider context of Hindu society they are located within the hierarchical ritual system. This leaves open the question of hierarchy among subcastes and between genders. Perhaps in some respects they share a similar contradiction with the Buddhists, in that they both apparently have an egalitarian soteriology while participating in ritual hierarchy.

One can see how difficult it is to separate out what is frequently designated "religion" in literature. Sikhs are different from Hindus at the soteriological level and also in terms of ethnicity and political goals. But they seem to share some of the same ritual principles centered on caste and hierarchy.

Fuller (1992, 50) points out that Muslim saints are frequently worshiped by Hindus. But the saints are also worshiped by Muslims. It may be true, as Fuller later says, that "Muslims in India have long decried the Hindu's reverence for images" (62). However, this decrying is part of the strict soteriology of Islam, which may moderate ritual in the case of strict followers but which presumably does not mean that Indian Muslims do not worship images at all. I suspect that it is the more educated Muslims who would strictly follow this injunction.

It would be difficult to separate Hindus and Muslims simply on the basis of different religions defined by relations with superhuman beings. I suggest that what distinguishes, for instance, Indian Christians, Muslims, and Sikhs is more their adherence to different soteriologies, which might be conceived in more traditional terms as *marga* and *moksha*. They might also be conceived as having a social service element or a political element, where *moksha* is collective and conceived in terms of ethnic or national liberation or, as in the case of Ambedkar Buddhists and Dalits, as liberation of the scheduled castes from untouchability and hierarchy. Here we can see that soteriology, politics, and ritual may be different elements combining in different ways and degrees in any given institution or movement. Soteriologically speaking, these different minorities have different conceptions. Buddhists try not to participate in *balutedari* duties such as scavenging or in festivals dominated by the higher castes; they are highly politicized and conceive of politics as part of what is meant by Buddhist liberation. They also are, by definition, a scheduled caste, which means that they cannot be analyzed without taking into account this ritual identity. In the case of Indian Muslims, they are de facto defined in caste and subcaste terms, yet simultaneously their identity may be defined in ethnic terms and in Kashmir connected to the soteriological goal of an independent state.

Conclusion

What I would hope to illustrate is that religion is too clumsy as a concept to fine-tune these distinctions. What counts as religion and what counts as nonreligion is fraught with confusions. The fact that "religion" may be used to categorize different minorities in the census does not guarantee that it is a useful analytical category. On the contrary, it may be a contributory cause in the confusion over who deserves rights to reservations or in what sense an identity is shared and in what sense it is not. And it seems to me that Fuller has taken a step backward here. I suggest if one went through his book and took any particular usage of the terms "religion," "religious," "socioreligious," and "religion and society" one could find alternative terms that would render the meaning clearer.

And in fact Fuller himself provides them again and again, most notably the concept of hierarchical complementarity based on the ritual principles of pure–impure. For example, the unclear term "socioreligious" occurs in what is otherwise a lucid discussion of the distinction between substantial and relational deities. Fuller shows that some high vegetarian deities such as Minakshi and Sundareshvara, who are served by Brahman priests, are conceived by the lower castes as dependent on nonvegetarian village deities such as Chellattamman. Such relational dependence of the high on the low symbolizes—at the level of divinity—the hierarchical complementarity of the relations between Brahmans and lower castes. In contrast, the Brahman priests of the Minakshi temple virtually deny any such dependence of the vegetarian god on the meat-eating goddess and—in effect—conceive of the high god as substantial, that is, as self-dependent due to his own inherent qualities. The relationship with the meat-eating goddess is seen by the Brahmans as incidental and unimportant. Implicitly this also constitutes a denial of the complementarity in the relationship between Brahmans and lower castes. By analogy with their vegetarian deity, the Brahmans do not see themselves as being involved in a dependent, complementary relationship with those who are hierarchically inferior to them.

These different perceptions are illustrated by the following description. Once a year the meat-eating village goddess Chellattamman's movable image is brought before the vegetarian god Sundareshvara's central shrine. Brahman priests from the Minakshi temple perform Chellattamman's "coronation." After this annual ritual, the goddess's image is taken back to her temple by her own non-Brahman priests and animal sacrifices are performed to her. From the viewpoint of the devotees of the village goddess, this is an important ritual, a wedding that demonstrates the dependence of the god on the goddess and thus the element of complementarity in the hierarchical relationship between Brahmans and lower castes. But from the point of view of the Brahman priests in the Minakshi temple, this ritual is incidental and contingent and does not have great significance. Fuller says: "Unlike little village deities, great deities such as Minakshi and Sundareshvara, who are worshipped in major temples by Brahmana priests in charge of a completely vegetarian cult, do not symbolize the complementary hierarchical relationships of caste" (1992, 98).

Is this then a context where the term "socioreligious," with its implied distinction between the religious realm, defined in terms of deities, and the social realm of caste relations might become useful? Is the implication here that, though the lower castes view all the gods and goddesses as mutually interdependent and thus as symbolic of the complementarity between high and low castes, the denial of this complementarity by the Brahmans justifies treating the high vegetarian deities as a separate religious realm that is over and above the social relations of caste?

I do not think this is Fuller's intention for several reasons. For one, it makes the sociological analysis arbitrarily dependent on a high-caste theological view rather than a lower-caste view. It would seem highly strained and artificial to assert that, because the Brahmans view their deities as substantial, the word "religious" should be reserved by the anthropologist to describe it. Fuller says: "Thus worship of the village deities, not the great deities, predominantly legitimates in religious terms the caste hierarchy whose summit is occupied by Brahmanas" (99). However, he immediately adds: "In the end, the ritual representations of both categories of deity converge to legitimate Brahmana superiority within caste society" (99). It seems difficult, therefore, to find any sense in which concepts of divinity can be thought of independently of caste relations and thus any useful sense in which we have two distinct spheres, the religious and the social, or a useful distinction between Hinduism as a religion and caste society. Surely, the key term in the homologous relationships is complementary hierarchy, which is fundamentally a ritual relationship. Presumably, this principle can be found at every level of the ritual hierarchy. Indeed, time and again Fuller (1992, 93, 96) shows the reader how the principle of hierarchy and the importance of the distinction between the pure–impure opposition in the structuring of the caste system is constructed and reconstructed through rituals of worship and sacrifice. I cannot see that the term "socioreligious," or the idea of Hinduism as a partly autonomous realm, can be justified by his analysis.

Notes

1. This article is based on a chapter of my recently published book *The Ideology of Religious Studies* (2000). The use of the terms "ritual," "politics," and "soteriology" to stand for the analytical distinctions proposed here was partly prompted by a discussion with Julia Leslie of SOAS, London. Discussions with Eleanor Zelliot and Iwao Shima also led me to make further clarifications. I am grateful to these and other colleagues for their critical comments, though they are not responsible for any part of the argument itself.

2. One legitimate criticism often made of western scholars is that, by uncritically applying English-language or generally western categories to the analysis of nonwestern societies, they invite various orientalist distortions into their representations of the other. Thus, for example, though I sometimes use the term "supernatural," I would not want to convey the impression that the western distinction between nature and supernature is universal or typical for India. The terms "Hinduism" and "religions" are arguably essentializations which produce serious distortions. The problem is how to by-pass "religion" as a major distortion and find a more sensitive way to talk about "Ambedkar Buddhism" which itself needs deconstructing. It might be claimed that some of my own analytical categories, such as soteriology, ritual, economics, and politics, are themselves problematic western concepts, and it is certainly arguable that politics and economics, like "society," emerged as part of modern ideology, just as "ritual" was identified with Catholicism and backwardness. Perhaps there will always be distortion and even misrepresentation in the attempt to construct any research object, and that these distortions and misrepresentations are even more dangerous when applied by members of hegemonic societies to less powerful ones. However, my defense is that the terms I use, defined as I have defined them, do not carry the same degree of ideological baggage as "religion" and its constitutional separation from the secular, and provide a more nuanced way of representing social realities here and there.

BIBLIOGRAPHY

Alavi, H. 1987. "Pakistan and Islam: Ethnicity and Ideology." In *State and Ideology in the Middle East*, ed. H. Alavi and F. Halliday, 65–111. London: Macmillan.

Alper, H. P., ed. 1989. *Understanding Mantras*. Albany: State University of New York Press.

Ambedkar, B. R. 1936. *Annihilation of Caste*. Jalandhar: Bheema Patrika Publications.

—1945. *What Congress and Gandhi Have Done to the Untouchables*. Bombay: Thacker.

Andersen, Walter K., and Sridhar K. Damle. 1987. *The Brotherhood in Saffron: The Rashtriya Swayamsevak Sangh and Hindu Revivalism*. Boulder: Westview Press.

Appadurai, Arjun. 1981. *Worship and Conflict under Colonial Rule: A South Indian Case*. Cambridge: Cambridge University Press.

Appadurai, Carol Breckenridge. 1976. "The Minakshi-Sundaresrarar Temple of Madurai: A History of Mythic Life and Ritual Exchange in South India since 1800." Ph.D. diss. Madison: University of Wisconsin.

Babb, Lawrence A. 1975. *The Divine Hierarchy: Popular Hinduism in Central India*. New York: Columbia University Press.

—1986. *Redemptive Encounters: Three Modern Styles in the Hindu Tradition*. Berkeley: University of California Press.

Bailey, Greg. 1989 "On the De-Construction in Indian Literature: A Tentative Response to Vijay Mishra's Article." *South Asia*, New Series, 12(1) (June): 85-102.

Baird, Robert D. 1971. *Category Formation and the History of Religions*. The Hague: Mouton.

—1993. "On Defining 'Hinduism' as a Religious and Legal Category." In *Religion and Law in Independent India*, ed. Robert D. Baird, 41–58. New Delhi: Manohar.

Balagangadhara, S. N. 1994. *"The Heathen in his Blindness ...": Asia, the West and the Dynamic of Religion*. Leiden: Brill.

Ballard, R. 1992. "New Clothes for the Emperor: The Conceptual Nakedness of the Race Relations Industry in Britain." *New Community* 18(3): 481–92.

Ballard, R., ed. 1994. *Desh Pardesh: The South Asian Presence in Britain*. London: C. Hurst.

Banerjee, A. 1992. "Comparative Curfew: Changing Dimensions of Communal Politics in India." In *Mirrors of Violence: Communities, Riots and Survivors in South Asia*, ed. V. Das, 37–68. Delhi: Oxford University Press.

Banks, M. 1994. "Jain Ways of Being." In *Desh Pardesh: The South Asian Presence in Britain*, ed. R. Ballard, 231–50. London: C. Hurst.

Barot, R. 1987. "Caste and Sect in the Swaminarayan Movement." In *Hinduism in Great Britain: The Perpetuation of Religion in an Alien Milieu*, ed. R. Burghart, 67–80. London: Tavistock.

Barrows, John Henry. 1893. *The World's Parliament of Religions: An Illustrated and Popular Story of the World's First Parliament of Religions*. 2 vols. Chicago: Parliament Publishing Co.

Basham, A. L. 1954. *The Wonder That Was India*. London: Sidgwick and Jackson.

—1975. *The Wonder That Was India*. Calcutta: Rupa and Co.

Basu, T., *et al*. 1993. *Khaki Shorts and Saffron Flags: A Critique of the Hindu Right*. Hyderabad: Orient Longman.

Baumann, G. 1996. *Contesting Culture*. Cambridge: Cambridge University Press.

Bayly, Christopher A. 1985. "The Pre-History of 'Communalism'? Religious Conflict in India, 1700-1860." *Modern Asian Studies* 19(2): 177–203.

—1988. *Indian Society and the Making of the British Empire*. Cambridge History of India. Cambridge: Cambridge University Press.

Bhandarkar, R. G. 1965 [1913]. *Vaisnavism Saivism and Minor Religious Systems*. Varanasi: Indological Book House.

Bhartrhari. 1977. *Bhartriharis* Vakyapadiya. Ed. Wilhelm Rau. Wiesbaden: Deutsche Morgenlandische Gesellschaft.

Bhaskara, Laugaksi. 1934. *The* Arthasamgraha *of Laugaksi Bhaskara*. Ed. A. B. Gajendrakar and R. D. Karmarkar. Bombay: A. B. Gajendragadkar.

Bhattacharyya, Sibajiban. 1990. *Gadadhara's Theory of Objectivity: Visayatavada, Part I*. Delhi: Indian Council of Philosophical Research in association with Motilal Banarsidass.

Bhave, Sadashiv. 1988. "Bhakti in Modern Marathi Poetry." In *The Experience of Hinduism*, ed. Eleanor Zelliot and Maxine Berntsen. Albany: State University of New York Press.

Biardeau, Madeleine. 1991. *Hinduism: The Anthropology of a Civilization*. Delhi: Oxford University Press.

Bowen, D. 1987. "The Evolution of Gujarati Hindu Organisations in Bradford." In *Hinduism in Great Britain: The Perpetuation of Religion in an Alien Milieu*, ed. R. Burghart, 15–31. London: Tavistock.

Burghart, R. 1987. *Hinduism in Great Britain: The Perpetuation of Religion in an Alien Milieu*. London: Tavistock.

Caland, Willem, ed. 1915. *De Open-Deure tot het Verborgen Heydendom door Abraham Rogerius*. Werken Uitgegeven door De Linschoten-Vereeniging, 10. The Hague: Martinus Nijhoff.

—1926. *Ziegenbalg's* Malabarisches Heidenthum. Verhandelingen der Koninklijke Akademie van Wetenschappen te Amsterdam. Afdeeling Leterkunde. Nieuew reeks, 25/3. Amsterdam: Uitgave van Konenklijke Akademie.

Caldwell, Robert. 1881. *A Political and General History of Tinnevelly*. Madras: E. Keys.

Canda Baradai. 1992. *Prithiraja Rasau*. Osnabruck: Biblio Verlag. Photo reprint of the Bibiotheca Indica, Calcutta edition of 1873–1886.

Carey, S. 1987. "The Indianization of the Hare Krishna Movement in Britain." In *Hinduism in Great Britain: The Perpetuation of Religion in an Alien Milieu*, ed. R. Burghart, 81–99. London: Tavistock.

Carmody, Denise Lardner, and T. L. Brink. 2002. *Ways to the Center: An Introduction to World Religions*. 5th ed. Belmont, CA: Wadsworth/Thomson Learning.

Carnall, Geoffrey. 1997. "Robertson and Contemporary Images of India." In *William Robertson and the Expansion of Empire*, ed. Stuart J. Brown, 210–30. Cambridge: Cambridge University Press.

Centre for Contemporary Cultural Studies. 1982. *The Empire Strikes Back*. London: Hutchinson.

Chandra, Bipan. 1984. *Communalism in Modern India*. Delhi: Vani Educational Books.

Chatterjee, Partha. 1986. *Nationalist Thought and the Colonial World: A Derivative Discourse*. Minneapolis: University of Minnesota Press.

Chattopadhyaya, Brajadulal. 1998. *Representing the Other? Sanskrit Sources and the Muslims (Eighth to Fourteenth Century)*. Delhi: Manohar.

Chattopadhyaya, Sudhakar. 1970. *Evolution of Hindu Sects up to the Time of Samkaracarya*. New Delhi: Munshiram Manoharlal.

Bibliography

Civis. 1818. "Letter to the Editor." *The Asiatic Journal and Monthly Register* 5 (Jan.–June): 105–8.

Crawfurd, John. 1820. "On the Existence of the Hindu Religion in the Island of Bali." *Asiatick Researches* 13: 128–70.

Dalmia, Vasudha. 1995. "The Only Real Religion of the Hindus: Vaisnava Self-Representations in the Late Nineteenth Century." In *Representing Hinduism: The Construction of Religious Traditions and National Identity*, ed. Vasudha Dalmia and Heinrich von Stietencron, 176–210. London: Sage.

Dalmia, Vasudha, and Heinrich von Stietencron, eds. 1995. *Representing Hinduism: The Construction of Religious Traditions and National Identity*. London: Sage.

Das, Veena. 1990. "Introduction: Communities, Riots, Survivors—The South Asian Experience." In *Mirrors of Violence: Communities, Riots and Survivors*, ed. Veena Das, 1–36. Delhi: Oxford University Press.

Dass, Nirmal. 1991. *Songs of Kabir from the Adi Granth*. Albany: State University of New York Press.

De Bary, William T., *et al.*, eds. 1958. *Sources of Indian Tradition*. New York: Columbia University Press.

Dharampal-Frick, Gita. 1994. *Indien im Spiegel deutscher Quellen der Fruhen Neuzeit (1500-1750). Studien zu einer interkulturellen Konstellation*. Fruhen Neuzeit, 18. Tübingen: Niemeyer.

—1995. "Shifting Categories in the Discourse on Caste: Some Historical Observations." In *Representing Hinduism: The Construction of Religious Traditions and National Identity*, ed. Vasudha Dalmia and Heinrich von Stietencron, 82–98. London: Sage.

Dhavamony, Mariasurai. 1971. *Love of God according to Saiva Siddanta*. Oxford: Oxford University Press.

Dirks, Nicholas. 1989. "The Invention of Caste: Civil Society in Colonial India." *Social Analysis 5*.

—1992. *Colonialism and Culture*. Ann Arbor: University of Michigan Press.

Dirks, R. 1996. "Recasting Tamil Society: The Politics of Caste and Race." In *Caste Today*, ed. C. Fuller, 263–95. Delhi: Oxford University Press.

Doniger, Wendy. 1991. "Hinduism by Any Other Name." *Wilson Quarterly* 15(3): 35–37, 40–41.

Duara, Prasenjit. 1991. "The New Politics of Hinduism." *Wilson Quarterly* 15(3): 42–45, 47–50.

Dube, Saurabh. 1998. *Untouchable Pasts: Religion, Identity, and Power among a Central Indian Community, 1780-1950*. Albany: State University of New York Press.

Duff, Alexander. 1988 [1839]. *India and India Missions: Including Sketches of the Gigantic System of Hinduism Both in Theory and Practice*. Delhi: Swati Publications.

Dumont, Louis. 1980. *Homo Hierarchicus: The Caste System and Its Implications*. Chicago: University of Chicago Press.

Durkheim, E. 1915. *Elementary Forms of the Religious Life*. Trans. Joseph Ward Swaine. New York: Free Press.

Dwyer, R. 1994. "Caste, Religion and Sect in Gujarat: Followers of Vallabhacharya and Swaminarayan." In *Desh Pardesh: The South Asian Presence in Britain*, ed. R. Ballard, 165–90. London: C. Hurst.

Eaton, Richard M. 1996. *The Rise of Islam and the Bengal Frontier, 1204-1760*. Berkeley: University of California Press.

—1998. "(Re)imag(in)ing Otherness: A Postmortem for the Postmodern in India." Unpublished essay.

Eck, Diana. 1983. *Banaras: City of Light*. London: Routledge and Kegan Paul.

Edney, Matthew. 1997. *Mapping an Empire: The Geographical Construction of British India, 1765-1843*. Chicago: University of Chicago Press.

Eliot, Charles. 1954 [1921]. *Hinduism and Buddhism: An Historical Sketch*. 3 vols. New York: Barnes and Noble.

Ellwood, Robert S., and Barbara A. McGraw. 1999. *Many Peoples, Many Faiths: Women and Men in the World Religions*. Upper Saddle River, NJ: Prentice Hall.

Embree, Ainslie T. 1962. *Charles Grant and British Rule in India*. New York: Columbia University Press.

—1990. *Utopias in Conflict: Religion and Nationalism in Modern India*. Berkeley: University of California Press.

Erndl, Kathleen. 1993. *Victory to the Mother: The Hindu Goddess of North India in Myth, Ritual, and Symbol*. New York and Oxford: Oxford University Press.

Ernst, Carl W. 1992. *Eternal Garden: Mysticism, History, and Politics at a South Asian Sufi Center*. Albany: State University of New York Press.

Fellows, Ward J. 1998. *Religions East and West*. Fort Worth: Harcourt Brace College Publishers.

Fernandes Trancoso, Goncalo. 1973. *Tratado do Pe. Goncalo Fernandes Trancoso sobre o Hinduismo (Madure 1616)*. Ed. Jose Wicki. Lisbon: Centre de Estudos Historicos Ultra-marinos.

Ferro-Luzzi, Gabriella Eichinger. 1989. "The Polythetic-Prototype Approach to Hinduism." In *Hinduism Reconsidered*, ed. G. D. Sontheimer and H. Kulke, 187–95. Delhi: Manohar.

Fisher, Mary Pat. 2002. *Living Religions*. 5th ed. Upper Saddle River, NJ: Prentice-Hall.

Fitzgerald, Timothy. 1990. "Hinduism and the 'World Religion' Fallacy." *Religion* 20: 108–18.

—1996. "From Structure to Substance: Ambedkar, Dumont and Buddhism." *Contributions to Indian Sociology* n.s. 30(2): 273–88.

—1997a. "A Critique of 'Religion' as a Cross-Cultural Category." *Method and Theory in the Study of Religion* 9(2): 91–110.

—1997b. "Ambedkar Buddhism in Maharashtra." *Contributions to Indian Sociology* n.s. 31(2): 226–51.

—2000. *The Ideology of Religious Studies*. New York: Oxford University Press.

Franco, Eli, and Karin Preisendanz, eds. 1997. *Beyond Orientalism: The Work of Wilhelm Halbfass and Its Impact on Indian and Cross-Cultural Studies*. Amsterdam: Rodopi.

Frawley, D. 1995. *Arise Arjuna: Hinduism and the Modern World*. New Delhi: Voice of India.

Frietag, S. B. 1989. *Collective Action and Community: Public Arenas and the Emergence of Communalism in North India*. Berkeley: University of California.

Frykenberg, Robert. 1977. "The Silent Settlement." In *Land Tenure and Peasant in South Asia*, ed. Robert Frykenberg, 37–53. New Delhi: Orient Longman.

—1979. "Conversion and Crises of Conscience under Company Raj in South India." In *Asie du Sud, Traditions et changements*, ed. Marc Gaborieau and Alice Thorner, 311–21. Paris: Centre national de la recherche scientifique.

—1982. "On Roads and Riots in Tinnevelly: Radical Change and Ideology in Madras Presidency During the Nineteenth Century." *South Asia* 4: 34–52.

—1986. "New Light on the Vellore Mutiny." In *East India Company Studies: Papers Presented to Professor Sir Cyril Philips*, ed. Kenneth Ballhatchet and John Harrison, 207–31. Hong Kong: Asian Research Service.

—1987. "The Concept of 'Majority' as a Devilish Force in the Politics of Modern India: A Historiographic Comment." *Journal of the Commonwealth History and Comparative Politics* 25(3): 267–74.

—1989. "The Emergence of Modern 'Hinduism' as a Concept and as an Institution: A Reappraisal with Special Reference to South India." In *Hinduism Reconsidered*, ed. G. D. Sontheimer and H. Kulke, 29–49. Delhi: Manohar.

—1991. Review of Gauri Viswanath, *Masks of Conquest: Literary Study and British Rule in India. American History Review* 97: 272–73.

—1993a. "Constructions of Hinduism at the Nexus of History and Religion." *Journal of Interdisciplinary History* 23(3): 523–50.

—1993b. "Hindu Fundamentalism and the Structural Stability of India." In *Fundamentalisms and the State: Remaking Polities, and Militance*, ed. Martin E. Marty and R. Scott Appleby, 233–55. Chicago: University of Chicago Press.

—1994. "Fundamentalisms in South Asia: Ideologies and Institutions in Historical Perspective." In *Accounting for Fundamentalisms: The Dynamic Character of Movements*, ed. Martin E. Marty and R. Scott Appleby, 589–614. Chicago: University of Chicago Press.

—1996. *History and Belief: The Foundations of Historical Understanding*. Grand Rapids: Eerdmans.

—1997. "The Emergence of Modern 'Hinduism' as a Concept and an Institution: A Reappraisal with Special Reference to South India." In *Hinduism Reconsidered*, ed. Gunther-Dietz Sontheimer and Hermann Kulke, 82–107. New Delhi: Manohar.

Frykenberg, Robert, ed. 2003. *Christians and Missionaries in India: Cross-Cultural Communication since 1500*. London: RoutledgeCurzon.

Frykenberg, Robert, and Judith M. Brown, eds. 2002. *Christians, Cultural Interactions and India's Religious Traditions*. London: RoutledgeCurzon.

Fuller, C. J. 1992. *The Camphor Flame: Popular Hinduism and Society in India*. Princeton: Princeton University Press.

Gaeffke, Peter. 1977. "Muslims in the Hindi Literature." In *Beitrage zur Indianforschung*, vol. 4, 119–26. Berlin: Museum fur Indische Kunst.

Gandhi, M. K. 1936. "A Vindication of Caste." In *Annihilation of Caste*, ed. B. R. Ambedkar, 134–42. Jalandhar: Bheema Patrika Publications. First published in *The Harijan*, July 11, 18, and August 15, 1936.

Gaur, Albertine. 1967. "Bartholomaus Ziegenbalg's *Verzeichnis der Malabarischen Bucher [1708]*." *Journal of the Royal Asiatic Society for 1967*: 63–95.

Geertz, C. 1973. *The Interpretation of Cultures*. New York: Basic Books.

Germann, Wilhelm, ed. 1867. *Genealogie der Malabarishen [sic] Gotter: Aus eigenen Schriften und Briefen der au der zusammengetragen und verfasst von Bartholomaeus Ziegenbalg, weil. Propst an der Jerusamels-Kirche in Trankebar*. Madras: Printed for the Editor at the Christian Knowledge Society's Press.

Gethin, R. 1986. "The Five Khandas: Their Treatment in the Nikayas and Early Abhidhamma." *Journal of Indian Philosophy* 14: 37–39.

Gold, Daniel. 1991. "Organized Hinduisms: From Vedic Truth to Hindu Nation." In *Fundamentalisms Observed*, ed. Martin E. Marty and R. Scott Appleby, 531–93. Chicago: University of Chicago Press.

Golwalkar, M. S. 1939. *We or Our Nationhood Defined*. Nagpur: Bharat.

Gonda, Jan. 1963. *Der jungere Hinduismus*. Volume 2 of *Die Religionen Indiens*. Stuttgart: W. Kohlhammer.

Gopal, Sarvepalli. 1989. *Radhakrishnan*. New Delhi: Oxford University Press.

Gore, M. S. 1993. *The Social Context of an Ideology: Ambedkar's Political and Social Thought*. New Delhi: Sage Publications.

Grant, Charles. 1970. *Observations of the State of Society among the Asiatic Subjects of Great Britain particularly with respect to Morals; and on the means of improving it. — written chiefly in the Year 1792*. In volume 5 (*Colonies: East India*, pp. 3–92) of *Irish University Press Series of British Parliamentary Papers*. Shannon: Irish University Press.

Grant's work was first published in 1797 and then republished in *Parliamentary Papers 1812-13* and in *Parliamentary Papers 1831-32.*

Great Britain 1827. *Parliamentary Proceedings.* "Sacred Petition of Calcutta (1827)."

Great Britain. 1846. *Parliamentary Proceedings.* "Proceedings at the Public Meetings of the Hindu Community, Held in the Rooms of Patcheapah's Institution, On Wednesday, 7 Oct. 1846."

Guna. 1984. *Asiatic Mode: A Socio-Cultural Perspective.* Delhi: Bookwell Publications.

Hacker, Paul, 1978a. "Aspects of Neo-Hinduism as Contrasted with Surviving Traditional Hinduism." In *Kleine Schriften*, ed. Lambert Schmithausen, 580–607. Wiesbaden: Steiner.

—1978b. *Kleine Schriften*, ed. Lambert Schmithausen. Wiesbaden: Steiner.

Halbfass, Wilhelm. 1988. *India and Europe: An Essay in Understanding.* Albany: State University of New York Press.

—1991. *Tradition and Reflection: Explorations in Indian Thought.* Albany: State University of New York Press.

—1992. *On Being and What There Is: Classical Vaisesika and the History of Indian Ontology.* Albany: State University of New York Press.

Hall, S. 1996. "Introduction: Who Needs Identity?" In *Cultural Identity*, ed. S. Hall and P. du Gay, 1–17. London: Sage.

Hardy, Peter. 1972. *The Muslims of British India.* Cambridge: Cambridge University Press.

Harper, Susan Billington. 1991. "Azariah and Indian Christianity in the Late Years of the Raj." D.Phil. thesis. Oxford: University of Oxford.

Hawley, John Stratton. 1991. "Naming Hinduism." *Wilson Quarterly* 15(3): 20–34.

Heesterman, J. C. 1974. "Die Autoritat des Veda." In *Offenbarung, geistige Realitat des Menschen: Arbeitsdokumentation eines Symposiums zum Offenbarungsbegriff in Indien*, ed. Gerhard Oberhammer, 29–40. Vienna: Indologisches Institut der Universitat Wien.

Hess, Linda, and Shukdev Singh. 1983. *The Bijak of Kabir.* San Francisco: North Point Press.

Hiltebeitel, Alf. 1991. "Of Camphor and Coconuts." *Wilson Quarterly* 15(3): 26–28.

Hinnells, John, and Eric Sharpe, eds. 1971. *Hinduism.* London: Routledge Kegan Paul.

Hopfe, Lewis M. 2001. *Religions of the World.* Rev. Mark R. Woodward. 8th ed. Upper Saddle River, NJ: Prentice-Hall.

Hopkins, Thomas J. 1971. *The Hindu Religious Tradition.* Encino, CA: Dickenson Publishing Co.

Imam, Z. 1975. *Muslims in India.* Bombay: Orient Longman.

Inden, Ronald. 1986. "Orientalist Constructions of India." *Modern Asian Studies* 20: 401–46.

—1990. *Imagining India.* Oxford: Blackwell.

Irschick, Eugene F. 1994. *Dialogue and History: Constructing South India, 1795-1895.* Berkeley: University of California Press.

Isaacs, Harold R. 1965. *India's Ex-Untouchables.* New York: John Day Co.

'Isami, 'Abd al-Malik. 1967–1977. *Futuhu's salatin: Or, Shah namah-I Hind.* Trans. Agha Mahdi Husain. 3 vols. Bombay: Asia Publishing House.

Jackson, R., and E. Nesbitt. 1993. *Hindu Children in Britain.* Stoke on Trent: Trentham Books.

Jaffrelot, Christophe. 1993. "Hindu Nationalism: Strategic Syncretism in Ideology Building." *Economic and Political Weekly*, March 20–27: 517–24.

Joshi, L. S. 1948 [1940]. *A Critique of Hinduism.* Trans. G. D. Parikh. Bombay: Modern Age Publications.

Kabir. 1982. *Kabir-bijak.* Ed. Gangasarana Sastri. Introduction Sukadev Simha. Varanasi: Kabiravani Prakasan Kendra.

Kadam, K. N. 1988. "The Birth of a Rationalist." In *The Experience of Hinduism: Essays on Religion in Maharashtra*, ed. E. Zelliot and M. Berntsen, 280–90. Albany: State University of New York Press.

Bibliography

Karn, V. 1997. *Ethnicity in the 1991 Census*. Vol. 4. London: HMSO.

Kaye, John. 1859. *Christianity in India: An Historical Narrative*. London: Smith, Elder.

Ketkar, S. V. 1988 [1911]. *Hinduism: Its Formation and Future*. Delhi: Caxton.

Khan, Paunchkouree. 1848. *The Revelations of an Orderly*. Benares: Recorder Press.

Killingley, Dermot. 1993. *Rammohun Roy in Hindu and Christian Tradition: The Teape Lectures 1990*. Newcastle upon Tyne: Grevatt and Grevatt.

King, Christopher. 1974. "The Nagari Pracharini Sabha (Society for the Promotion of the Nagari Language and Script) of Benares, 1893-1950: A Study in the Social and Political History of the Hindi Language." Unpublished paper. Madison: University of Wisconsin.

King, Richard. 1999. *Orientalism and Religion: Postcolonial Theory, India and "the Mystic East."* London: Routledge.

Klostermaier, Klaus K. 1994. *A Survey of Hinduism*. 2nd ed. Albany: State University of New York Press.

—1998. *A Short Introduction to Hinduism*. Oxford: One World Publications.

Knott, K. 1986. *Hinduism in Leeds*. Leeds: University of Leeds.

—1987. "Hindu Temple Rituals in Britain: The Reinterpretation of Tradition." In *Hinduism in Great Britain: The Perpetuation of Religion in an Alien Milieu*, ed. R. Burghart, 157–79. London: Tavistock.

—1994. "The Gujarati Mochis in Leeds: From Leather Stockings to Surgical Boots and Beyond." In *Desh Pardesh: The South Asian Presence in Britain*, ed. R. Ballard, 213–30. London: C. Hurst.

Krishnamurti, J. 1978. *The Wholeness of Life*. London: Victor Gollancz.

Kulke, Herman. 1985. "Maharajas, Mahants, and Historians: Reflections on the Historiography of Early Vijayanagar and Sringeri." In *Vijayanagara—City and Empire: New Currents in Research*, ed. Ann Libera Dallapiccola with S. Zingel-Ave. Lallemant, 120–43. Stuttgart: Steiner.

Küng, H., and H. von Stietencron. 1987. *Christentum und Weltreligionen II: Hinduismus*. Gütersloh: Gütersloher Verlagshaus Mohn.

Lach, Donald F. 1965. *Asia in the Making of Europe*. Vol. 1, in two parts. Chicago: University of Chicago Press.

Laine, J. 1983. "The Notion of 'Scripture' in Modern Indian Thought." *Annals of the Bhandarkar Oriental Research Institute* 64: 165–79.

Larson, Gerald J. 1995. *India's Agony over Religion*. Albany: State University of New York Press.

Laws of Manu. 1991. Wendy Doniger, with Brian K. Smith, trans. London: Penguin.

Lelyveld, David. 1978. *Aligarh's First Generation*. Princeton: Princeton University Press.

Lévi-Strauss, Claude. 1972 [1963]. "The Bear and the Barber." In *Reader in Comparative Religion: An Anthropological Approach*, ed. William A. Lessa and Evon Z. Vogt, 181–89. New York: Harper & Row.

Liebau, Kurt, ed. 1998. *Malabarische Korrespondenz. Tamilische Briefe an deutsche missionare*. Sigmaringen: J. Thorbecke.

Lieten, G. K. 1994. "On Casteism and Communalism in Uttar Pradesh." *Economic and Political Weekly* 29(14): 777–81.

Lincoln, Bruce. 1996. "Theses on Method." *Method and Theory in the Study of Religion* 8(3): 225–27.

Lipner, Julius J. 1986. *The Face of Truth: A Study of Meaning and Metaphysics in the Vedantic Theology of Ramanuja*. London: Macmillan and the State University of New York Press.

—1989. "Religion and Religions." In *Radhakrishnan: Centenary Volume*, ed. G. Parthasarathi and D. P. Chattopadhyaya. Delhi: Oxford University Press.

—1992. "On 'Hindutva' and a 'Hindu-Catholic,' with a Moral for Our Times." *Hindu-Christian Studies Bulletin* 5: 7.

—1993. "Seeking Others in Their Otherness." *New Blackfriars*, March: 152–65.

—1994. *Hindus: Their Religious Beliefs and Practices*. London: Routledge.

—1996. "Ancient Banyan: An Inquiry into the Meaning of 'Hinduness.'" *Religious Studies* 32: 109–26.

—1999. *Brahmabandhab Upadhyay: The Thought of a Revolutionary*. Delhi: Oxford University Press.

Lipner, Julius J., ed. 1997. *The Fruits of Our Desiring: An Enquiry into the Ethics of the* Bhagavadgita *for Our Times*. Calgary: Bayeux Arts.

Llewellyn, J. E. 1996. "Hindu Fundamentalism: The Once and Future Oxymoron." *Critical Review of Books in Religion* 9: 83–104.

—2002. "(Foot)Notes on *Orientalism and Religion*." *Method and Theory in the Study of Religion* 14(2): 234–48.

Lochtefeld, James G. 1996. "New Wine, Old Skins: The Sangh Parivar and the Transformation of Hinduism." *Religion* 26(2): 101–17.

Lord, Henry. 1630. *A Discoverie of the Sect of the Banians. Containing their History, Law, Liturgie, Casts, Customs, and Ceremonies. Gathered from their Brahmanes, Teachers of that Sect: As the particulars were comprized in the Booke of their Law, called the Shaster: Together with a display of their Manners, both in times past, and at this present*. Also in the same volume, *The Religion of the Persees. As it was Compiled from a Booke of theirs, contayning the Forme of their Worshippe, written in the Persian Character, and by them called their Zunduvaslaw. Wherin is shewed the Superstitious Ceremonies used amongst them. More especially their Idolatrous worshippe of Fire*. London: Printed by T. and R. Cotes, for Fra. Constable. Copy in the Houghton Library, Harvard. Paged [A] 1–14, [B] 1–95 (text 1), and [C] 1–10, [D] 1–53 (text 2).

Lorenzen, David N. 1972. *The Kapalikas and Kalamukhas: Two Lost Saivite Sects*. Berkeley: University of California Press. Second edition with two new appendices. Delhi: Motilal Banarsidass, 1991.

—1991. *Kabir Legends and Ananta-das's* Kabir Parachai. Albany: State University of New York Press.

—1995. "The Historical Vicissitudes of Bhakti Religion." In *Bhakti Religion in North India: Community Identity and Political Action*, ed. David N. Lorenzen, 1–32. Albany: State University of New York Press.

—1996. *Praises to a Formless God: Nirguni Texts from North India*. Albany: State University of New York Press.

—1999. "Who Invented Hinduism?" *Comparative Studies in Society and History* 41: 630–59.

—2003. "Europeans in Late Mughal South Asia: The Perceptions of Italian Missionaries." *Indian Economic and Social History Review* 40(1): 1–31.

Lorenzen, David N., ed. 1995. *Bhakti Religion in North India: Community Identity and Political Action*. Albany: State University of New York Press.

Lorenzen, David N., and Benjamin Preciado Solis. 1996. *Atadura y liberacion: las religiones de la India*. Mexico: El Colegio de Mexico.

Lutgendorf, Philip. 1997. "Imagining Ayodhya: Utopia and Its Shadows in a Hindu Landscape." *International Journal of Hindu Studies* 1(1): 19–54.

Lutyens, M. 1988. *The Open Door*. London: John Murray.

Malamoud, Ch. 1977. *Le Svadhyaya*. Paris: Institut de civilisation indienne.

Manrique, Sebastiao. 1649. *Itinerario de las missiones que hizo el padre F. Sebastian Manrique*. Rome: Francisco Caballo. A new edition by Luis Silveira was published in Lisbon in 1946. An English translation was published by the Hakluyt Society, Oxford, in 1927.

Manu. 1972–1985. *Manusmrti*. Ed. J. H. Dave. 6 vols. Bombay: Bharatiya Vidya Bhavan.

Bibliography

Marco della Tomba. 1878. *Gli Scritii del Padre Marco della Tomba: Missionario nelle Indie Orientali*. Ed. Angelo de Gubernatis. Florence: Le Monnier.

Marriot, McKim. 1989. "Constructing an Indian Ethnosociology." *Contributions to Indian Sociology*, n.s., 23(1): 1–39.

Marshall, Peter J., ed. 1970. *The British Discovery of Hinduism in the Eighteenth Century*. Cambridge: Cambridge University Press.

Marshall, Peter J., and Glyndwr Williams. 1982. *The Great Map of Mankind*. Cambridge: Harvard University Press.

Matilal, B. K. 1985. *Logic, Language and Reality: An Introduction to Indian Philosophical Studies*. Delhi: Motilal Banarsidass.

—1989. "Dharma and Rationality." In *Rationality in Question: On Eastern and Western Views of Rationality*, ed. S. Biderman and B.-A. Scharfstein. Leiden: E. J. Brill.

Matthews, Warren. 1999. *World Religions*. 3rd ed. Belmont, CA: Wadsworth Publishing.

McCutcheon, Russell T. 1997. *Manufacturing Religion: The Discourse of Sui Generis Religion and the Politics of Nostalgia*. Oxford: Oxford University Press.

McLeod, Hew. 1995. "Caste (Sikh)." In *A New Dictionary of Religions*, ed. John R. Hinnells, 93. Oxford: Blackwell.

Metcalf, Barbara. 1982. *Islamic Revival in British India*. Princeton: Princeton University Press.

Metcalf, H., T. Modood, and S. Virdee. 1996. *Asian Self-Employment*. London: Policy Studies Institute.

Michaelson, M. 1987. "Domestic Hinduism in a Gujarati Trading Caste." In *Hinduism in Great Britain: The Perpetuation of Religion in an Alien Milieu*, ed. R. Burghart, 32–49. London: Tavistock.

Mines, M. 1981. "Islamic and Muslim Ethnicity in South Asia." In *Ritual and Religion among Muslims in India*, ed. I. Ahmad. Delhi: Manohar.

Modood, T. 1992. *Not Easy Being British: Colour, Culture and Citizenship*. Stoke on Trent: Runnymede Trust and Trentham Books.

Mohanty, J. N. 1992. *Reason and Tradition in Indian Thought: An Essay on the Nature of Indian Philosophical Thinking*. Oxford: Clarendon Press.

Monier-Williams, Monier. 1877. *Hinduism*. London: Society for Promoting Christian Knowledge.

—1889. *Buddhism in Its Connexion with Brahmanism and Hinduism and Its Contrast with Christianity*. London: J. Murray.

—1993 [1877]. *Hinduism: Hinduism and Its Sources*. New Delhi: Orientalist. Photo-reprint, probably of 1919 edition.

Morris, Henry. 1904. *The Life of Charles Grant*. London: Murray.

Mudaliar, Chandra Y. 1974. *The Secular State and Religious Institutions in India: A Study of the Administration of Hindu Public Trusts in Madras*. Wiesbaden: Steiner.

Muir, J. 1976. *Original Sanskrit Texts on the Origin and History of the People of India*. Reprint of the 1870–1874 revised edition. New Delhi: Oriental Publishers.

Mujahid, Abdul Malik. 1989. *Conversion to Islam: Untouchables' Strategy for Protest in India*. Chambersburg, PA: Anima Books.

Murr, S. 1983. "Les conditions d'emergence due discour sur l'Inde au Siecle des Lumieres." *Purusartha* 7: 233–84.

Murr, S., ed. 1987. *L'Inde philosophique entre Bousset et Voltaire*. Vol. 1: *Moeurs et coutumes des Indiens (1777)*. Vol 2: *L'indologie du Pere Courdoux*. Paris: Ecole francaise d'Extreme Orient.

Nandy, Ashis. 1983. *The Intimate Enemy: Loss and Recovery of Self under Colonialism*. Delhi: Oxford University Press.

Nardella, Umberto. 1989. "La conoscenza dell'Hindi e Urdu in Italia nei secoli XVIII eXIX." In *La conoscema dell'Asia e dell'Africa in ltalia nei secoli XVIII e XIX*, ed. Aldo Gallotta and Ugo Marazzi. Vol. 3, tome I. Naples: Istituto Universitario Orientale.

Neill, Stephen. 1984. *A History of Christianity in India: The Beginnings to A.D. 1707*. Cambridge: Cambridge University Press.

Nesbitt, E. 1994. "Valmikis in Coventry: The Revival and Reconstruction of a Community." In *Desh Pardesh: The South Asian Presence in Britain*, ed. R. Ballard, 117–41. London: C. Hurst.

Neufeldt, R. 1980. *F. Max Muller and the Rg-Veda*. Calcutta: Minerva Associates Publications.

Neusner, Jacob. 1983. "Alike and Not Alike: A Grid for Comparison and Differentiation." In *Take Judaism, for Example*, ed. Jacob Neusner, 227–35. Chicago: University of Chicago Press.

—1995. "Is There a Theology of Rabbinic Judaism?" *Temenos* 31: 239–51.

Nigosian, S. A. 2000. *World Religions: A Historical Approach*. 3rd ed. Boston: Bedford/St. Martin's.

Norton, George. 1848. *Native Education in India*. Madras: Pharoah and Co.

Nowikowski, S., and R. Ward. 1979. "Middle-Class South Asians in Manchester." *New Community* 7(1).

Nye, M. 1993. "Temple Constructions and Communities: Hindu Constructions in Edinburgh." *New Communities* 19(2): 201–208.

—1995. *A Place for Our Gods: The Construction of an Edinburgh Temple Community*. Richmond, Surrey: Curzon Books.

Oberhammer, G. 1974. "Die Uberlieferungsautoritat im Hinduismus." In *Offenbarung, geistige Realitat des Menschen. Arbeitsdokumentation eines Symposiums zum Offenbarungsbegriff in Indien*, ed. Gerhard Oberhammer, 41–92. Vienna: Indologisches Institut der Universitat Wien.

Oberoi, Harjot S. 1994. *The Construction of Religious Boundaries: Culture, Identity, and Diversity in the Sikh Tradition*. Chicago: University of Chicago Press.

O'Connell, Joseph. 1973. "The Word 'Hindu' in Gaudiya Vaisnava Texts." *Journal of the American Oriental Society* 93: 340–44.

Oertel, H. 1930. *Zur indischen Apologetik*. Stuttgart: W. Kohlhammer.

O'Flaherty, W. D. 1973. *Asceticism and Eroticism in the Mythology of Siva*. Oxford: Oxford University Press.

Oman, John Campbell. 1903. *The Mystics, Ascetics, and Saints of India: A Study of Sadhuism, with an Account of the Yogis, Sanyasis, Bairagis, and Other Strange Hindu Sectarians*. London: T. F. Unwin.

Omvedt, Gail. 1976. *Cultural Revolt in a Colonial Society: The Non Brahman Movement in Western India, 1873 to 1930*. Bombay: Scientific Socialist Education Trust.

—1980. *We Will Smash This Prison: Indian Women in Struggle*. London: Zed.

—1991. *Violence Against Women: New Theories and New Movements in India*. Delhi: Kali for Women.

—1993. *Reiventing Revolution: New Social Movements and the Socialist Tradition in India*. Armonk, NY: M. E. Sharpe.

—1994. *Dalits and the Democratic Revolution*. Delhi: Sage India.

—1995. *Dalit Visions: The Anti-Caste Movement and the Construction of an Indian Identity*. Hyderabad: Orient Longman.

Orwell, George. 1991. "Reflections on Gandhi." In *The Oxford Book of Essays*, ed. John Gross, 501–9. Oxford: Oxford University Press.

Pandey, Gyanendra. 1990. *The Construction of Communalism in Colonial North India*. Delhi: Oxford University Press.

—1992. *The Construction of Communalism in Colonial North India*. Delhi: Oxford University Press.

Bibliography

Parpola, A. 1981. "On the Meaning and Etymology of the Sacred Syllable *Om.*" *Studia Orientalia* 50: 195–213.

Patterson, O. 1974. "Context and Choice in Ethnic Allegiance." In *Ethnicity and Experience*, ed. N. Glazer and D. Moynihan, 305–49. Cambridge, MA: Harvard University Press.

Petech, Luciano, ed. 1952–1956. *I Missionari Italiani nel Tibet e nel Nepal*. 7 vols. Il Nuovo Ramusio, 2. Rome: La Libreria dello Stato.

Pollock, Sheldon. 1993a. "Deep Orientalism? Notes on Sanskrit and Power beyond the Raj." In *Orientalism and the Poscolonial Predicament*, ed. Carol A. Breckinridge and Peter van der Veer, 76–133. Philadelphia: University of Pennsylvania Press.

—1993b. "Ramayana and Political Imagination in India." *Journal of Asian Studies* 52(2): 261–97.

Presler, Franklin A. 1987. *Religion under Bureaucracy: Policy and Administration for Hindu Temples in South India*. Cambridge: Cambridge University Press.

Prinja, N. K. 1996. *Hindu Dharma: A Guide for Teachers*. Norwich: Religious and Moral Education Press for Vishwa Hindu Parishad.

Radcliffe-Brown, A. R. 1952. *Structure and Function in Primitive Society*. London: Cohen and West.

Radhakrishnan, Sarvepalli. 1968 [1927]. *The Hindu View of Life*. London: George Allen and Unwin.

Radhakrishnan, Sarvepalli, and Charles A. Moore, eds. 1957. *A Sourcebook of Indian Philosophy*. Princeton: Princeton University Press.

Raheja, G. G. 1988. "India: Caste, Kingship, and Dominance Reconsidered." *Annual Review of Anthropology* 17: 497–523.

Rajamanickam, S. 1972a. *The First Oriental Scholar*. Tirunelveli: De Nobili Research Institute, St. Xavier's College.

Rajamanickam, S., ed. 1971. *Adaptation (Narratio Fundamentorum quibis Madurensis Missionis Institutum caeptum est et hueusque consisit, 1619)*. Trans. J. Pujo. Palayamkottai: De Nobili Research Institute.

Rajamanickam, S., ed. 1972b. *Roberto de Nobili on Indian Customs (Informatio de quibusdam moribus nationis indicae, 1613)*. Trans. Peter Leonard. Palayamkottai: De Nobili Research Institute.

Rajarama, N. S., and D. Frawley. 1995. *Vedic Aryans and the Origins of Civilization*. St. Hyacinthe, Quebec: World Heritage Press.

Rajshekar, V. T. 1987. *Dalit: The Black Untouchables of India*. Atlanta: Clarity Press.

Ram-Prasad, C. 1993. "Hindutva Ideology: Extracting the Fundamentals." *Contemporary South Asia* 2(3): 285–309.

Ratcliffe, P. 1996. *Ethnicity in the 1991 Census*. Vol. 3. London: HMSO.

Rattansi, A. 1994. "Introduction." In *Racism, Modernity and Identity*, ed. A. Rattansi and S. Westwood. Cambridge: Polity.

Renou, Louis. 1960. *Le destin du Veda dans l'Inde*. Etudes vediques et panineennes, 6. Paris: E. De Boccard.

—1965 [1960]. *The Destiny of the Veda in India*. Trans. Dev Raj Channa. Delhi: Motilal Banarsidass.

Richards, Glyn. 1988. "Modern Hinduism." In *The World's Religions*, ed. Stewart Sunderland, *et al.*, 705–13. London: Routledge.

Robertson, William. 1791. *An Historical Disquisition concerning the Knowledge which the Ancients had of India*. London: Strahan and Cadell.

Rogers, John D. 1994. "Post-Orientalism and the Interpretation of Premodern and Modern Political Identities: The Case of Sri Lanka." *Journal of Asian Studies* 53(1): 10–23.

Rosel, J. 1982. *Die Hinduismusthese Max Webers*. Münich: Weltforum.

Ross, Alexander. 1696 [1653]. *Pansebeia: or, A View of All Religions in the World ... The Sixth Edition, Enlarged and Perfected by Alexander Ross.* London: Printed for M. Gillyflower and W. Freeman.

Roy, Rammohun. 1978. *The English Works of Raja Rammohun Roy with an English Translation of "Tuhfatul Muwahhidin."* New York: AMS Press. Reprint of the 1906 edition.

Rudolph, Lloyd I., and Susanne Hoeber Rudolph. 1967. *The Modernity of Tradition.* Chicago: University of Chicago Press.

—1987. *In Pursuit of Lakshmi: The Political Economy of the Indian State.* Chicago: University of Chicago Press.

Russell, Jeffrey. 1991. "Inventing the Flat Earth." *History Today* 41: 13–19.

Said, Edward. 1978. *Orientalism.* New York: Pantheon Books.

—1979. *Orientalism.* New York: Vintage Books.

—1991. *Orientalism.* Harmondsworth: Penguin.

Sangharaksita. 1957. *A Survey of Buddhism.* Boulder, CO: Shambala.

—1986. *Ambedkar and Buddhism.* Glasgow: Windhorse.

—1988. *The History of My Going for Refuge.* Glasgow: Windhorse.

Savarkar. V. D. 1942 [1922]. *Hindutva.* Poona: S. R. Date.

—1989. *Savarkar Commemoration Volume.* Bombay: Savarkar Darshun Pratishthan.

Schmitlhenwer, Peter. 1991. "Charles Philip Brown: The Legacy of an East India Company Servant and Scholar of South India." Ph.D. diss. Madison: University of Wisconsin.

Searle-Chatterjee, M. 1981. *Reversible Sex Roles: The Special Case of Benares Sweepers.* Oxford: Pergamon.

—1990. "The Muslim Hero as Defender of Hindus: Myth Reversals and Ethnicity among Benares Muslims." In *Person, Myth and Society in South Asian Islam.* Special volume of *Social Analysis* 28, July.

—1993. "Religion Division and the Mythology of the Past." In *Living Banaras*, ed. B. Hertel and C. Humes, 145–58. Albany: State University of New York.

—1994a. "Caste, Religion and Other Identities." In *Contextualizing Caste*, ed. M. Searle-Chatterjee and U. Sharma, 147–69. Oxford: Blackwell.

—1994b. "Urban 'Untouchables' and Hindu Nationalism." *Immigrants and Minorities* 13(1): 12–25.

Sen, K. M. 1961. *Hinduism.* Harmondsworth: Penguin Books.

Sharma, Arvind. 1986. "What is Hinduism? A Sociological Approach." *Social Compass* 33(2-3): 177–83.

—2002. "On Hindu, Hindustan, Hinduism and Hindutva." *Numen* 49: 1–36.

Shulman, David. 1985. *The King and the Clown in South Indian Myth and Poetry.* Princeton: Princeton University Press.

Simha, Sivaprasad. 1988. *Kirtilata aur Avahattha Bhasa.* 3d ed. Delhi: Vani Prakasan.

Smart, Ninian. 1973. *The Phenomenon of Religion.* London: Macmillan.

—1974. "Truth and Religions." In *Truth and Dialogue: The Relationship between World Religions*, ed. John Hick, 45–58. London: Sheldon Press.

Smith, Brian K. 1987. "Exorcising the Transcendent: Strategies for Defining Hinduism and Buddhism." *History of Religions* 27: 32–55.

—1989. *Reflections on Resemblance, Ritual, and Religion.* New York: Oxford University Press. Reprint 1998. Delhi: Motilal Banarsidass.

—1992. "Canonical Authority and Social Classification: Veda and *Varna* in Ancient Indian Texts." *History of Religions* 32(2) (Nov.): 103–25.

—1993. "How Not to Be a Hindu: The Case of the Ramakrishna Mission Society." In *Religion and Law in Independent India*, ed. Robert D. Baird, 333–50. New Delhi: Manohar.

—1994. *Classifying the Universe: The Ancient Indian Varna System and the Origins of Caste.* New York: Oxford University Press.

—1996. "Re-envisioning Hinduism and Evaluating the Hindutva Movement." *Religion* 26: 119–28.

—1998. "Questioning Authority: Constructions and Deconstructions of Hinduism." *International Journal of Hindu Studies* 2: 313–39.

—1999. "Authority, Power, and the Definition of 'Religion.'" Special edition on *Definitions of Religion in the Context of Social-Scientific/Historical Research. Historical Reflections/ Reflexions historique* 25(3) (Fall): 411–22.

—2000. "Who Speaks for Hinduism?" *Journal of the American Academy of Religion* 68(4) (December): 741–49.

Smith, John D. 1980. "The Two Sanskrit Epics." In *Traditions of Heroic and Epic Poetry*, vol. 1, ed. A. T. Hatto. London: Modern Humanities Research Association.

Smith, Jonathan Z. 1982. *Imagining Religion: From Babylon to Jonestown.* Chicago: University of Chicago Press.

—1983. "No Need to Travel to the Indies: Judaism and the Study of Religion." In *Take Judaism, for Example*, ed. Jacob Neusner, 215–26. Chicago: University of Chicago Press.

Smith, Wilfred Cantwell. 1963. *The Meaning and End of Religion: A Revolutionary Approach to the Great Religious Traditions.* New York: Macmillan.

—1978. *The Meaning and End of Religion: A Revolutionary Approach to the Great Religious Traditions.* London: SPCK.

—1991. *The Meaning and End of Religion: A Revolutionary Approach to the Great Religious Traditions.* Minneapolis: Fortress.

Sontheimer, Gunther-Dietz, and Hermann Kulke, eds. 1997 [1989]. *Hinduism Reconsidered.* New Delhi: Manohar.

Southwold, M. 1978. "Buddhism and the Definition of Religion." *Man* 13(3): 362–79.

Spear, Percival. 1949. *India, Pakistan, and the West.* London: Oxford University Press.

Staal, Frits. 1989. *Rules without Meaning: Ritual, Mantra and the Human Sciences.* New York: Peter Lang.

Stanley, John M. 1988. "Gods, Ghosts, and Possession." In *The Experience of Hinduism: Essays on Religion in Maharashtra*, ed. E. Zelliot and M. Berntsen, 26–59. Albany: State University of New York Press.

Stephens, Thomas (also Stevens). 1945. *Doutrina Crista em Lingua Concani par Tomas Estevao, S. J. Impressa em Rachol (Goa) em 1622.* Introduction and notes by Mariano Saldanha. Lisbon: Agencia Geral das Colonias.

Stietencron, Heinrich von. 1988. "Voraussetzungen westlicher Hinduismusforschung und ihre Folgen." In "*... aus der anmuthigen Gelehrsamkeit*," Eberhard Muller, ed., 123–53. Tübingen: Attempto.

—1989. "Hinduism: On the Proper Use of a Deceptive Term." In *Hinduism Reconsidered*, ed. Gunther D. Sontheimer and Herman Kulke, 11–27. Delhi: Manohar.

—1995. "Religious Configurations in Pre-Muslim India and the Modern Concept of Hinduism." In *Representing Hinduism: The Construction of Religious Traditions and National Identity*, ed. Vasudha Dalmia and Heinrich von Stietencron, 51–81. London: Sage.

—1997. "Hinduism: On the Proper Use of a Deceptive Term." In *Hinduism Reconsidered*, ed. Gunther-Dietz Sontheimer and Hermann Kulke, 32–53. New Delhi: Manohar.

Stowe, Harriet Beecher. 1982. *Three Novels.* New York: Library of America.

Streefland, P. 1979. *The Sweepers of the Slaughterhouse.* Assen: Van Gorcum.

Svaminathan, V. 1970/1972. "On Aumkara-Mandanamisra and Sankaracarya." *Journal of Oriental Research* (Madras) 40/41: 105–16.

Sweetman, Will. 2002. "Hinduism: An Implicit or Explicit Religion?" *Implicit Religion* 5(1): 11–16.

Sweetman, Will, ed. 1999. *A Discovery of the Banian Religion and the Religion of the Persees: A Critical Edition of Two Early English Works on Indian Religions.* Lampeter: Edwin Mellen Press.

Talbot, Cynthia. 1995. "Inscribing the Other, Inscribing the Self: Hindu-Muslim Identities in Pre-Colonial India." *Comparative Studies in Society and History* 37(4): 692–722.

Tavakoli-Targhi, Mohammad. 1996. "Orientalism's Genesis Amnesia." *Comparative Studies of South Asia, Africa and the Middle East* 16(1): 1–14.

Taylor, D. 1987. "The Community of the Many Names of God: A Saivite Ashram in Rural Wales." In *Hinduism in Great Britain: The Perpetuation of Religion in an Alien Milieu,* ed. R. Burghart. London: Tavistock.

Thapar, Romila. 1985. "Syndicated Moksha?" *Seminar* 313: 14–22.

—1989. "Imagined Religious Communities: Ancient History and the Modern Search for a Hindu Identity." *Modern Asian Studies* 23(2): 209–31.

—1996. "The Tyranny of Labels." IX Zakir Husain Memorial Lecture. New Delhi: Zakir Husain College.

Trautmann, Thomas R. 1997. *Aryans and British India.* Berkeley: University of California Press.

—1998. "Hullabaloo about Telugu." Unpublished paper.

Trevelyan, Ernest John. 1908. *Hindu Family Law, as Administered in British India.* London: W. Thacker and Co.

Trivedi, P. 1984. "To Deny Our Fullness: Asian Women in the Making of History." *Feminist Review* 17(2): 37–50.

Van Buitenen, J. A. B. 1959. "Aksara." *Journal of the American Oriental Society* 79: 176–87.

—1974. "Hinduism." *The New Encyclopaedia Britannica, Macropaedia* 20: 519–58.

Van der Veer, Peter. 1994. *Religious Nationalism: Hindus and Muslims in India.* Berkeley: University of California Press.

Van der Veer, Peter, ed. 1995. *Nation and Migration.* Philadelphia: University of Pennsylvania Press.

Vertovec, S. 1992. "Community and Congregation in London Hindu Temples: Divergent Trends." *New Community* 18(2): 251–64.

—1995. "Hindus in Trinidad and Britain: Ethnic Religion, Reification and the Politics of Public Space." In *Nation and Migration,* ed. P. van der Veer, 132–56. Philadelphia: University of Pennsylvania Press.

Vivekananda. 1970–73. *Complete Works.* 8 vols. Calcutta: Advaita Ashrama.

Waardenburg, J. 1973. *Classical Approaches to the Study of Religion.* The Hague: Mouton.

Wagle, N. K. 1997. "Hindu-Muslim Interactions in Medieval Maharashtra." In *Hinduism Reconsidered,* ed. Gunther-Dietz Sontheimer and Hermann Kulke, 134–52. New Delhi: Manohar.

Ward, K. 1993. *Images of Eternity.* Oxford: Oneworld Publications.

Washbrook, D. A. 1988. "Progress and Problems: South Asian Economic and Social History, c. 1720-1860." *Modern Asian Studies* 22: 57–96.

Weber, Max. 1967. *The Religion of India: The Sociology of Hinduism and Buddhism.* Trans. H. Gerth and Don Martindale. New York: Free Press.

Werbner, P. 1987. "Barefoot in Britain: Anthropological Research on Asian Immigrants." *New Community* 14(1/2).

—1991. "The Fiction of Unity in Ethnic Politics: Aspects of Representation and the State among Manchester Pakistanis." In *Black and Ethnic Leaderships in Britain: The Cultural Dimensions of Political Action,* ed. P. Werbner and M. Anwar, 113–45. London: Routledge.

Wezler, A. 1982. "Manu's Omniscience: The Interpretation of Manusmrti II, 7." In *Indology and Law: Studies in Honour of Professor J. Duncan M. Derrett,* ed. J. Duncan M. Derrett,

Bibliography

Gunter-Dietz Sontheimer, and Parameswara Kota Aithal, 79–105. Wiesbaden: F. Steiner Verlag.

Wicki, Josef, ed. 1948–1972. *Documents Indica.* 12 vols. Rome: Monumenta Historica Soc. Iesu and Institutum Historicum Soc. Iesu. Sixteenth-century documents mostly written by Jesuits, mostly in Portuguese.

Wilson, H. H. 1972. *Religious Sects of the Hindus.* Varanasi: Indological Book House. First published in *Asiatic Researches*, 1828 and 1832.

Wink, Andrew. 1986. *Land and Sovereignty in India: Agrarian Society and Politics under the Eighteenth-Century Maratha Svarajya.* Cambridge: Cambridge University Press.

Young, Richard Fox. 1981. *Resistant Hinduism: Sanskrit Sources on Anti-Christian Apologetics in Early Nineteenth-Century India.* Vienna: De Nobili Research Institute.

Younger, Paul. 1972. *Introduction to Indian Religious Thought.* Philadelphia: Westminster Press.

Yule, Henry, and Arthur Coke Burnell. 1968. *Hobson-Jobson: A Glossary of Colloquial Anglo-Indian Words and Phrases.* New ed. New York: Humanities Press.

Yule, Henry, and Arthur Coke Burnell, eds. 1886. *Hobson-Jobson: A Glossary of Colloquial Anglo-Indian Words and Phrases and of Kindred Terms, Etymological, Historical, Geographical, and Discursive.* London: John Murray.

Zaehner, R. C. 1966. *Hinduism.* New York: Oxford University Press.

—1969. *The Bhagavad Gita.* Oxford: Oxford University Press.

—1971. *Hinduism.* Oxford: Oxford University Press.

Zelliot, Eleanor. 1982. "A Medieval Encounter between Hindu and Muslim: Eknath's Drama-Poem Hindu-Turk Samvad." In *Images of Man: Religious and Historical Process in South Asia*, ed. Fred W. Clothey, 171–95. Madras: New Era Publications.

—1992. *From Untouchable to Dalit: Essays on Ambedkar Movement.* New Delhi: Manohar.

Ziengenbalg, Bartholomeus, and Johann Ernst Grundler. 1714. *Siebende Continuation des Berichts derer koniglichen danischen Missionarien.* Halle: Zu Verlegung des Waysen-Hauses.

Ziolkowski, Eric J. 1990. "Heavenly Visions and Worldly Intentions: Chicago's Columbian Exposition and World's Parliament of Religions (1893)." *Journal of American Culture* 13: 11–12.

Zupanov, Ines G. 1999. *Disputed Mission: Jesuit Experiments and Brahmanical Knowledge in Seventeenth-Century India.* New Delhi: Oxford University Press.

INDEX OF AUTHORS

Index of Authors

Index of Authors

INDEX OF SUBJECTS